WITHDRAWN

I cannot tell the truth.
I can only say what I know.

—Native of James Bay, 1979c.

In this series

The Whaling Question
  (The Inquiry by Sir Sidney Frost of Australia)
The Condor Question: Captive, or Forever Free?

The best thing that can happen to a condor nest is that nobody finds it. —CARL KOFORD

The Condor Question
CAPTIVE OR FOREVER FREE?

What does it cost the earth?

There is but one ocean, though its coves have many names;
a single sea of atmosphere, with no coves at all;
the miracle of soil, alive and giving life, lying thin
on the only earth, for which there is no spare.
. . .

. . . We seek a renewed stirring of love for the earth.
We plead that what we are capable of doing to the earth
is often what we ought not to do.
We urge that all people now determine
that a spacious untrammeled wildness shall remain whole,
to testify that this generation had love for the next,
and reverence for a greater wisdom than our own.
. . .

. . . We would celebrate a new renaissance.
The old one found a new world to exploit.
The new one has discovered the earth's limits.
Knowing them, we may learn anew
what compassion and beauty are.

Ali Pearson

We may see that progress is not the accelerating speed
with which technology multiplies and subdues the earth,
nor the growing number of things we possess and cling to,
It is a way and a pace leading toward truth,
sustaining love, letting us be more content and serene,
at less cost to the earth. —DAVID R. BROWER

. . . *they move finished and complete,*
gifted with extensions of the senses
we have lost or never attained,
living by voices we shall never hear.
They are not brethren. They are not underlings;
they are other nations, caught with ourselves
in the net of life and time, fellow prisoners
of the splendor and travail of the earth.

—Henry Beston

SAN FRANCISCO

The Condor Question
CAPTIVE OR FOREVER FREE?

With *contributions by* DAVID and KENNETH BROWER
DAVID DeSANTE, JOSEPH S. DIXON, ANNE and PAUL EHRLICH
JERRY EMORY, CARL KOFORD, A. STARKER LEOPOLD, EBEN and
IAN McMILLAN, ALDEN H. MILLER, RUSSELL PETERSON
DAVID PHILLIPS, ROLAND CASE ROSS, DICK SMITH
LOWELL SUMNER, SANFORD WILBUR, and others.

Edited by DAVID PHILLIPS and HUGH NASH

FRIENDS OF THE EARTH

Acknowledgement

We are grateful to Jerry Emory, Mark Palmer, Greg Serrurier, Katy Slichter, and Steve Rauh for their assistance in conducting interviews that appear in this book. Mrs. Suzanne Koford and Helen Green helped transcribe interview material and Ali Pearson and Tim Bowles generously contributed map graphics and text illustrations. Steve Herman, Ray Dasmann, John Taft, Fred Eissler, and Bob Wilkinson helped initiate the project and review the manuscript. Texts from the *Condor Journal* ©1968 by Dick Smith are reprinted by permission of Capra Press, Box 2068, Santa Barbara, California. This book would not have been possible without all their help.   —D.P. and H.N.

ISBN: 0-913890-48-0
Library of Congress Card Number: 81-68548

Designed by David Brower
Cover illustration and design by Terry Down
Text illustrations by Ali Pearson and Tim Bowles

Foreword

THIS BOOK IS many things. First it is a loving portrait of an extraordinary creature: the California condor. In reading this book, you will see, through the eyes of various authors who have known it well, the majestic soaring flight, the complex life history, and intriguing behavior of these remarkable birds. You will come to appreciate their role in the ecological system of the central and southern California mountains where they range widely as scavengers, disposing of carcasses and helping to recycle nutrients—one of nature's indispensible services. And you will discover how tragically vulnerable to human disturbance condors are.

This book thus also is a plea to save the California condor, whose numbers are not known with precision but quite clearly are too low to ensure long-term survival. Still, concern about the condor's survival is nothing new; it goes back at least seventy years. Unfortunately, this concern has too often inspired efforts in the condor's behalf that have been more threat than help. The most experienced students of the condor quickly learned that the birds are excruciatingly sensitive to human interference. The mere appearance of a person within several hundred yards of a nesting site may cause interruption of feeding or incubating behavior long enough to result in loss of the chick, for instance.

More recently, well-meaning biologists relatively inexperienced with condors and heedless of the warnings issued years before by others more knowledgeable, have sought to photograph and film the birds' behavior, not hesitating to invade nests in the process. Further, they have attempted to weigh and measure the chicks and even plan to operate on adults to determine their sex and to attach radio transmitters to them in order to monitor their far-flung foraging flights.

Most outrageous of all, a formal "Recovery Plan" of the U.S. Fish and Wildlife Service aims to capture a substantial portion of the remaining condor population for breeding in captivity, returning the progeny to the wild at some unspecified but far-off future date. One wonders whether a better plan could be devised to *hasten* the extinction of the California condor! Indeed, the death of a chick at the very start of the program from pure fright at being manhandled by investigators came as no surprise to those familiar with this giant vulture. But the event demonstrated to a startled world the incompatability of condors with this space-age technology intended to "save" them.

So this book, more than being a plea to save the condor, is a telling exposé of the wrongheadedness of the Condor Recovery Plan. It is clear that the condor is threatened principally because of destruction and deterioration of its habitat. It has been a victim, like other birds at the top of the food chain, of persistent pesticides, of poisons intended for rodents and coyotes, of heedless hunters, and, possibly not least, of harrassment by insensitive scientists and just plain curious people. Development and recreational activities have rendered useless numerous nesting and roosting sites. Although habitat preservation is supposed to be a major part of the Recovery Plan, no serious effort has yet been made in that direction. Instead, the plan calls for removing the birds from it for breeding under managed conditions.

But what assurance is there that captive breeding of condors can be successfully accomplished? A bird bred and raised in captivity is a quite different creature from one raised in the wild. What assurance is there that a captive-bred condor could survive on its own in the wild?

Finally—and this is the crux of the issue—what assurance is there that twenty or forty years hence, in the absence of wild condors as justification for preserving their habitat, there will be any habitat remaining to receive the captive birds? The condors are only one prominent species among many thousands that occur within its range and are part of the same ecosystem. But, because the condors are both prominent and endangered, that range is still partially protected. If the condors are removed, what is to stop the farmers, foresters, drillers, miners, developers, ORV drivers, and the rest from destroying the area, pushing to extinction countless populations (if not entire species) of plants, small mammals, reptiles, insects and other inconspicuous organisms? If their habitat is destroyed, the condors will be one more relic of Earth's former biological diversity, a forlorn shadow of its present glory languishing in zoos until final extinction overtakes them.

This book is a plea to save the condor in a sane, sensible, and reasonable fashion—not through inappropriate technological gimmickry and harrassment. There is a way to do it right that is both less costly and will protect other species as well: leave the condor alone and protect its habitat. It remains to be seen whether *Homo sapiens* can summon that much wisdom, however. We hope that this book will mark a turning point in treatment of the condor. The one thing we hope it will not be is an epitaph.

ANNE AND PAUL EHRLICH

The California Condor is America's rarest large bird. Only a concerted, cooperative effort by all the land agencies involved, state and federal, and the people of California, can ensure the perpetuation of this great bird which has come down to us unchanged through eons of time. All it needs is elbow room and to be left alone. What space we leave or fail to leave for it will be a measure of the level of our civilization.

—CARL W. BUCHHEISTER
President, National Audubon Society
May 5, 1965

Contents

Ali Pearson

Introduction

ALMOST EVERYONE WANTS to save the California condor from extinction, but the effort to do so is plagued by what Joseph Walker, in a letter to *The New York Times*, on May 11, 1981, described as cognitive dissonance—the belief in two or more mutually exclusive ideas. He noted, for example, the belief that the way to reduce the likelihood of nuclear war is to build more nuclear weapons. He wondered whether, like the village in Vietnam, America will be destroyed in order to be saved. We narrow that concern to the California condor, and suspect on sound grounds that the attempt to save the condor by breeding it in captivity will destroy the bird.

In early 1979, the United States Fish and Wildlife Service (USFWS) revised the California Condor Recovery Plan to embark on a controversial, last-ditch effort to breed the severely endangered condor in captivity. The capturing of condors had been proposed and rejected in the mid-1960s but emerged again in a document entitled *The Contingency Plan for Captive Breeding of California Condors*. It recommended that all free-flying condors be captured for marking with radiotransmitters and that most—perhaps all—condors be removed from the wild for experiments with captive breeding. It was frequently claimed that condors were no longer breeding in the wild—a false claim. Opponents of the Plan believed there was not enough evidence to justify captive breeding. Though it is clear that the condor population has declined radically in historic times, year-to-year population trends are not clear, and there is no proof that the condor population is presently in decline. We suspect that population counts have been juggled to give an illusion of steep decline and to allege urgency.

[17]

To many, the proposed capture program has become synonymous with abandonment of the wild condor population; the program gambles on high-technology manipulation of a species which has proved extremely sensitive to human disturbance.

The proposed handling would be substantial (see the permit application, *Federal Register*, June 3, 1981, excerpted in Appendix 1).

The permit requests authority to enter active and inactive nests, to remove eggs and nestlings, and to capture nestlings, preflight immature and adult condors between now and the year 2015.

During the first three-year period, nine condors would be removed from the wild for captive breeding and twelve free-flying condors and all preflight immatures would be captured for marking. Despite the death due to weighing and measuring of one of the two condor chicks known to have hatched in 1980, the permit would allow the weighing and measuring of all young condors.

From each trapped bird, 17cc of blood would be drawn from a wing or neck vein for various tests. Three developing feathers would be plucked for use in feather pulp sexing and two grams of feather material from up to twenty contour feathers would be taken for heavy metal analysis.

Condors would be captured using cannon or rocket nets at baited trap sites. Monitoring of radioed condors would be from ground vehicles, a small airplane, and an array of ten to twelve mountaintop radio receivers, erected to provide "automatic, unmanned coverage" of the condor range. Birds retained for attempts at captive propagation would be transported to zoo facilities in San Diego for long-term captivity, each pair of condors to be confined in pens twelve meters square and five meters high.

The plan would cost 25 million dollars over the next three decades—the most expensive program ever devised for an endangered species.

The question we pose here is not whether this approach is ultimately too costly to the people, but whether it would be too costly to the species. In a misguided attempt to save the condor, the capture program could push the condor to extinction.

The breeding population in the wild could easily be reduced below the required genetic minimum, and the zoo population could succumb to human-caused disasters.

In what follows we provide a selection from the writings of a group of biologists and naturalists whose work has essentially been ignored. Some have spent their entire lives in condor country. Others have made the study of condors a major part of their professional lives. They dispute the premise upon which the capture program is based: that everything else has been tried and thus captive breeding is the only hope. They provide convincing evidence that the tragedy has been and continues to be the neglect of the condors' essential habitat and the failure to protect them adequately in the wild.

A close look at the Condor Recovery Program indicates that the new-found enchantment with captive breeding commands virtually all attention, research effort, and funding. Meanwhile the destruction and degradation of critical condor nesting, feeding, roosting, and watering areas continues virtually unchecked. The effort to confront clear threats—such as indiscriminate shooting—languishes, owing to lack of funds. Factors largely ignored are disturbance, harassment, poisoning with rodenticides, and conversion of prime habitat; these continue to contribute to the decline of the condor population.

To find examples of the unbalanced and misdirected nature of the recovery effort, one has only to compare the remedial actions outlined in the Condor Recovery Plan with the priorities of the present "hands-on" program. The comparison is presented in table form as Appendix II. This table includes the specific recommendations of Friends of the Earth.

Land Acquisition

Within the past one hundred years, California condors ranged from Canada's Vancouver to Baja California, but as their population declined they have withdrawn to a relatively small area northeast of Santa Barbara. Though condors still range over many thousands of square miles, the strictest habitat protection is necessary in nesting and roosting areas. The Condor Recovery Plan identified numerous parcels of private land key to safeguarding the wild condor population, but little or no action has been taken, and land prices continue to soar. The Reagan Administration, as of this writing, has directed that the Land and Water Conservation Fund, traditionally the major source of federal funds for purchase of habitat for endangered species, be diverted from this use. Acquisition of important condor-use areas, which might have been possible in a recovery effort fundamentally committed to habitat protection, now appears highly unlikely. The condor and ultimately mankind is the loser, for even if the breeding program should prove succesful there would no longer be suitable habitat in the present range to return condors to.

Little or no effort has been made to establish ties with private organizations and land trusts committed to acquisition of important habitat, nor has the recovery effort attempted to utilize easements and tax-incentives to ensure compatability between development and the survival of the condor.

Management of Federal Lands

Much of the critical condor habitat is on federally owned lands, yet the effort to manage these areas in ways that benefit condor survival has been lackluster at best. The Sespe-Frazier Roadless Area surrounds the Sespe Condor Sanctuary on three sides and is five times larger. It is acknowledged to be of critical importance to the condor and, even exclusive of considerations of the condor, warrants designation as a Wilderness Area. During the recent Roadless Area Review and Evaluation program (RARE II) more than seventy percent of those members of the public who responded felt that the area ought to be classified as Wilderness. Such designation would protect watersheds and ecosystems and reduce such disruptions as road constructions, offroad vehicle use, dam construction, and resource exploitation. Though the Recovery Plan indicates the need to develop fire-management plans to benefit condors and stresses the importance of minimizing animal damage control programs on the Los Padres National Forest, no progress has been made in either direction. In 1980 the California Fish and Game Commission, upon the recommendation of Friends of the Earth, the Sierra Club, and several other organizations, endorsed the proposal for wilderness designation for the Sespe-Frazier Roadless Area. The Condor Recovery Team has not provided appreciable assistance to this important first step in the protection of condor habitat.

Law Enforcement

Condors have been shot at for many years; direct and circumstantial evidence has led researchers who have devoted much time to studying condors in the wild to conclude that indiscriminate shooting in condor use areas is a major problem. The Recovery Plan suggests restrictions on firearms use in certain areas, increases in law enforcement patrols, and the relocation of problem campgrounds. The attitude of those now in charge of the condor recovery effort seems to be that until condors with radiotelemetry devices are found shot, and shooting is thus proved to be the cause of death, no major effort can be launched to reduce the threat. Law-enforcement capability has been quietly and drastically reduced. No US Fish and Wildlife Service agent has primary responsibility for condor protection. Patrols are infrequent, sign posting is negligible, and use of firearms proliferates. Recommendations from three generations of condor experts have been largely ignored. Each year of inaction brings further conflict between recreationists' chance to play and the condor's chance to survive.

Research

The focus of research in the proposed program is on breeding condors in captivity. Experiments are proceeding with capture methods, double clutching of captive Andean condors (forcing a condor to lay two eggs by removing one for incubation), and studies of the effects of radiotelemetry devices on captive and free-flying vultures. Though this augments the general body of knowledge of condors, important and long-neglected studies pertaining to the survival in the wild of the California condor has been given lower priority. Independent biological assessments are badly needed, not only of condor population dynamics and productivity, but also of condor food and water, which should be tested for contamination, and of surrogate species, especially the turkey vultures from the same area. The impact of 1080 and other rodenticides has yet to be carefully studied; ways need to be found to reduce the threat posed by ground application of these poisons. Many historic nest sites have not been checked for evidence of reproductive activity and nesting success. Intensified observation is needed, by methods that do not disturb the condors, to provide better data on the present status of the wild population, unburdened by the trauma engendered by hands-on biological technicians.

Habitat

In all, a fundamental problem with the present recovery effort is the fragmentation of responsibilities for habitat work between the Fish and Wildlife Service, the Forest Service, Bureau of Land Management, and the California Department of Fish and Game, advised by the California Fish and Game Commission. Independent evaluation of the effort, by the National Audubon Society and other cognizant organizations, is essential. Far too often conflicts between condor recovery and resource exploitation go unchecked. Plans for dams, hydro facilities, offroad vehicle parks, oil and gas leases, uranium mines, and urban development are proliferating in the condors' last redoubt—all this while the Recovery Team concentrates on hands-on technology for saving condors in cages.

As attention shifts to the building of a captive condor population, new threats to the habitat are ignored—the threats resulting from removing the condors, the very symbol of habitat protection, from the habitat itself. As plans for firing cannon nets proceed, and for traumatizing birds that cherish solitude, one must ask how we will ever provide comprehensive habitat protection for condors if they are taken out of the wild when it has already been so difficult protecting it with the birds there to help us.

The arguments for an ecosystem approach to the conservation of the wildlife are as important to the condor as they are to all the Earth's endangered plants and animals. Captive breeding cannot realistically be looked to to avoid the extinction of from 500,000 to 2,000,000 species of plants and animals by the year 2000 as projected by the *Global 2000 Report to the President*.

William Conway, Director of the New York Zoological Society, recently estimated that if all United States zoos were to allocate half their space to captive propagation, 150 species at most could be maintained, at a cost of some twenty-five billion dollars in the next twenty years. This is not only horrendously expensive and a logistic nightmare, but in our view spends a lot of time and energy taking us where we don't want to be.

Though a number of species have been propagated in captivity, a look at the actual contribution of captive breeding to the recovery of endangered wildlife reveals few conspicuous successes and a multitude of uncertainties, unresolved problems, and tragic losses. The whooping crane program is often used to justify the capture of California condors. However, the record of that program more aptly demonstrates that habitat protection rather than captive propagation is responsible for the success thus far. Since most female whooping cranes lay two eggs but usually only fledge one young, beginning in 1967 the "extra" eggs have been taken either to be raised in captivity or to be placed in the nests of a closely related species, the sandhill crane, for an experiment in cross-fostering. Fifty eggs were taken from the wild to form a captive flock and more than eighty have been placed in sandhill crane nests thus far. Though survival of the transplants is about three times worse than that of the main wild population, about seventeen whoopers are now mixed in with the sandhill crane flock and about twenty survive in captivity. The effects of this cross-fostering on the mating, breeding, and migration of whooping cranes are unknown as released birds are not yet sexually mature. Survival of eggs laid by captive whoopers has been low. From fifty-three eggs laid from 1975-1978 only six birds survive. Even less success has been achieved in placing eggs from captive birds into sandhill crane nests. From some thirty-seven eggs transferred, no more than three now survive.

No captive raised bird has ever been used to supplement the natural wild population—yet through habitat protection and what the Whooping Crane Recovery Plan terms "conventional management procedures" the flock has increased from a low of fifteen to the current total of approximately eighty. The manipulative intervention has played no part in this recovery; the success rightly belongs to the program to protect wintering habitat, educate the public, and reduce losses during migration. This lesson falls on deaf ears when it comes to the condor program.

Attempts to generalize to the proposed condor capture program from the management of whooping cranes makes little
sense. Condors lay only one egg every other year. The young
condor remains at the nest site for some fifty-eight weeks and
takes five or six further years—many of these in the company
of its parents—to mature. Condors are thus critically unlike the
whoopers: no captive flock could possibly be built without reducing the population of wild condors and thus their reproductive potential. Moreover, no wild whoopers were removed for
the Recovery Program, whereas the Condor program calls for
removal of at least one-third of the existing world population.
Cross-fostering whoopers with sandhill cranes has provided a
potentially successful method of re-establishing a geographi-
cally separate population. No such surrogate exists, however,
for the condor. Cross-fostering is impossible.

The dissimilarities in population characteristics between the
peregrine falcon and the California condor again provide little
evidence that captive propagation is in the best interest of the
wild condor. More than four hundred and seventy captive-
raised peregrine falcons have been released to the wild since
1973 in one of the most ambitious captive breeding efforts ever
attempted. Only three pairs of captive-raised birds are known
to have successfully hatched chicks thus far. The point here is
not to denigrate that effort, but rather to indicate the dangers in
generalizing from the peregrine to the condor. Condors have
much lower reproductive potential. A condor capture program
would have far fewer initial pairs, and reintroduction would
most likely be considerably more difficult. Hundreds of captives could not be released every year to experiment with.

No California condor has ever successfully raised young in
captivity. The one attempt to release a California condor, Topa
Topa, failed. The condor was attacked by wild condors and
nearly perished. He is now on public display at the Los Angeles
Zoo. Though the Andean condor has been bred in captivity,
the fate of re-introduced birds is largely unknown. Three of the
twelve captive-raised birds released in South America this year
have died and one other failed to assimilate into the wild population and had to be returned to captivity. Neither the captive-

raised birds nor the wild Andeans under observation were known to court or breed in 1981.

It would seem illogical, and premature, to judge captive breeding successful as a recovery technique until a captive, when released, breeds successfully in the wild and its young prove the success by themselves breeding. This extended test requirement would seem to be especially important with the condor, considering how long the period of juvenile dependency lasts.

Apart from the shaky biological basis for captive breeding of condors, the wild condor must be seen as an integral part of a total ecosystem. Protection of the condor and its ecosystem is possible, but only if given the proper emphasis rather than focusing on the removal of condors from the wild. The ultimate survival of the condor is at stake, for even if captive breeding proved successful, simply releasing pen-raised birds would be futile without a wild population and protected habitat.

The evidence to date suggests that handling, capture, and captive breeding are the problem, not the answer for the California condor.

— DAVID PHILLIPS

As long as you're talking about a handful of people, working in a laboratory or in the field where nobody can see them, and you're expecting to influence public opinion, the Forest Service, and all these other agencies, I don't think you're going to get the job done. I don't care who these people are; one or two people wandering into a planning department office or coming before a board of supervisors never got that far. They don't have any more political wallop than a . . . than a condor. The only way to do it, if you're really going to change things around, is to take advantage of the power you have in all the citizen's groups that you can get behind you, and mount a real campaign. If I were going to try to change zoning regulations in Tulare County, I wouldn't send any biologist over there—except as an expert witness. I'd have two hundred people from the Sierra Club and Audubon Society sitting there and talking to the supervisors. Until we have that kind of wallop behind this program, you people are going to be on the defensive from here to kingdom come. You're going to say, "Oh, we can't do anything about the Forest Service." I know what we can do about the Forest Service; we've done it already on the San Rafael Wilderness. They came in with a half measure, and we got them to double the acreage because we brought political power to bear. As long as you've got to worry about how many gallons of gas you can get for that tank because you have only so much money, you're not going to have a program that gets off the ground. I think captive breeding is the end result of biologists' working by themselves under a cloak of secrecy because they're afraid of a condor backlash, instead of getting out and fighting like hell. . . .

—Fred Eissler

1 KENNETH BROWER

Night of the Condor

Although he was born in San Francisco in 1944, Kenneth Brower's early memories are mostly of wild country. For twenty years he has been writing about it and its inhabitants, wild or primitive. He has been the naturalist-editor of books in the Sierra Club's exhibit-format series about the Big Sur coast, the West Ridge of Everest, Navajo country, Kauai, Baja California, and the two volumes on the Galapagos Islands. For the Friends of the Earth series he has edited books on Maui, the Big Sur and Navajo country, and has written three: *Earth and the Great Weather: The Brooks Range, Micronesia: Island Wilderness*, and *Wake of the Whale*. He has published two books with Holt, Rinehart and Winston—*With Their Islands Around Them* and *The Starship and the Canoe* (the latter also having appearing in a Bantam paperback and in editions in the United Kingdom and Poland), and with the University of Louisiana Press on Micronesia. His work has also appeared in *The Atlantic Monthly, Audubon Magazine, Country Journal, Paris Review, Reader's Digest,* and *Omni,* where an edited version of "Night of the Condor" appeared in 1979.

Ali Pearson

Night of the Condor

D R. CARL KOFORD led the way past tall, gray rows of museum cases, then up a flight of stairs and past more museum cases. We were in a scientific mausoleum—the Museum of Vertebrate Zoology of the University of California at Berkeley—and the Navy-gray cases filled the place. The air was cool and smelled faintly of napthalene. At the far end of the room, bone-white atop the Navy gray, too big to fit inside, was the skull of a gray whale. Dr. Koford turned hard right, into an aisle between two Navy-gray rows. He did not have to pause to read the number. He knew this aisle by heart.

"You can tell the condor case," he said, nodding upward. "It's the biggest one." He was right. The case labeled "Cathartidae" was twice as long as the others. He reached high to undo the hasps.

Koford was a trim, graying man, retired now but youthful in his movements and expression. He wore an old red-checked shirt with frayed holes in one shoulder. His face was pleasantly weathered from a life spent observing animals in the field— vicuñas in South America, monkeys in Puerto Rico, prairie dogs on the prairie, and, at the beginning of his career, condors in southern California.

He removed the front panel, setting it on the floor. An invisible cloud of napthalene escaped the case and enveloped us. Inside the case were four horizontal trays, and Dr. Koford rolled out the lowest. For an instant I felt like a relative called down to the morgue to identify the victim. Clearly, though, the corpse on the tray was no kin to me. The bird was enormous—

in life, condors weigh twenty pounds or more—and it lay on its
back. There were two others supine behind it. I studied the
great hooked beak, designed to tear at carcasses. I ran my
finger along a foot, which, uncurled, would have had the span
of a woman's hand. With a fingertip I tested the pinpoint of a
talon, designed to hold a carcass down while the beak tore.
There were, I knew, only about thirty condors left in the wild.
It occurred to me that sometime early in the next century,
perhaps sooner, the only California condors left on the planet
might lie supine on trays like these.

I read the labels. The condor's scientific names were felici-
tous. The condor and the other American vultures belong to
the family Cathartidae, from the Greek *kathartes*, "a cleanser,"
from *katharos*, "pure." The etymology recalled the dignity in
what might sometimes seem a grisly profession. The vultures
are responsible for a catharsis of the landscape. Their job is to
take things down to the bone again. The condor's generic name
was *Gymnogyps*, its specific name *californianus*. *Gymnogyps* de-
rives from *gyps*, Greek for vulture, and *gymnos*, "naked." The
condor's head and neck are naked of feathers, an adaptation
that allows the bird to clean itself more easily after the grisly
work.

"This one is a juvenile male shot near Pasadena in 1908,"
Koford said, fingering a tag tied to the foot. "And this one was
taken in 1886." Over his shoulder, I read the Victorian hand-
script on the second tag. This bird has been dead nearly a
century. Time had desiccated it. Hefting the body, I found it
nearly weightless. Dr. Koford rolled out another tray. He bur-
rowed with his fingers in the downy neck of another young
bird, as if searching for something there. "This one is still
pretty downy," he said. "It was probably killed the same year it
came out of the nest." (Growing up in condors is the reverse of
growing up in men. Condor necks are feathery in adolescence,
naked in adulthood.) "The big mortality takes place in the first
months out of the nest. They're such lousy fliers at first."

He demonstrated how the young bird defends itself in the
nest. Putting his head down, he hissed and hit at me awk-
wardly with his wingtips. Then he looked embarrassed. He
had forgotten himself for a moment and had become a condor.

Several detached flight feathers lay at the foot of one bird, and Koford now picked up two of them. "Individual feathers are over 24 inches long," he said. Holding a feather in either hand, he extended his arms, pointing the feather tips outward. "The length of the wing bones is about the same as in a human's arms, so this would be the wingspread."

"Eight feet?" I estimated, too quickly.

"Nine," he said. He stood with his wings extended. He had forgotten himself again. For a moment, there in the narrow, Navy-gray aisle, he soared.

Riding the wind currents above their chaparral-covered California hills, condors make a musical whistling as air spills past their pinions. "As if," Peter Kaplan has written, "all the grace and freedom of flight were expressed in a few singing notes." The singing is audible one hundred yards away, and is more pronounced and harmonic in adults than in juveniles, almost as if the wind-song were music that required learning. Diving, the condor makes a roar like escaping steam, audible half a mile away.

The distinctive feature of condor flight is high stability in soaring. The condor's "loading"—its ratio of body weight to wing surface—is heavy, nearly twice that of the turkey vulture. Turkey vultures can ascend more quickly, but in any kind of turbulence they wobble markedly in comparison. Sailing on their thermals, condors hold rock steady. Human observers, even experienced ones, often mistake condors for transport planes, and planes for condors. Condors can soar for an hour without flapping. They can glide without turning for eight minutes or more and can cover ten miles on one tack.

It is possible to appreciate the catharsis performed by the condor yet still shudder a little. It would be difficult to invent a more perfect symbol for death. The condor is archetype for the Grim Reaper. Perching, the bird is dark, ruffed, and broad-shouldered, as if wearing a black cape. The head is naked as a skull. The beak and talons are cruelly curved, the eye blood-red. Soaring, the condor extends the incredibly long fingers of its pinions—the eight black sabers on each wingtip.

Gymnogyps is a survivor of an epoch when the scale of life was larger. In the Pleistocene, condors appear to have been more abundant in North America than black vultures or turkey vultures. The smaller vultures, perhaps, were unable to compete with condors at the giant corpses of that period's megafauna. Condors waited on musical wings for mammoths and glyptodonts and chlamytheres to die. They watched *Megatherium*, the giant ground sloth, and *Tapirus*, the giant tapir, as those antediluvian creatures struggled in the La Brea tar. Sometimes on landing they became trapped themselves. Standing in their circles, shuffling and pecking for position, they awaited their turns to feed on American camels, hippopotamuses, and lions, on dire wolves, saber-toothed cats, and hyenoid dogs. They broke off their soaring and dove to avoid passes by their giant Pleistocene cousin, *Teratornis*, a supercondor weighing fifty pounds, perhaps the largest bird ever to fly. *Teratornis* died out with the Pleistocene. *Gymnogyps* had the last laugh.

In historical times the California condor ranged as far north as British Columbia, as far south as Baja California. The Spaniards saw them along the California coast and called them "royal eagles." Lewis and Clark saw them in large numbers at the mouth of the Columbia River, and called them "buzzards." Today that former domain has shrunk to several counties in southern California. When, forty years ago, Carl Koford began his study of condors, the population he estimates was sixty birds. A subsequent study showed that in the period 1946–1963, the number fell by a third—forty birds survived. The most recent study estimates thirty. The condor appears to be going the way of *Teratornis*.

In February of this year, the U.S. Fish and Wildlife Service (USFWS), after consultation with the National Audubon Society, circulated a draft proposal for meeting the condor crisis. Its first recommendation was that "all free-living condors should be trapped, individually marked, and fitted with radio transmitters." A number of the trapped birds would be bred in captivity and their offspring returned to the wild.

There were other recommendations—that the condor census be standardized, that condor food items be analyzed, that pesticide levels be checked in similar birds—and Carl Koford favors many of these steps, but to the first he is strongly opposed.

"It's absolutely unnecessary, and probably harmful, and may

wipe these birds out far sooner than would happen without interference."

Condors live 30 to 40 years, he points out, so there is no danger of immediate disappearance. There is reason to hope that the condors will recover naturally, he believes. The use of DDT has diminished recently, and as a consequence the brown pelican, for one, is coming back from the edge of extinction. Use of compound 1080 to poison mammals is decreasing in the condor's range, and deer hunters there are fewer. USFWS itself estimates, he notes, that there are 6 or 7 immature birds among the 30 survivors, an encouraging increase over the 4 immatures estimated in 1974. Capture will be traumatic for the birds, both physically and mentally. There is no guarantee that they will breed in captivity, or that zoo-propagated birds will be knowledgeable enough about the subtleties of condorhood to survive in the wild. We have time enough, he thinks, to take a number of more appropriate steps before resorting to measures so drastic and untried.

"There is a great deal of learned behavior in condors," he says. "How are these released birds going to know about avoiding storms, and attacks by eagles, and how to compete with other birds at the carcass? There's no precedent to suggest they can do it. I keep ducks. If I put a new duck in with three other ducks, sometimes they kill it. Or like hatchery-raised trout. Trout raised in a hatchery don't act like other trout. They're in the wrong part of the stream; they're eating the wrong food. A released bird is only half a bird."

The USFWS and the Audubon Society dismiss Koford's objections. They are convinced that the condor's plight is desperate and requires desperate efforts at salvation. The dismissal of Koford would be a simpler matter if only he were something other than the world's foremost expert on this small tribe of huge birds. But he is nothing other. His *The California Condor* remains the major work in the field, and nearly the only one.

When Koford was twenty-four, an age when he should have been drinking beer with his buddies and running around in Model-As, he was living instead in a cave half a mile from the caves where his condors lived. He was shooting horses to see if the condors were interested in the cadavers. He was traveling the semi-deserts of upper and lower California, questioning

vaqueros about condors they had seen. He was photographing
the remains of animals after condors had finished with them.
Mostly, for three years of his life, he was watching. He watched
the ponderous, hopping run of condor take-off, one foot striking the ground slightly ahead of the other, the bird covering 15
to 40 feet before it was airborne. He watched condors in flight:
the double dip they execute to prevent a stall or lose altitude;
the flex-glide, in which the dihedral angle of the wings di-
minishes or becomes negative and the bird gains speed. He
watched immatures tilt their tails too frequently, overcontrol-
ling, and he watched them nearly turn themselves over in attempting turns. He watched birds descending and he noted
how early their landing gear came down—the feet dropping
ten minutes and one thousand feet above the ground. He
watched the characteristic yawn of condors on landing. He
watched them stretch themselves, like human joggers, before
taking off in the mornings, and he noted that they seldom
stretched during the rest of the day. Koford counted. "For a
single adult, the greatest number of side stretches that I noted
was 6 during a period of 65 minutes," he would write. Gazing
into condor eyes, he noted that the nictitating membrane
blinked every 2–5 seconds. Koford listened. He heard the
"muffled crash" of feathers against rock when condors landed.
He heard the condor's grunt, "like a supressed human
belch"—a sound in perfect harmony with Cathartid diet.

A rare thing happens about twenty pages into *The California
Condor*—something especially rare in scientific mongraphs.
The condor comes alive. Koford's descriptions of condor
anatomy and behavior are lean, clear-eyed, free of jargon, in-
stantly visualizable. They are literature. You *see* the bird. If the
day ever comes when all that remains of condor flesh and
feathers lies on museum trays, then all that remains of condor
movement and culture will lie between the covers of Koford's
book.

I knew what I felt about the bold USFWS plan for condors
before meeting Dr. Koford, before hearing his wishful alternatives, his emotion-charged views on the bird with which he
spent his youth. I knew he was right.

The line, "All free-living condors should be trapped . . .
and fitted with radio transmitters," was enough for me. I did

not have to read further, to the part about laparotomies and the other indignities that would be performed on the birds.

Of all the bird-men debating the issue, Koford's view of what a condor is is the subtlest and most complex, and thus, I think, has the best chance of being right.

Something seems to happen, often, to men for whom wildlife becomes a profession. The USFWS and Audubon people have become so concerned with the problem of the bird that they have lost sight of what a *bird* is. What use to us is a great soarer that has been handled, marked, laparotomized, popcorned by zoo crowds, and radio-tagged? What use is such a bird to itself? What the world does not need is a flying Pleistocene radio station.

Having dreamed up a neat bit of technology with an application to biology—a miniature transmitter—we are compelled to try it out. It *is* neat, but it will never tell us as much about condors as the human eye, with a patient brain behind it, the instruments Koford used back in 1939.

I suspect, along with Koford, that capture will do more harm than good, that condors will breed themselves better than humans can breed them. To think otherwise is another instance of *hubris* in the species that has brought condors low.

And what if nothing can bring the birds back? What if *Gymnogyps*, watching Los Angeles sprawl toward its last hills, has simply decided it is time to go? Perhaps feeding on ground squirrels, for a bird that once fed on mastodons, is too steep a fall from glory. If it is time for the condor to follow *Teratornis*, it should go out unburdened by radio transmitters.

Departing, the condor might do us a final service, in the manner of mineshaft canaries. They might open our eyes. When the *vultures* watching your civilization begin dropping dead from their snags, it is time to pause and wonder.

The California condor is a majestic bird seen in its natural rugged environment as it sweeps in superbly controlled flight over crests of ridges and great slopes of tangled chaparral. The air passing through its wing tips sets up a steady whine as it is pressed into service to keep the great glider aloft. The condor passes overhead, the sound recedes, and the bird now circles and scans with keen eyes the ground below and the activities of its fellow condors. Here is a picture long to be remembered, a heritage from the past displaying the acme of a specialization for flight which we are still privileged to view as part of our natural esthetic resource.

Pessimism has long prevailed about the ability of the Calfornia condor to survive as man takes more thorough control of the country within its range. The condor can not live with man, some people have said; though harmless, it can not survive the changes brought about by him; it is a passing remnant of the Pleistocene. But through several decades of such an attitude of defeatism the condor has hung on as though to prove it could, yet threatened at every turn with extinction and indeed doomed should a few unfortunate accidents take place and a further invasion of its stronghold be allowed. Man will certainly fail to save the California condor unless he tries to save it, and the trying is eminently worth while as anyone with even the most rudimentary appreciation of nature will agree who has actually watched wild condors living in their native mountains.

—ALDEN MILLER

California Condors, Forever Free?
Conservation
Interview, Fall of 1979

THE DEFINITIVE source on condor behavior and biology is *The Cali-*
fornia Condor. In the early 1940's, Dr. Carl Koford immersed himself
for three years in thorough observational study of condors in the
wild, then wrote the book. From that point till his death in 1979, he
became the most informed biologist on the condor as well as an out-
spoken opponent of the capture program. Dr. Koford's further observational studies of wildlife species are unsurpassed in many respects.
He spent two years in the Peruvian highlands and published a
monograph on the vicuna. Later he studied the ecology of prairie
dogs on the Great Plains, bats in Panama, rhesus monkeys introduced on Carribean Islands, feral goats on the Galapagos, monkeys
in Japan and Uganda, Jaguars and Ocelots in South America, and
pumas in California. In the course of other projects he observed grif-
fon vultures in Africa and India, king vultures in Panama, and Andean condors in Peru and Chile. For his work on condors, he won the
annual Terrestrial Ecology award of the Wildlife Society. He received
a Ph.D. in Zoology from the University of California, Berkeley. Kenneth Brower's "Night of the Condor" (chapter 1) is a dual profile—of
Carl and the condor.

"Forever Free" first appeared in the newsletter of the Santa Monica
Bay Audubon Society in 1979. "Conservation" is excerpted from *The*
California Condor (Dover, 1953).

Tim Bowles

California Condors, Forever Free?

SUPERBLY FITTED to soar dozens of miles from mountain roosts to distant scattered food supplies, the huge California condor symbolizes wildness in a landscape increasingly modified by man. Must we further dilute the natural scene by manhandling the birds and injecting cage-raised stock into condor society?

Such action is proposed in a recent (January 1979) plan of the U.S. Fish and Wildlife Service entitled "Draft Recommendations for Implementing the California Condor Contingency Plan." This Draft, based largely on a scientific Advisory Panel Report (Audubon Conservation Report No. 6, 1978), proposes many unarguably beneficial measures such as studies of condor nestings, experiments with turkey vultures, and analysis of food supplies for contaminants. But it also proposes some drastic, artificial procedures such as: Trap all free-living condors. Mark them with metal wing bands, plastic streamers, throat-skin tattoos and radio transmitters. Hold them at least three days for sex determination, possibly including tranquilizer injections and laparotomy. For a captive group, take nine birds during the first two years and ultimately all wild condors. Retain all captured immatures and take most eggs and nestlings over a period of five years. Eventually release birds in recent and former condor range.

The plan is to attract birds down to a carcass and catch them with a clap-trap (spring-loaded clamshell net) or cannon-projected net. Even with great care the trapped birds will suffer physiological and psychological stress, and some will be injured in their struggles. Transport and holding for sexing will increase risks of exposure to avian diseases. After examination, some will be released. But even a minor injury to wings could affect the flight and other abilities of the released birds, and monitoring for a few hours or days may not reveal all the adverse effects. As in other social animals, confinement can induce loss of social rank after release and may cause fighting.

The intended capture area, Tejon Ranch in the Tehachapi Mountains, is the present center of condor activity and therefore seems to be the most harmful site to cause disturbance. Birds escaping capture may be frightened so that they hesitate to descend to other food, which is then claimed by competitors. Further, even during incubation, each parent can spend periods of up to 24 hours away from its nest and travel widely, as I found out during a nesting study in 1939 ("The California Condor," 1953). Some smaller African vultures feed more than 40 miles from their cliff nests. And in every month of the year there is danger of capturing or injuring an adult with distant dependent young. The proposed winter capture period, November to March, overlaps both the period of fledging (starting in September) and of laying (starting February). Even during the biennial breeding "holiday" of an adult, its capture may break up an established pair.

Inasmuch as condors retain immature plumage until about their sixth year, removal of all immatures for a period of five years will prevent addition of any new breeding stock to the wild population until at least 1990, when young hatched in 1984 become adult. Every immature represents the total survival resulting from several nestings; hence, loss of even one will significantly reduce the potential for new breeders to add several young to the population over succeeding decades.

The efficiency and permanence of the intended marking gadgets are unproven for use on mountain-dwelling birds that may live more than 30 years. Returns on banded African vultures have been poor, even over periods of less than two years. Rugged topography and cave-roosting habits will interfere with line-of-sight radio transmissions, even though signals will presumably be monitored from aircraft. Colored streamers on condors might affect social relations, as the orange head, red throat, and white wing patches apparently function as signals during some aggressive and sexual displays.

Nesting condors are sensitive to disturbance, although the dangers may not be obvious. In early stages, I think that a single flushing of an adult could lead to nest desertion. Flushing during incubation endangers the egg by breakage or cooling, and later disturbance exposes the nestling to ravens, delays its feeding, and may induce premature fledging. If parents sometimes closely approach a photographer near a nest, it is because of apprehension for the safety of their nestling, not a sign of tameness. For some active nests, absence of a nestling late in the season has been taken to mean fledging success, whereas the actual fate of the young was unknown. At least two fledglings have been found dead below nest caves. And where a nesting has survived many disturbances, as at the one I observed on more than 100 days in 1939, the site was not used in subsequent years. Eleven nestings were reported in 1966-1967, mostly in the Sespe Sanctuary, but increased searching effort in 1968 revealed only one, far distant. Further, the fact that in one cliff condors nested in four successive years suggests to me that the first three young died before the next nesting season. Several people had visited the site each year, and some photographed the chick at close range. The Contingency Plan of 1976, prepared by a Recovery Team, did not recommend any nest invasions. All nests should remain inviolate.

In a breeding program supervised by Ray Erickson at Patuxent, eight young Andean condors have been raised from 21 eggs over a period of eight years. But it seems doubtful that cage-breeding of California birds will be so "easy." In Peru and Chile, I have observed Andean condors, and compared to our birds they are tougher, better adapted for walking and running, and they have far broader ecological tolerances as shown by their vast breeding range, over 3000 miles long including low and high elevations, wet and dry sites. There are still good numbers in Argentina and Chile. The Andean condor spends far more time in sexual activities, has a longer breeding season, a shorter interval between nestings, and apparently a shorter period of juvenile dependency, according to a 2-year field study by Jerry McGahan. At least 15 California condors have been kept for periods of two to 40 years in zoos but only one is known to have laid eggs, of which none proved fertile. Have any Andean condors hatched in captivity nested successfully?

Forced laying of more than one egg every other year, the natural rate, by removing the egg or nestling, imposes on the female physiological stresses which may shorten her reproductive life and decrease her lifetime egg production. The prolific Andean condor in San Diego Zoo laid for only eleven years. Taking eggs in the wild, with the idea of stimulating re-laying in the same season (i.e., double-clutching), if successful, would advance the fledging date into the most severe part of winter, with consequent danger to both juvenile and parents.

If condors are not surviving well in the wild, why should we expect released cage-raised birds to do better? In the wild they must forage skillfully, know the landscape and air currents, seek appropriate shelter at night and in storms, cope with aggressive eagles, and compete with established condors. All poultry raisers know the difficulties of adding to an established flock a new bird; it is generally rejected if not killed. The release of over 100 captive-raised peregrine falcons in the U.S. since 1973 has resulted in poor survival and no known nesting (Peregrine Fund Newsletter No. 6, 1978). Recent Florida small vulture experiments consisting of taking nestlings from parents, holding the birds for two weeks or so, and releasing them near a roost, are of scant value in predicting socialization of condors released in wild environment. Further, the added birds cannot benefit the population unless they survive to maturity, breed, and produce young that in turn survive and reproduce. The need is to enlarge the wild *breeding* population; it seems unlikely that captive-raised condors will be good breeders.

Actually this Draft does not state the need for any captures; rather, it aims to supply captive methodology, roughly similar to that used to build a captive flock of whooping cranes. Year to year changes in numbers and in proportion of immatures are uncertain. The Contingency Plan of 1976 concluded that there were "well over 40" condors and that most adults were not even attempting to nest, but the Panel Report of 1978 stated that a reasonable number was between 20 and 30, and that breeding rate was about normal for that number. An official "minimum" estimate of 53 condors in 1969 was revised downward in 1974 to only 39, using the same data and interpretive rules. The Panel found available data too meagre for reliable numerical estimation of population characteristics.

A decrease of roughly ten birds during the past dozen years

could have been caused by many factors including shooting, nest area disturbances, consumption of poisoned food, and seasonal food shortages, all remedial without captures. The estimated decline may be partly caused by decrease in the concentration of large numbers at sites where they can be counted. Group size reflects food distribution and weather; it is not necessarily proportional to the total population size. The Panel concluded that population monitoring had been inadequate, and discovery of all nestings improbable. Perhaps the best indicator of welfare, as in many game species, is the proportion of immatures. The Draft estimates that there are at present six or seven immatures, a number which indicates a pronounced increase over the estimates of four in 1974 and five in 1975. In the light of this encouragement, why should we intervene?

To summarize, the Draft Recommendations emphasize trapping, marking, propagation and release. But these dramatic artificial methods seem too expensive and controversial for efficient action. And their overall benefits are doubtful, whereas their esthetic and biological harm to the wild population seems certain. Further, if we remove most of the condors from the wild, how will we be able to study them to find the environmental troubles that led to decrease? When the health of an individual fails, the normal course of action is to review life history, examine current condition and symptoms, diagnose cause of abnormalities, prescribe remedies, and monitor the course of treatment. The condor population is like a delicate organism, and the same course is logical. But the capture plan largely neglects the first three steps and prescribes heroic measures which have ugly side effects. If we bring condors to depend on captive reproduction, we will invalidate the argument that certain mountain areas are crucial for protection of nest sites, and developers will press for use.

The Draft omits mention of many welfare influences; presumably these will be incorporated in a revised overall Recovery Plan. How can we assure that no condors will be shot? How can we reduce competition with golden eagles, which are dominant over condors at food, fly earlier and later in the day, nest earlier in the year in some of the same cliffs, are strongly territorial, and sometimes chase condors in the air. Golden eagles outnumber condors in much of the condor range and usurp much potential condor food. Black bears have also increased and they take condor food in the mountains. To what extent are condors feeding on deer, which have decreased greatly since the mid 1960s? Has food supply been enlarged by the increased hunting for feral pigs? There are more than 7,000 in San Benito County alone. What can be done to reduce the aerial broadcast of compound 1030 poisoned grain to kill ground squirrels on private lands in condor range? Poisoning will probably resume in May of this year. A recent USFWS-EPA report confirmed that after such poisoning, many dead squirrels, coyotes, bobcats, and rabbits were exposed on the surface. Have condors been eating these recently, as they did formerly? Are water supplies adequate in summer, and bathing pools accessible; the pools were an important feature of major condor roosts in the past. What is the extent and effect of ectoparasites? Bedbugs infested my studied nestling and may have caused it to leave the nest cave prematurely. How can we induce more condors to use the western portion of their range? Would a managed herd with artificial predation be feasible as a means of supplying clean food to condors? Is it practicable to determine seasonal distribution of feeding condors and their food by means of aerial surveys?

To judge the true condition of the condor population and to plan wisely for its future, the first need is for a complete list of verified facts about the bird and its environment. For examples, we need tabulations of all individual nest histories; up-to-date maps of occurrence by locality, season, frequency, and type of activity; description of seasonal distribution, quality, and quantity of potential and actual food supplies, and of factors influencing these; surveys of use of compound 1080 and other dangerous pesticides in condor feeding range; analyses of observed relations between condors and other animals; compilation of comparative data on population dynamics of other large carrion-feeding birds; lists of legal violations and their outcomes; and appraisal of turkey vulture habits and welfare in condor range. Intensive new work will help to fill-in information gaps. It may be feasible to identify all immatures individually and to keep track of their annual travels and survival rates. Once the relevant data are available, scientists and administrators can use these as a basis to advise additional specialized research and to formulate sound conservation policy.

Do we want to replace wild condors with cage-bred hand-raised birds? A wild condor is much more than feathers, flesh, and genes. Its behavior results not only from its anatomy and germ plasm but from its long cultural heritage, learned by each bird from previous generations through several years of immature life. A cage-raised bird can never be more than a partial replicate of a wild condor. If we cannot preserve condors in the wild through understanding their environmental relations, we have already lost the battle and may be no more successful in preserving mankind.

Aldo Leopold said that the recreational value of wildlife is inversely proportional to its artificiality. Condors are nesting in the wild; several immatures are striving toward adulthood. We can insure their eventual maturity and consequent growth of the wild population through elimination of damage by human activities, preservation of sufficient condor habitat including its organisms, and wise application of sound biological knowledge. Let us keep condors forever free.

Conservation

I NASMUCH as the condor has persisted in spite of apathy and predictions of its early extinction, let us be optimistic and assume that the species will persist indefinitely if we will give it aid. In the course of the past 60 years, the attitude of those who have written about condors has been mainly one of pessimism and of resignation to the approaching extinction of the species. An article written by Cooper in 1890 was entitled, "A Doomed Bird." Beebe (1906) stated: "Its doom is near; within a few years at most, the last individual will have perished." Loye Miller (1937) wrote that the condor had developed a "strong candidacy for the pluperfect status" and asked (1942), "Is it not a species with one foot and even one wing in the grave?" Sheldon (1939) wrote that the condor had "outlived its time" and that it was "on the trail of the dodo." Many of the older generation hold this pessimistic view.

Grinnell, in a letter written in 1937 to a prominent ornithologist, criticized this pessimistic viewpoint and pointed out that of course the condor was doomed to extinction if human attitudes toward it did not change and if nothing were done, but that one could adduce evidence that the human race itself was also doomed. Pessimism leads to apathy and defeatism. The major obstacle to all attempts to aid the condor has been the lack of interest of persons capable of effective action.

Major mortality and welfare factors

Wanton shooting. — A condor seems to be a tempting target for a man or boy with a gun. Cooper (1890) and Stephens (1919) gave shooting as one of the main reasons for the decrease in the numbers of condors. E. T. Mendenhall and J. B. Dixon, of San Diego County, told me that in the late 1800's it was the ambition of every boy to shoot a condor. W. Lee Chambers (1936) had a sporting goods store near Santa Monica from 1896 to

1905. At about that time the first high-powered sporting rifles came into use and there was much indiscriminate shooting. Two condors which had been shot were brought into Chambers' store about 1905. In December, 1908, an immature condor was shot near the Finley nest by a constable (Finley, 1928). About 1910, the Peyton brothers found a wounded condor which had been shot (specimen). Boys shot two condors near Santa Paula in 1916 (specimens).

In 1925, the San Diego Natural History Museum was given a freshly mounted condor by an anonymous party with the stipulation that no questions be asked. In 1927, a hunter drove into Santa Barbara with a condor, which he had shot, tied to his car (specimen). In 1929, a young condor, shot through the wing, was found near Fillmore. This bird survived for 10 years at the Zoo in San Diego. About 1932, a condor which had been shot was found near Lebec by Harold Bowhay of Bakersfield. The bird died in captivity. In 1940, a hunter told me of the location of a condor which he said had been shot. I found the carcass, but it was too decomposed to allow verification of the cause of death.

In 1944, a rancher flushed a large group of condors near Porterville. One struck a wire fence and was injured. The rancher shot it and the specimen was mounted. Another rancher admitted to me that a few years ago he shot several times at a large bird in the belief that it was a golden eagle before he saw that it was a condor. A sheep rancher, who killed two golden eagles in San Luis Obispo County about 1946, said that he would shoot any condors which he saw near his sheep. He refused to be convinced that condors were not predatory. This was the only rancher that I found to bear malice toward condors.

It is not improbable that, on the average, at least one condor is shot each year. There are several thousand hunters on some ranger districts on the Los Padres National Forest in the first week of the deer hunting season. Many of these hunters are from distant areas and they have not heard of condors. Those sportsmen who are acquainted with condors generally state that they would not shoot one but that they believe that many other hunters would shoot anything. On a few occasions I saw men shooting with rifles at turkey vultures in areas within the range of condors.

Collecting. —I know the present location of 130 skins or mounted specimens of the condor. Those institutions having five or more such specimens are: American Museum of Natural History (18), U.S. National Museum (16), Los Angeles County Museum (14), Museum of Comparative Zoology (14), California Academy of Sciences (11), Chicago Museum of Natural History (7), Museum of Vertebrate Zoology (7), British Museum (5). Most of these specimens were collected for "scientific purposes." One collector, Frank Arundell, assisted in the shooting of 10 condors for museum specimens about 30 years ago. E. B. Towne acquired about 13 condors from various hunters. In 1884 and 1885, H. W. Henshaw gathered about nine specimens, all apparently from hired hunters (Harris, 1941).

Perhaps the highest price ever paid for the skin of a condor was the £45 received by W. C. Blake (1895) from Rothschild. About 1917 a well known museum in California refused to pay a collector more than $200 for collecting three condors. The last legally taken specimens were procured about 1920. In all, approximately 200 condors or their eggs have been taken as specimens. Undoubtedly collecting activity has contributed significantly to the decline of the condor in some areas.

Poison. —For nearly 100 years, most of the published accounts of condors have included the statement that many condors were killed by feeding on carcasses which had been poisoned for the purpose of killing carnivores. Alexander Taylor (1859) related that condors were often killed by feeding on meat which had been poisoned with strychnine. Beebe (1906) stated that "hundreds" of condors had perished from poison. Henshaw (1920) wrote that "hundreds fell victims of the poisoned meat which the sheep herders put out for the purpose of killing the bears, cougars, and coyotes which preyed upon the sheep." As late as March 14, 1949, the Los Angeles Times stated that many condors had died from eating poisoned meat which had been set out for coyotes. Cooper (1890), Stephens (1919), and others have considered poisoning to be one of the main causes for a decrease in the number of condors in the late 1800's.

The only reported "observation" which indicates that a condor may have died from eating poisoned bait is given in a mimeographed pamphlet by Fry (1926). He claims that in 1890 he saw two dead condors which a sheepherder had found near a poisoned carcass. Bleitz (1946) states that arsenic was found in the remains of a chick which died in the nest. As the body of this bird lay for a week in a cabinet which was normally used for specimens preserved with arsenic, and as arsenic is rarely used as a poison for squirrels or carnivores, the poison found in the specimen was probably acquired after death.

An intensive program of control of ground squirrels by means of grain poisoned with thallium sulphate was commenced in the foraging range of the condor about 1926. Many birds and mammals which fed on the poisoned squirrels were killed by the poison. Among the carnivorous birds reported to be killed were ravens, red-tailed hawks, golden eagles, and turkey vultures (Linsdale, 1931). Many persons became alarmed about the possible effect of the poison on condors. One letter (November 20, 1935) from a government official to an inquiring citizen stated that, on the basis of experiments on "raptorial birds," a condor would have to eat 20 squirrels at a feeding to be seriously affected and it would have to eat five squirrels a day for two or three months to accumulate a lethal dose. If this information is correct for condors, it is probable that some condors have acquired a lethal or near lethal dose of thallium.

The fact that the bodies of condors killed by poison have not been found in poisoned areas is not evidence that such poisoning does not occur, for it is unlikely that the birds would die at the site of feeding. Grinnell (letter June 1, 1935) pointed out that although thallium might not kill a condor, the poison might weaken the bird so that it would succumb during periods of food scarcity or severe weather, and that the poison might affect the endocrine system.

Commencing in 1945 a new poison replaced thallium in much of the feeding range of the condor. This poison is Compound 1080 (sodium flouroacetate). Joseph Keyes and others of the Fish and Wildlife Service watched for the effects of this poison on condors and other birds during trial applications in Kern County. So far, neither condors nor turkey vultures have been found to be killed by eating squirrels poisoned with 1080. Experiments on the toxicity of 1080 have been carried out (National Research Council, 1948). For a ground squirrel, the minimum lethal dose of 1080 is about .5 milligrams per kilogram of body weight as against 25 milligrams for thallium.

The results of experiments on the feeding of Compound 1080 to eagles and vultures were as follows (*ibid.*: 3):

Bird	Number	Dosage	Per cent killed
Golden eagle	8	5.0 mg./kg.	50
Turkey vulture	7	20.0 mg./kg.	71
Black vulture	10	15.0 mg./kg.	50

Judged by these results, a turkey vulture would have to eat as much as 40 times its own weight in poisoned squirrels before it would probably be killed. The amount would be less if the contents of the cheek pouches and stomach were eaten or if the squirrel had ingested more than the minimum lethal dose. At least in rats, "the ingestion of sub-lethal doses of 1080 has shown no significant cumulative effect" (National Research Council, 1948). Perhaps, then, the use of Compound 1080 is less dangerous to condors than the use of thallium. Again, however, the physiological effect of the ingestion of sublethal doses of this poison over a long period might well be harmful to condors.

In southern California, ranchers poison coyotes and other carnivores by putting out chunks of pork containing capsules of strychnine. It is conceivable that occasionally a condor eats one of these baits. To a limited degree, strychnine poisoned grain is used to poison squirrels. This poison acts very fast so that a high proportion of the squirrels die outside of their burrows where they are accessible to carnivorous birds. So far as I know, its effect on vultures has not been tested. We can only discover the true dangers of poison by experimentation on living condors, and none can be spared for this purpose.

Trapping.—A condor was caught in a coyote trap set by a state trapper on Tejon Ranch in February, 1939. One toe of the bird was nearly pulled off. The toe was amputated and the bird was released (P. S. Sprague, letter March 2, 1939). Early in 1941, a trapper for Kern County found a condor in one of his traps and released it (B. L. Fox, letter March 13, 1941). In November, 1947, an immature condor was found in a coyote trap by Lester Arnold, game warden of Kern County. The trap had been set by the carcass of a cow. The leg of the bird was broken and the bird was so badly injured that it could not be saved. It died and was sent to the Los Angeles County Museum (L. Arnold, letter February 13, 1949). Eben McMillan told me that two condors were caught in traps near Avenales Ranch about 1935. One bird died and the other was released.

Doubtless there have been several other instances of the trapping of condors in recent years, for the trapping campaign is intensive in many areas which condors frequent. Most trappers would not advertise the fact that they had caught a condor. Normally trappers employ a double set and use liquid scent rather than bait. After a coyote is caught, it usually springs the second trap, so that condors which feed on trapped coyotes are not usually in danger. Traps set near carcasses are dangerous to condors, but the normal practice is to set the trap in a trail which leads to a carcass, not at the carcass itself.

Accidents.—Inasmuch as condors alight in a rather clumsy fashion, it is probable that they often injure their wings. About 1934, some boys found an emaciated young condor with a broken wing. The bird died in captivity and it is now mounted in the courthouse at Ventura. Early in 1941, I found a dead juvenile on a high grassy ridge near Fillmore. The humerus of the bird was broken but there was no other apparent injury. When found, the bird lay a few yards from a slender vertical pipe which had been used as a surveying marker. I believe that the condor had collided with the pipe in soaring low over the ridge.

At one nest, I found a nestling in an apparently retarded state of development. It left the nest in late fall and its remains were found several hundred feet from a point below the nest. One wing of the bird had been broken apparently before the bird left the nest, and had healed in an irregular manner. Daggett (1898) tells of an immature condor with a broken wing which was captured. While confined in a cage at the National Zoological Park, a young condor (U.S.N.M. 804) suffered four fractures of wing and leg bones, without apparent cause, during one summer and autumn.

In early June one parent arrived at nest 1 with a severe leg injury. The bird could scarcely walk and it generally stood with the injured leg off the ground. It spent long periods in sitting on the nest cliff. Four months after the injury was noticed, this bird still walked with a limp. In June, 1941, an adult condor was found dead in a water tank on the Still Ranch near Annette. Presumably the bird had entered the tank to drink and had been unable to get out. Oil workers near Maricopa told Robinson (1939) that about 1927 several condors were killed by wading into pools of oil "in the belief that it was water."

Starvation. —Condors which are unable to fly well because of injury or sickness probably die of starvation or thirst. On the other hand, condors weakened by starvation may be killed by other agencies. For these reasons, there is no record of a condor which has died solely of starvation. The majority of the condors observed by me seemed to be able to find food on every day when the weather was suitable. I encountered no emaciated condors, but a nesting adult observed by H. M. Hill (MS) in June seemed to be thin and light in weight.

From the standpoint of food, winter is the most critical period for condors. The hours of the day which are suitable for soaring are few. Storms preclude foraging on some days. Juveniles are entirely dependent and must be fed. Many condors gather in the principal nesting region so that adults with young must compete with other condors. Livestock is withdrawn to the lower parts of its range. There are no carcasses of poisoned squirrels. Cold probably increases the need for food.

Fire. —The roosting and nesting areas of condors have often been swept by fire. About 1917, a fire burned from the Piru River to the Sespe River and included some nesting and roosting sites. Another fire swept the lower Sespe region about 1928. In 1933, a fire in central Ventura County burned off the area about a nesting site known to Sidney Peyton. I found burned sticks in one nest. In 1939, fire swept the area of the condor roosts at McChesney Mountain. In 1941 there were two brush fires within half a mile of nest sites in the Sespe region. On the Los Padres National Forest, where many condors roost and nest, about 90 per cent of the fires are caused by man (F. P Cronemiller, verbal).

Some effects of fire are of benefit to condors. Animals suitable for food may be killed. Areas of thick brush where condors could not find food or reach it are opened up by fire. Many of the favorite perches and roosts of condors are fire-killed conifers. Fire apparently has not caused condors to abandon any roosting area permanently.

As most fires occur in summer when young condors are still in the nest, young could be suffocated by smoke. After they leave the nest, flightless juveniles could be burned by fire. The thick chaparral which protects some nesting areas from disturbance by man is removed by fire.

The main purpose of the Los Padres National Forest is the protection of the watershed from fire. Adequate protection requires the construction of roads, trails, and firebreaks. In some areas, this construction has made the roosts and nests of condors easily accessible to man and construction work has disturbed the birds. Thus, there is a conflict between those who would protect the condors from man and those who would protect the forest from fire. The increased use of aerial patrol for fire detection on the national forests has decreased the amount of travel on roads and trails by forest personnel and has increased efficiency of fire protection. It is hoped that new methods will decrease the necessity for expansion of the system of roads and trails on the national forests.

Roads and trails. —In many roosting and nesting areas, the natural closure by brush and ruggedness has been eliminated by the development of roads and trails. Dynamiting and the noise of heavy machinery and trucks can seriously disturb condors at a long distance. The construction of an aqueduct along the upper San Luis Rey River in the early 1900's probably contributed to the cessation of nesting there. On Breckenridge Mountain a public road passes within a few hundred yards of trees in which condors roost, and there are many summer homes nearby. Condors have been seen over each of the four United States highways which pass out of the southern San Joaquin Valley, and I have seen condors on the ground within a few hundred feet of some State highways. Several years ago it was planned to place a dam in lower Sespe Canyon and to build a resort at Sespe Hot Springs. Fortunately for the condors, these plans did not materialize.

Some of the changes in roads and trails during the past 30 years have decreased the accessibility of areas inhabited by condors. At one time there was a road for several miles up lower Sespe Canyon and there was a resort in the lower part of the canyon. Floods demolished the road so that the area became accessible only by a makeshift foot trail. A recently constructed truck trail has partly reopened this area to travel. Many trails and firebreaks which were made in the 1930's have disappeared because of the growth of chaparral. If the present trends in government economy continue, it is doubtful that these trails will ever be restored.

During the period of active field work, little logging was being done in the range of the condor. This activity has increased with the rise in the price of lumber and logging has occurred near at least one nest (Tulare County). Extensive operations have been carried out on Bear Mountain, Kern County, where condors roost. As these operations are of the selective type which results in minimal disturbance of the forest, and as roosting trees are generally poor for lumber, the main harm of logging has been in the increased development of roads and the consequent influx of people.

Oil development.—Exploration and drilling for oil and gas have had an adverse effect upon condors in several important areas. Many oil workers are from out of the state and they have little knowledge of, or respect for, California game laws. Men working far from towns are none too apt to observe bird protective regulations. Roads to the drilling sites make condors accessible to persons who shoot from automobiles and to well-meaning but not harmless photographers and sightseers. In the vicinity of Bakersfield, Maricopa, and McKittrick, oil fields occupy large areas which would otherwise be used for grazing.

The discovery of oil in the Cuyama Valley has encouraged the mineral leasing of a great deal of land in the Los Padres National Forest. In Sespe Canyon there are several oil wells in operation. One long-abandoned derrick is located within half a mile of current nesting site. A few years ago a well was drilled at the foot of a small canyon in which at least three formerly-used nesting sites are located. The region where most of my nesting observations were made was accessible because of a road which had been built for the purpose of hauling oil drilling equipment but which was little used.

During World War II an oil exploration company built a road into the center of a principal winter roosting and nesting canyon. This road passes within a few hundred yards of four nest sites known to me. For three years before the installation of a locked Forest Service gate, this road gave easy access to the area to photographers and others who disturbed the nesting birds. In the last few years this road has been seldom used and much of it has been destroyed by erosion. Although a large proportion of the important condor nesting area in Ventura County has been leased from time to time, most of the interest has been in buying and selling leases rather than in drilling and production.

Photographers. —Condors have been photographed a great deal. In 1906, Bohlman and Finley took about 250 photographs of two adult condors and their young one. Although the photographs were taken on slow glass plates, they surpass any series of still pictures of the condor which have been taken with modern high-speed equipment. J. R. Pemberton took several thousand feet of colored 16-millimeter motion pictures of condors between 1936 and 1941. Ed N. Harrison and Telford Work have each taken hundreds of feet of motion pictures as well as many colored still photographs of condors. John H. Storer photographed condors in slow motion in order to study their flight. Don Bleitz has taken a good series of colored still pictures and I have taken a few hundred pictures in black and white. Several other persons have many photographs of condors. Just about every activity except the mating display and copulation has been adequately photographed.

The activities of photographers have been far from harmless to condors. The failure of some nests known to me was probably due, at least in part, to the activity of these men. Even with great care, a party which I assisted kept the nesting adult from the egg or chick on some occasions. Other photographers were much less solicitous of the welfare of the birds and some of their activities were literally cruel. Even when photographing a large bird with a telephoto lens, one must be comparatively close to the subject. The use of a blind does not preclude disturbance. Few men are qualified to judge whether a condor is acting in a normal undisturbed fashion. There is little to be gained by attempting to obtain more photographs of these birds.

Minor mortality and welfare factors

Sickness and disease.—Cooper (1890) encountered a torpid adult condor perched on a hillside in May, 1872. He approached close to the bird but it did not move except to open its bill. There was no external evidence of disease, injury, or recent feeding. Wilson (1928) captured an adult condor which could not fly. The bird disgorged some food and did not fly after it was released, but it was gone by the next day. On January 1, 1937, on Tejon Ranch, Perry Sprague captured an adult condor which could not fly. The bird was put in a pen. It disgorged everything shortly after eating. About 10 days later it died in an emaciated condition.

A condor in the New York Zoological Park died in 1913 of indigestion. According to Lee Crandall, the bird was sick for a long time but it showed improvement for a short time after it was given bicarbonate of soda in its drinking water. Rett (1946) examined the remains of an adult condor which had been found dead near a water trough. The processes of the femur and tibia of one leg were eaten away almost entirely by a disease similar to osteomyelitis.

Eating foreign objects.—As condors peck and nibble at various indigestible objects, it is not surprising that they sometimes swallow harmful materials. A condor at the New York Zoological Park died in 1906 from eating an elastic band. Dissection of a condor which died at the National Zoological Park in 1905 revealed a small stick protruding through the wall of its stomach. A condor died after 10 years in the zoo at San Diego from eating a strip of rubber which it had pulled from a hose. According to the keeper, Karl Koch, this bird had been very ill on a previous occasion but it had been cured by pushing a hose down its throat and thus apparently freeing some obstruction.

Storm.—Rett (1938) examined two condors which were found dead near the carcass of a horse after a hailstorm. The condition of the bodies suggested that the birds had been killed by hailstones. It is conceivable that if a period of severe cold should immediately follow a period of wet fog or rain, condors roosting in the open could be rendered flightless by the formation of ice in their feathers. Storms may prevent foraging and thus facilitate starvation. Stormy winds might increase the possibility of flight accidents.

Killing for quills. —In accounts of the condor, it has often been stated that many condors were shot so that their quills could be made into containers for carrying gold dust. The main support for the idea that this practice was common is the account of condors in Lower California by Anthony (1893). He wrote: "Every Indian and Mexican gold miner is provided with from one to six of the primary quills of this species for carrying gold dust. . . . All [only two recorded] of the dead birds that I saw in Lower California had been killed for their quills alone." J. D. Reyes, resident of Cuyama Valley since 1887, told me that the quills of condors and other large birds were formerly used for carrying gold dust and that they were sold for a dollar each.

Two persons told me that a certain man, who collected condors in Ventura County about 1900, shot condors to get feathers to use for bee brushes. Sidney Peyton, an experienced bee keeper, assures me that a condor feather would make a very poor bee brush.

Indians. —Among some tribes of Indians in southern California there was an annual mourning ceremony or feast at which a condor or other large bird was killed. According to Kroeber (1925), among the Luisenos the nests of eagles and condors were personal and hereditary property, and the young were sometimes taken from the nest and reared. An account of an annual feast at which a condor was killed and skinned is given in Boscana's "Chinigchinich" (Harris, 1941). Scott gives a similar account from his own inquiries (*in* Bent, 1937). At the Rincon Indian Reservation, Scott (MS) saw two dancing skirts made of the large feathers of condors. Edward Davis of Mesa Grande has a similar skirt which the Indians made for him. In parts of the present area of San Diego County the taking of young condors for ceremonial purposes was once common.

Lassoing. —Some published accounts of the condor include the report that vaqueros used to lasso the birds for sport. I heard similar stories from ranchers and old-timers. Stephens (1899) gives an account of the lassoing of an adult condor at a carcass. The bird appeared stupid. It could run but apparently it could not fly. A vaquero rode up and lassoed it. The bird died, presumably from being choked by the rope. Bryant (1917) tells of another condor which was lassoed near a carcass. This bird died in Golden Gate Park six months later. I did not encounter any condors on the ground which could be approached close enough to lasso. Not improbably the birds which were caught in this manner were unable to fly because of sickness or injury.

"Penning."—Shields (1895) tells of hearing from an old-timer that condors were caught in former days by placing a carcass within a small pen so that a condor which alighted at the carcass would not have room to take off. I do not know of a first-hand account of this practice. Probably the story was borrowed from the account by Darwin (1909) of a similar method employed to capture South American condors in Chile.

False information.—False and harmful information about condors has often been printed, especially in newspapers. In the Los Angeles Times for July 6, 1934, there was a large drawing showing how a condor is "capable of carrying a fawn in its talons." The accompanying article was based on information from E. I. Dyer (1935) and others who wished to avoid erroneous and sensational publicity. The Newhall Sentinel for September 2, 1937, stated that a condor could easily pick up a sheep. These falsehoods encourage certain persons to shoot at condors.

The misinformation about the high value of eggs has often been repeated. Overemphasis of rarity leads egg collectors, photographers, and curious persons to seek condors and consequently to disturb them. The publication of false information cannot be stopped merely by making accurate information available. A few years ago an inquiring reporter for a national weekly magazine was furnished with accurate information on the status of the condor. The printed version featured, as fact, the oft published but unsubstantiated conjecture that condors had become rare because of eating poisoned baits.

Impractical proposals

"Artificial" feeding.—Feeding of condors by providing carcasses near their roosts is not practical except as an experiment. To provide a constant supply of food would entail much labor, expense, and waste. It would be difficult to insure that condors would get the meat and that other animals would not. Constant feeding at one locality would attract carnivores which might harm the feeding condors. A constant supply of food at one locality might keep condors from utilizing "natural" sources of

food and perhaps would cause numbers to concentrate in one area where they could be wiped out by some disaster. By association with humans the birds might lose some of the cautiousness which is necessary to their survival.

Transplanting.—The trapping of condors for release in areas which they formerly inhabited is not practical in such a mobile species. For any promise of success, one would have to trap a mated pair. Not only would this be difficult, because the sexes look alike, but there is no season when such a pair might be taken without danger of causing the death of their young. Probably a transplanted pair would try to return to the site of their nest or young. This plan does not seem feasible.

Actually condors transplant themselves through wandering, and when vagrants find suitable conditions at some extralimital location, they might remain and breed. The nesting in 1950 in Tulare County, more than 100 miles from the nearest previously known nest site, may be an example of this kind of extension in range. The amount of extralimital wandering and the tendency to repopulate formerly inhabited areas should increase if the total population increases in size.

Breeding in captivity.—Breeding condors in captivity should be attempted only after all efforts to maintain the natural population have failed. South American condors have been bred in a large cage at the Zoo in San Diego and have even been induced to produce one young every year instead of in alternate years. In some years the egg has been taken soon after laying and hatched in an incubator, and the parent birds raised a second chick in the same year. Possibly the same avicultural feat could be accomplished with California condors although courting activities in captives of this species are unknown. It is extremely doubtful that a condor raised by hand and lacking the experience gained by being raised in the wild could survive for long if released. Release of captive condors might well introduce zoo diseases into the wild population.

The beauty of California condor is in the magnificence of its soaring flight. A condor in a cage is uninspiring, pitiful, and ugly to one who has seen them soaring over the mountains. Condors are so few that their recreational value is one of quality rather than of quantity. As Leopold (1936) points out, the recreational value of wildlife is in inverse proportion to its artificiality. The thrill of seeing a condor is greatly diminished when the birds are being raised in captivity. Our objective should be to maintain and perhaps to increase the natural population of condors.

Recommendations

Protection by law.—About eighty years ago Cronise (1868) wrote that the condor should be protected by law from "reckless slaughter." Cooper (1890) stated that there was a law protecting the condor but that few persons knew of it. The present California law protects the condor as a nongame bird. Although the condor is excepted from scientific collectors' permits, permission was given in 1950 to the San Diego Zoo to take two young condors for the purpose of attempting to breed them in captivity. The Zoo personnel were unable to find a nest outside of the condor sanctuaries. In 1952 the California Fish and Game Commission granted the Zoo a permit to "trap and cage one pair."

The section of the Fish and Game Code (1963) under which the condor is protected is 3511. "Fully protected birds are: California condors (*Gymnogyps californianus*) . . . . Fully protected birds may not be taken at any time and no provision of this code or any other law shall be construed to authorize the issuance of permits or licenses to take any fully protected bird and no such permit or license heretofore issued shall have any force or effect for any such purpose." (Added by Stats. 1957, Ch. 1972.) The penalty for violation is a fine of not over $500 or imprisonment for not over six months, or both. Apparently only one person has ever been punished for killing a condor. He shot a condor near Pasadena in 1908 and tried to sell it, but he was apprehended and fined $50 (Finley, 1928).

I discovered by inquiry among hunters, ranchers and others in the field that federal laws are respected far more than are state laws. As a striking and unique species, threatened with extinction, the condor is of national interest and is deserving of strict federal protection.

A start toward federal protection was made in 1942 when the "Convention on Nature Protection and Wild Life Preservation in the Western Hemisphere," sometimes known as the "Natural Resources Treaty," became effective. In the Annex to this convention, the California condor was listed among those species whose protection (Article VIII) "is declared to be of special urgency and importance," and the United States agreed to protect it "as completely as possible." Perhaps because of the intervention of World War II, however, no federal laws were passed to implement the good intentions of the treaty. However, the Convention has already had a beneficial effect in that persons who live in the range of the condor are proud of the fact that condors have received official national recognition.

More recently the California condor has received official international recognition as a threatened species. In 1949, the International Technical Conference on the Protection of Nature at Lake Success included the condor in a list of 13 birds of the world which are "in need of emergency action if they are to be saved from extinction" (UNESCO, 1950). Of course mere recognition does not help the birds directly, but it focuses attention on the need for action, and it may lead to the passing of effective laws prohibiting the disturbance of condors or their nests.

Protection by closures.—The nesting and roosting areas of condors must be protected from disturbance by man. All the recently used nest sites known to me are within national forests, or, in one case, an Indian reservation. Three important roosting areas are outside of the national forests but these are not easily accessible by road and they are closed to the public by the surrounding landowners.

In 1937, an area of about 1200 acres surrounding Sisquoc Falls, Santa Barbara County, was closed to all travel and use by the United States Forest Service. This closure was in large measure due to the efforts of Robert E. Easton and the National Audubon Society. In order to make this closure effective, regulation T-9 of the rules and regulations governing the National Forests was modified so as to prohibit persons from going on areas closed for the protection of rare species. The amendment consisted of adding the following paragraph:

"(I) The unauthorized going or being upon any area which has been closed by the Chief, Forest Service, for the perpetuation and protection of (a) rare or vanishing species of plants or animals, (b) special biological communities, or (c) historical or archeological places or objects of interest; also the unauthorized going or being upon any area so closed for scientific experiments and investigations, or for other purposes where controlled use is necessary in order to insure proper treatment and protection. The boundaries of each area shall be defined by the Regional Forester and indicated in so far as practicable by posting notices along such boundaries and on roads and trails leading into such areas."

Previous to 1941 there were many deer hunters in the Sisquoc River region in late summer, but the permits required of hunters stipulated that they were not to enter the closed area and apparently there was no trespassing. The protection of this area has not been altogether effective in preventing the disturbance of condors there, for a well-used trail passes along the edge of the sanctuary and through a stand of large pines where condors often roost. This trail is much used by fishermen in spring. The disturbance of condors in this area has been greatly lessened by the recent practice of closing a large part of the forest to travel during the summer, including the deer hunting season, in order to reduce the danger of fire. The fire closure and the relative inaccessibility of the area seem, so far, to have afforded condors adequate protection in that region.

Partly as a result of the findings of this study, the Forest Service, in 1947, closed to public travel and use a large area around the lower Sespe River. Access corridors were provided for fishermen, ranchers, and oil well operators. The Forest Service provides a special condor patrolman for eight months of the year, the National Audubon Society contributing the cost of the first four months, and the Forest Service that of the last four months. This area, the Sespe Wildlife Preserve, includes most of the condor nesting sites and the principal winter roosts. As all the area was normally closed in summer because of the danger of fire, the closure did not result in any appreciable loss of recreational area to the public. Inasmuch as the laying of eggs commences in February and as most juvenile condors cannot fly well by the following January, a year around patrol by a permanent warden is recommended.

The creation of the Sespe Wildlife Preserve was not entirely effective in protecting nesting condors from disturbance, for the Forest Service had no power to prevent issuance of oil and gas leases within the preserve by the Department of the Interior. New oil discoveries in the general region stimulated oil and gas prospecting. The Forest Service recommended disapproval of applications for leases of land within the preserve. The applicants objected strongly. As a result, a public hearing was held by the Department of the Interior so that both conservationists and oil interests could present their views. The final outcome was the issuance, by the Secretary of the Interior, Oscar L. Chapman, of Public Land Order 695. This order states that 55 square miles of land in the Los Padres National Forest are "withdrawn from all forms of appropriation under the public-land laws, including the mining laws, and" with certain exceptions "the mineral-leasing laws, and reserved as a condor sanctuary, under the jurisdiction of the Forest Service."

Within the 16 square miles where the concentration of nests is especially great no entry to the surface of the ground is permitted, but oil and gas may be tapped by directional drilling from outside the area. Within the remaining 39 square miles oil and gas deposits may be developed and extracted "subject to the condition that no lessee shall use or invade, for any purpose, the surface of any such lands within one-half mile of a condor nest active within three years." Valid mineral leases in effect as of the date of the Withdrawal Order were not affected thereby, but all such, covering approximately half of the "closed" area, will have matured by late 1955; no extensions thereof, let alone new leases, will be granted without inclusion of the restrictive regulations called for by the Order. Many geologists believe that actual drilling operations will not prove feasible.

Many persons oppose every closure of public land. Sheldon (1939) takes the extreme view that by setting up a condor sanctuary, the public sacrifices the recreational value of a large area "in exchange for the extremely doubtful preservation of a bird of no value, esthetically or otherwise." To a lesser degree, this view is held by some hunters and hikers. Stockmen who graze cattle on parts of the national forests resent further restriction of grazing land. Oil prospectors and speculators in mineral leases oppose the withdrawal of land from mineral entry.

The "natural" closure of certain areas by their inaccessibility should be maintained as far as possible or even augmented by the rerouting or cessation of maintenance of certain roads and trails. In 1936, the construction of a fire road to the vicinity of Sisquoc Falls was halted far short of that site through the efforts of the National Audubon Society and a few interested persons. The welfare of condors and other wildlife should be considered in the planning of roads and trails.

Education.—Condors cannot be made to stay on the national forests or within any area which might be closed for their protection. Most of the feeding areas are on private lands. Therefore, the only way of completely protecting condors from molestation is through the cooperation of people throughout the range of condors. Sensational publicity is harmful in that it causes persons who otherwise would have no direct influence upon condors to seek the birds and to disturb them. Educational efforts should be concentrated primarily upon those persons who may encounter condors. The interest and cooperation of these people can best be gained by helping them to understand something of the relation of the condor to its environment rather than by giving them a list of "don'ts." The principal groups of persons, within or near the range of condors, who should be informed and who have the opportunity to pass on this information to others, are as follows:

United States Forest Service supervisors, rangers, patrolmen, lookouts, and guards.

State and county forestry and fire department officials and lookouts.

County agricultural commissioners and their assistants.

Game wardens and trappers.

Ranchers upon whose property condors feed.

Sportsmen's organizations.

Teachers of conservation and biology.

Where school is held for forest guards, there is an excellent opportunity for enlisting their interest in condors. Some other important groups can be informed at local meetings of cattlemen's and wool growers' associations.

The most effective means of education is through personal contact with individuals. Many persons have little respect for signs and they do not bother to read printed matter which is given to them. On parts of the national forests where there are checking stations or where hunting or camping permits are required, there is an opportunity for forest officials to inform persons individually before they enter areas inhabited by condors. One man, truly interested in condors, can do a great deal toward educating others. If eventually it is possible to employ permanently a man to guard the interests of condors in the field, this man should spend much more time in visiting persons throughout the condor range and securing their cooperation than in patrolling nesting areas against intruders. With education and cooperation, little, if any, patrolling probably would be necessary.

Food. —Maintaining or augmenting the supply of food can best be accomplished through the education and cooperation of stockmen. At present there are a few ranchers who, because of their interest in condors, leave carcasses which are in suitable locations for the birds. If, through the cooperation of county health authorities, there were a system of special inspection of carcasses for disease, many more carcasses could be left on the range instead of being destroyed. Trappers have a constant supply of carcasses and means for transporting them. They should be encouraged to leave carcasses at sites suitable for feeding by condors. To secure the help of ranchers and trappers and to guide them in their efforts in behalf of the condor, the constant service of man well acquainted with the birds is needed.

Carcasses of poisoned animals must be regarded as dangerous to condors until they are proven otherwise. The agricultural commissioners in the principal counties where condors feed on poisoned squirrels must be kept alert to this danger. Additional research on the physiological effects of eating poisoned mammals could be carried out on turkey vultures. If the poison proves harmful, gassing or other means of killing squirrels in their burrows should be encouraged where condors forage and the use of quick-acting poisons which cause squirrels to die outside of their burrows should be discouraged. Here again the need for a permanently employed field man who is interested in condors and well versed in their ways is needed.

Interview, Fall 1979

CARL KOFORD was interviewed by Friends of the Earth in the Fall of 1979. A slightly edited version of the taped interview follows. The interviewers were David Phillips, of Friends of the Earth; Mark Palmer, of the Sierra Club; and Steve Rauh, of the Conservation Press. In what follows, they lose their identity to *"Questioner."* The interview, tragically, was Carl Koford's last.

Questioner: Your research, especially the condor book, has been highly praised for its thoroughness despite the rugged country you were working in.

Koford: It was not really bad country because there was water in the potholes, so you didn't have to carry water. Normally, you know, you drink a gallon a day in hot country. It was the brush—learning how to get through the scrub oak and stuff—that was difficult. We didn't have mountain boots or anything like that in those days, but I got some logging boots with hobnails and they worked pretty well on the rocks. I wore out two or three pairs of those.

This was a fellowship, not a full-time job. I spent some time at Berkeley taking some courses I needed. Then I expanded my field work to other parts of the condor range during 1940 and early '41, finding some additional condor nests. But I was in the Naval ROTC and was ordered to active duty in the middle of June, 1941, so I had to leave everything and go.

I came back in March 1946, went to the same places again, and found condors nesting in some of the same holes again. That was when I met the McMillan brothers and found out about the increase in numbers up in San Luis Obispo County. From then on I spent a lot of time with the McMillan brothers, and also up north of Bakersfield because they started the 1080 poisoning; I did very little work on the nesting after that. So I finished up my three years; I had just a few spotty observations from then up to 1950.

Questioner: Was Audubon pretty pleased with the way the fellowship worked out?

Koford: Well, no. John Baker was the president, and he apparently thought that I should spend all my time working on what he considered the conservation of the birds, not on their natural history. He thought I was largely wasting my time on that, although that was the stated purpose in my contract. Joseph Grinnell had been very careful in drawing up the contract. The only requirement was that I give Audubon a quarterly report on what I was doing. There was no requirement for a final report or anything else. I was just to study the natural history of the condor, the idea being that in order to have a good conservation program you have to have sound basic data. But John Baker was not happy with it; he wanted something readable and breezy. He was very disappointed that I didn't find out whether 1080 was killing condors or not. (Of course we still don't know, even yet.)

Baker's favorite was Robert Porter Allen, who, in the meantime, had published an Audubon report on the spoonbill—how glorious it was to see a spoonbill, and lots of flowery language, and so on. So I had to revise the original thesis somewhat for publication. I had my PhD by that time and had started some field work in Peru on the vicuna. The final revision of the manuscript was done in a hotel in Lima. I sent the manuscript back airmail to Dr. Miller sewed up in a sack—that's the way they do it in Peru. The airline lost the manuscript; it was lost for seven months. My brother is a lawyer, and we sued the airline for $50,000. Two weeks later they delivered the manuscript. It had been at the Oakland airport all along, but misplaced.

Since then, of course, I've been on other jobs and didn't intend to spend any more time on condors. I was working for the Public Health Service in Puerto Rico, raising monkeys, when National Audubon offered me the job of updating the condor report. They sent a fellow named Sandy Sprunt down there to talk to me about it. I recommended that Audubon get the McMillan brothers to work on it, because I thought the thing that needed to be done then was to appraise the public attitude toward the bird.

The McMillan brothers are not biologists, but self-trained and self-educated people who really know the country and the people. They were ranchers who could talk to the locals. They took on the job and spent what time they could at it. Then Alden Miller helped them with the writing and it was published in 1965 as the Miller-McMillan Report. They hadn't attempted to make any nesting surveys, though they did look at some of the old nests. Their study was primarily distributional, and on the basis of their records, they estimated that there were only about 40 condors left. But they estimated that reproduction was satisfactory because about one-third of the population had immature plumage. They decided that mortality must be mostly in the adult age classes, and from their observations, most of it was probably from shooting—with the possibility of 1080 poisoning also. They found dead condors where all the circumstantial evidence pointed to poisoning. But they weren't sure what kind of poison was involved, and this couldn't be established by tissue analysis.

This 1965 report on the decrease in condors excited the Audubon people again—and the Fish and Wildlife Service, which was starting its new Office of Endangered Species. They sent Fred Sibley down to start working on condors in 1966. Sibley's only previous experience with raptorial birds had been banding albatrosses in the South Pacific somewhere, but he was an energetic field man and he dove into this condor program. He had all the climbing gear—you know, all the ropes and slings and everything—and went climbing all over the country. That's apparently what he spent most of his time doing. But as far as I could tell, there was never even one day when he watched condors at one place all day to see when they came and went, or watched a nest all day to see what the birds' schedules were.

Then, because of the great decrease in condors, Sibley set out to make a nesting survey. He ran down all of the old-timers he could to find out where nests had been reported. I think he came up with a list of something like 32 sites where there had supposedly been condor nesting. He visited, went inside, measured, and photographed many nest sites—I think 27 were invaded. This was in 1966 and '67. Well, in 1968, the bottom fell out. Sibley could find only one nest! He had an assistant by that time, and he knew the country well, but he could only find one nest. Some people suggested that all this nest disturbance might have caused the cessation of nesting. Ian McMillan, especially, was very strong on that point.

Partly because of public outrage, probably, Sibley departed and was replaced by Sanford Wilbur, who had been working on duck refuges for the Fish and Wildlife Service. That was in 1969. Wilbur has been running the program since then. John Borneman, sent by the National Audubon Society, is principally a public relations man; he gives talks to schools and clubs, and he also does some of the condor observation. But there have been no additional nesting studies, except for sort of looking for nests: they go out to the old nest sites and see if it looks as if they'd been used. There's really no search for nests in the early part of the nesting cycle, though. There hasn't been any nesting study involving actually watching the birds for any length of time.

This is where the fall census comes in. I think it started in 1965. There was a board put together, a committee that included Ray Dasmann, Alden Miller, and some other people, to decide what should be done about the condor situation. They decided that one way to get numbers and age distribution was to make a count during a limited period—have a number of stations manned on the same day and count how many condors were seen. This was set up for October, and they initially had about 60 stations. They were all over the condor range, way up into Monterey County, and of course the people watching were eager, interested people, but not at all trained in condor observation. Fish and Game paid their transportation, furnished their cars and everything, so it was really Fish and Game that was running the survey. The watchers observed for two days and then tried to figure out how many birds their sightings represented. First they'd see three birds in one place, then several hours later someone would see five somewhere else, and you'd have to try to figure out whether any of them were the same birds or not. It's kind of difficult to do. They came up with an estimate of around 50.

The next year Fred Sibley was there and he more or less took charge of supervising and analyzing the census. This time the count was something like 56, but they began to insist that this was a minimum number. Then Ian McMillan stepped in and looked at the original data, and began to ask questions. He said, "Well, how do you know that these birds sighted in the morning were different from these sighted in the afternoon, and not the same?" This criticism caused a great stir, and there was a big battle at one of the Cooper Ornithological Society meetings. When McMillan got up to report that he questioned the data, people apparently knew he was going to; the opposition was lined up. Ben Glade from Fish and Game, and others, got up and argued with him in public. Ian McMillan is quite an arguer himself.

When Wilbur came on the job, the numbers and the population estimate and the analysis of the data were quite different. They came up with a count of something like 27 condors. Then Wilbur looked over the earlier data and revised the numbers down from 57, or whatever it was, down to 39—using the old Sibley data. So all those counts didn't mean very much.

Another event occurred while I was still in Puerto Rico: it must have been in the early '60s. We had generally refrained from publicizing condors because we figured it would attract people and we didn't want any more people than necessary. Actually, the obscurity—the fact that people didn't know the birds were there, or how many there were, or where to go, or where the roads were—kept people away. That was pretty much the Grinnell philosophy. But then in the early '60s, the National Audubon Society, when Carl Buchheister was president, decided to go the other way. They would have lots of publicity and make a lot of money, then use this money to support more condor research. The Forest Service put out maps of condor country, with little red dots where you could go to watch condors. They made big signs explaining about condors and put them up at Point Pinos and lots of other places. They had a special condor-watching place called Squaw Flat, just north of Fillmore outside the condor sanctuary, with a parking area and all that. This was shortly before the McMillans went on the job. I think the publicity did attract a lot of people who otherwise would never have bothered the condors at all.

The Sespe Wildlife Area was renamed the Condor Sanctuary, so it was on the maps and that's where everybody thought they could go to see condors—including people like

Roger Tory Peterson. He wrote in one of his books, "Well, the condors have their sanctuary now." As though a big sanctuary would take care of everything, even though the condors spent most of their time off the sanctuary foraging on private lands. That was one of the landmarks, the publicity.

Questioner: So you feel the publicity was a mistake, pretty much?

Koford: As far as I'm concerned, yes, because of what has happened since.

A few years later, after the McMillan report, they pulled in their horns quite a lot on publicity. They didn't put out those maps any more. They actually plowed up some of the roads in the Squaw Flat area to keep people from coming in there. And they have gotten a lot of firearms closures: in areas around condor zones you're not supposed to carry firearms. (There have supposedly been plenty of violations, but I've never heard of any convictions.) Aircraft are not supposed to fly below 3,000 feet over certain condor nesting places, but there have been lots of violations by military aircraft, helicopters, and everything else. That's a big problem nowadays. There are so many private planes, and lots of pilots don't even have a map, much less pay attention to restricted areas.

Questioner: What about oil drilling?

Koford: Well, Hopper Canyon was surrounded by oil wells that were producing high quality oil, but not in very large amounts. During World War II, they found oil in similar formations in Cuyama Valley. So the Hopper Canyon area became a hot property, thought very probably to have oil. People who held the leases for oil and gas wanted to sell. We had a meeting in Los Angeles in 1950, the first to discuss the problem, and we all got up and said our piece. There were lawyers for the oil people, who were crying about our boys dying in Korea for lack of oil. Hollywood ladies in floppy hats were telling us that the oil men were not bad, but good. Old-timers were telling us that God would take care of the condors. After the meeting, the oil people were very nice. They wanted to compromise, and did agree to certain restrictions: not drilling within a certain distance from active condor nests, using only slant drilling under the central part of the Hopper Canyon zone, and so on. It has been pretty much that way ever since. The Forest Service has continually turned down applications for sale of the leases, and the area of the sanctuary has been increased quite a bit by additions from year to year until it now includes a lot of Piru Canyon and parts up north.

There was another furor about the time that Sibley came on the job. In fact, it may actually have stimulated Fish and Wildlife to send him. There was a plan to dam Sespe Creek and make a big reservoir. That would have required a road through the wildlife area—what was later to become the condor sanctuary. The lake would not be on sanctuary land, but the access road would. Alden Miller, especially, thought this was extremely dangerous: it would bring in a lot of people with a lot of guns. So he fought hard against it. The water people wanted it, of course. And people like Sidney Peyton—an old-timer who had collected condor eggs back in the '20s, always considered himself a great authority, and was a very fine man—got on the side of the water people. Ed Harrison, who had taken a lot of movies of condors and therefore was a great condor expert, got on the side of the water and oil men. They said, "We'll put a cyclone fence on each side of the road, and we'll feed the condors: they'll be better off than they are now." Well, it finally came to a vote in the county and the plan was narrowly defeated. That was a major crisis at the time when Sibley came on the job. Apparently his main mission was to appraise the probable effects of the proposed dam and road on the condor population. He wrote an administrative report about that.

Questioner: Was the issue in the county the condor versus the dam, or was it the dam versus some economic alternative?

Koford: No, it was the condors versus the dam.

Questioner: So a majority in the county voted to preserve the condor?

Koford: Yes.

Questioner: Do you think that pressure for a dam might have influenced Fish and Game to compromise on the oil rigs—that they had fought one political battle and weren't prepared for another one?

Koford: The sanctuaries are not owned or controlled by the Fish and Wildlife Service; they belong to the Forest Service. It was the Forest Service that originally set aside the small Sisquoc sanctuary—only about 1,000 acres—and the Sespe wildlife preserve that became a sanctuary. That was all done by the Forest Service. There still hasn't been any compromise on the oil. But it keeps coming up periodically, and they're pretty sure there's several million dollars worth of oil under the sanctuary. They have put some wells right on the very edge of the sanctuary. Fish and Wildlife bought Hopper Ranch, next to the sanctuary where condors used to feed once in awhile. The oil people are still drilling their wells and building their roads even though it has been a federal game refuge for some time. But that's really academic now, because there are no condors around Hopper Canyon. The most they see at any time is about four birds, just flying through. There was one nesting there in 1976, I think.

One interesting thing came out in '76. That's when they put out the contingency plan, a rather short plan by Wilbur. His diagnosis at that time was that the condors were not breeding—that there was something wrong with them and they were not attempting to breed. This came out in July 1976. Well, in August of '76 they found a young condor fledged in Santa Barbara County, and in December of that year, they found one condor fledged in the condor sanctuary. This was rather embarrassing for them, and Wilbur is still arguing that they're not breeding. But there's really no evidence for that at all.

There was one other event: the phosphate mine business that caused some stir. But it was really of no particular importance. It was up on Pine Mountain, which is very seldom visited by condors. A few fly over it. Some people wanted to develop a phosphate mine there, and of course, the Forest Service didn't want it because it was on their land and it would be messed up. The Forest Service, unfortunately, sometimes seems to use condors as an excuse to fight off-road vehicles, mining development, and so on. Audubon went along with them, and took the attitude that it was harmful to condors. They got an economist on the job to analyze the phosphate economics. They were finally able to demonstrate to the company that it was a losing proposition. So the mine was never developed. But it got an awful lot of publicity, and a lot of people think to this day that the mine was right in the middle of the condor sanctuary. It was quite a long way off.

Questioner: What do you think would be the effect of a large-scale captive breeding program?

Koford: Of course captive breeding has a lot of bad things about it. If you study any animal well enough, you can understand what its habitat requirements are. I think what our goal should be is to understand what the habitat requirements are and to furnish them, even if we have to resort to some artificiality such as having a flock of sheep out there and knocking one off once in awhile to help feed the birds. Obviously, the birds have certain basic requirements. They have to have cliffs for nesting and trees for roosting. They have to have water nearby and proper food within cruising range. And it all has to be related to the position of the nest sites, so the birds have time to go out and feed and come back, and it has to be considered on a year-round basis.

We've just never studied the habitat enough to know what's needed. I think that's the way to go, to furnish what the birds want. We may have something pretty close to it develop by itself in the Mount Pinos area, because condors are roosting there and they have a food supply out there on the southern edge of the San Joaquin Valley. But apparently it's not a good area for nesting.

Questioner: What would it take to demonstrate conclusively that you could have a sustainable population in the wild? How much observation time would you need? If you had unlimited financial resources, how could you do it and how long would it take?

Koford: Well, I don't think you could ever demonstrate that it would work forever. All you could do was demonstrate that it was working at the time. But normally a study like that would take three years. In order to get any kind of measure of variations that occur from year to year, you have to have at least two years. And any factor you study is going to be either the same, less, or more the second year. You may think you have a trend, but you need at least one more year to see if there is a trend or not. If nesting is good one year but poor the next, well, you're not sure whether that's a trend. So I'd say at least three years.

One thing I suggested should be done is get the birds back in the western part of the range, and I think that Wilbur goes along with that now. For one thing, the sheep distribution has changed since there is a lot more irrigated pasture now. Instead of migratory sheep, we have resident sheep. In Camp Roberts alone—on the Monterey, San Luis Obispo County line—there are 10,000 sheep. They lamb there and they're there all year round—an excellent source of condor food potential. There are other big ranches that have alfalfa and have sheep. So there are far more sheep in the western range the year around, especially in winter when the condors would be nesting, than there were in 1950. There are nesting sites that were formerly used there: in southern Monterey County in the early 1900s, in the Panza Range in the 1920s and possibly since then, and in—what's that other spot?—well, near La Panza where the nest was in the late '60s. You'd want to get the birds back over there and using those areas.

Questioner: I'm curious what you think about the live trapping of birds.

Koford: You mean for release in parts of their former range?

Questioner: Yes.

Koford: I don't think it would work. Trapping itself is very likely to hurt the birds psychologically, if not physically. And our general experience with releasing any kind of trapped animals in a different place has been dismal. They just don't stay. Bears don't stay, lions don't stay, and I don't think condors would stay.

My idea would be to attract condors over gradually. Birds in the Mount Pinos area range over very close to the Santa Barbara County line. If we had some kind of feeding station there at the time of year when condors are around, they would start feeding there. Then put up another feeding station a few miles further over. And keep them happy when they're there, especially during the breeding season. Even if you had to make some air drops of carcasses in order to keep them fed, I think that would be the best way to go.

Questioner: I'd like to get back to captive breeding.

Koford: There are several things involved. First, the capture of the birds themselves and how much damage that would do— especially to those who are released again. Then, assuming there was successful breeding in cages, as there has been with the Andean Condor in Patuxent, whether there's any chance of the released birds' surviving and breeding. They'd not only have to survive, but they'd have to compete with golden eagles and turkey vultures for food, and they'd have to compete with the established condors for nesting and mates. Unless we can demonstrate with similar birds such as turkey vultures that it's feasible—or with Andean Condors, perhaps—I think it's foolish even to start in that direction.

Questioner: If you took a number of juveniles—they are planning to capture juveniles, mostly—if you took them and planned to release captive-raised birds into the wild in 20 to 40 years, would you have any remnant condor population left at that point?

Koford: Well, we don't know. But every condor you remove, regardless of its age, reduces the breeding potential of the remainder. If you take one condor out, you not only lose one condor, you lose all the progeny that condor would have had during its lifetime of 30 to 40 years. So even one condor taken could cause a tremendous difference.

If they take immatures instead of adults, that's less immediate harm. But as for eventual harm, in the statistics, I don't think it would make any difference. Adults—the ones in immature plumage—are not breeding: that's the reason for taking the young ones. There would be no harm to immediate nesting. But adults cannot be taken at any season without danger of their having a dependent young one or an egg in the nest.

Questioner: The Sierra Club's Condor Advisory Committee, of which you are a member, came up with a number of recommendations, most of which would involve very rigorous testing using substitute birds such as turkey vultures and Andean Condors, which would probably postpone actual capture of California Condors for as long as 3½ years. That has been adopted as Sierra Club policy. How do you feel about those recommendations?

Koford: I've been in favor of the turkey vulture research all along, for 20 years, and it has been horribly neglected. We don't even have the faintest idea what the effects of 1080 are on turkey vultures. So I think they should be used as research birds, but the demonstration should be done in the condor range with resident turkey vultures, not down in Florida with a different sub-species or tame birds.

Questioner: What do you consider the major argument against captive breeding?

Koford: That the wild population can't afford to lose any of its members.

At the National Audubon Society meeting in Estes Park a few months ago, someone told me he had heard Russell Peterson refer to the peregrine falcon program and the Mauritius kestril program as highly successful. Well of course, as we all know, the peregrine program is not entirely successful—even though the bird is more or less susceptible to domestication and they've been training them for two thousand years or more. How many birds did they have to sort through before they got their breeding stock? I understand that all the offspring have been produced by about 32 peregrines. They must have had to sort through a lot of birds to find the good breeders among them, so as an example for condors, it's worth almost nothing. The peregrine as a species is not endangered everywhere; it's only the eastern one, and we know what's wrong there. It is quite a different thing. They are trying to put peregrines in a habitat that doesn't already have peregrines. But with condors, you've got the additional problem of putting birds into an area where there is already an established population.

It's too bad we didn't get to Peterson earlier, because from his previous record, we thought he'd be a very reasonable person. But he seemed completely converted to defense of the capture program without any real knowledge.

Questioner: What do you think the motives are behind Audubon getting into captive breeding so heavily?

Koford: Well, we've heard talk that it has to do with fundraising. We haven't heard it directly from any Audubon people, but it seems fairly obvious. Especially if you've talked with Dick Plunkett; he is primarily a public relations man, and he's been the main one who's pushed the program all along.

The idea of capturing some birds and trying to raise them in captivity originated with Sanford Wilbur in about 1974. The recovery plan that was written in 1974 and approved in '75 said nothing about capturing any birds. Then the contingency plan came out about the same time, and that was based on captures. Right now we're waiting to see the revised recovery plan.

It seems obvious to me that with the number of immature birds that are being seen, consistently, there is no reason for being in such a hurry. As long as we have four or five immatures out there that are getting older—approaching sexual maturity—we've already got what we could accomplish in 20 years of a captive breeding program. So what's the rush in getting started?

Questioner: What do we have now in the way of recent observations of condors in the wild?

Koford: There have been several groups, most of them from Audubon societies, up on Mount Pinos recently, and they've had good luck seeing condors. Eben McMillan was up there with the Golden Gate Audubon Society (I think it was the 18th of last month) in August [1980]. They saw a minimum of six condors, and only two of them were surely adult. So they think that three or four were immatures. Then there's a girl from Los Angeles that I've never met, but she's doing some observations too, going up there on her own and sending me long reports. She has talked to John Borneman of the Audubon Society, and they're pretty sure there's a minimum of five immatures now—and that's just in the Mount Pinos area. So that's very good.

It was obvious to me ten years ago that the way to tell how the population was doing was exactly the same as for all other game birds. That is, just to analyze the nonbreeding population: see what age classes are present and how they survive from one year to the next. That's essentially what we're doing. If there are five immatures this year, then next year some of those should have reached the mature age class; there'll be others recognizable as first-year birds, and others in between.

Questioner: I think it would be helpful to talk a bit about how you came to be interested in the condor and what makes the condor special at this point—what the range of the species was, how far back it goes, and so on.

Koford: Do you want me to go two hundred years back? . . .

Questioner: I understand condors went back many thousands. . . .

Koford: Well, we don't know. We don't know.

Questioner: How far back do we have records of it?

Koford: We run into an additional problem here, because the Pleistocene condor is actually considered a different species, *Gymnogyps amplus,* based on some characteristics of the skull and on the length of the bones. The condor in the La Brea pits is this species *amplus*. The Pleistocene ended only about 10,000 years ago, and there are none of the modern *Gymnogyps* in that earlier period. So we don't really *know* it was the same bird. That's one of the confusing aspects. But if we consider them the same bird, why formerly, in Pleistocene times, they ranged clear to Florida and up to Washington. There are remains up in Shasta, in some of the caves there. Up on the Hood River, they found condor bones in Indian shell mounds. So the distribution was more or less transcontinental in the southern part of the United States back in the Pleistocene. There were additional vultures too, at that time, that have become extinct since. Such as *Teratornis*, which was larger than the condor—might have weighed 50 pounds.

We might clear up one point: it's often said in the title or subtitle of an article that the California condor is a Pleistocene relic, and there's something great about it. Well, the red-tailed hawk and the turkey vulture were there at the same time. In fact, the turkey vulture is known earlier in the fossil record than the condor. The condor is a fairly late comer.

Advancing a little farther, up to historical times, the first condors recorded were at Monterey in about the 1750s, by a monk who accompanied one of the sailing ship expeditions. Apparently the condors were pretty common along the coast then, feeding on whale remains, sea lion remains, and so on. Then Lewis and Clark found them at the mouth of the Columbia River in 1805. There's not the slightest doubt, because they have sketches of the head and detailed descriptions in their field notes. You can see those notes at the American Philosophical Society in Philadelphia. So condors were at the mouth of the Columbia River and up the Columbia a ways— perhaps up to The Dalles.

But then the range started to shrink southward, and there were records by Douglas, the botanist, in southern Oregon near Eugene up to about 1812. Then there are records around Eureka in the late 1800s—1895, somewhere in that neighborhood. There are specimens in the courthouse in Eureka. But then, this is all within the last 200 years. In this historical period of 200 years, we don't have any record of their breeding. Not only were there no nests or eggs or young found, but the Indians certainly would have had these birds in their legends and in their art, and so on—as they do in California—if they had been around a great deal. So there is a little argument as to whether those birds were migratory or just non-breeding birds that drifted up there during part of the year. Wilbur seems to think they were breeding up there, although there's no evidence whatever that they did.

Then there are other records in northern California, in the 1850s. Cooper, one of the early explorers there, found condors up in the Sacramento Valley. Then they shrank farther south. I don't remember exactly when the next records were, but essentially from 1900 on, there were none north of Santa Cruz, at the farthest. I don't think they even got that far—Monterey Bay was about it. Well, there was one record at Palo Alto in the early 1900s, of one bird; but the breeding, as far as we know, has always been confined to southern California. The northernmost breeding record is in Santa Cruz County. There has been nesting in San Benito County, the site of Pinnacles National Monument, and on south to San Diego County.

We don't know of any breeding in Baja California, although there were condors in the early 1900s in San Pedro Martir. There is an old book by Swan about birds of prey of the world, and he states that there was one egg, or one egg record from Baja. But there's no record of the egg, and not any reason to think that's true.

In the early 1900s, condors were still fairly numerous in San Diego County. They pulled out of there about 1912 or 1915. There were still occasional records clear up until the 1930s in Orange County, at Santiago Peak. But since I started in 1939, there have been no authentic records that far south. There have been some reports from the San Bernardino Mountains, but I really don't know if any of them have ever been verified. So the range, since the 1930s, has been pretty much the same as it is now. The *total* range, that is; but the numbers of birds using the various parts has changed radically, of course.

Starting in the 1930s, people noticed large numbers of condors in Sisquoc Canyon. That was apparently a main roost for them in the middle 1930s. And that's where the first motion pictures of condors were taken, in Sisquoc Canyon. That was about 1936, '37, '38. By 1939 there were occasional groups there, but the largest numbers were over in Ventura County, in winter—in the area where the large condor sanctuary is now. But there were no large numbers reported in the sanctuary area until about the middle '30s, and those only in winter. Apparently it was a winter congregating area, and because condors start to breed in winter, it was a main breeding area. That was the situation when I started my study. That was where most of the breeding was—in Ventura County where the present condor sanctuary is.

Questioner: Why did they leave the canyon area? Is that known?

Koford: No. It could have been a matter of food, because they were feeding in the '30s on sheep in the Cuyama Valley. The situation with sheep used to be that most of the country was unfenced. Sheep were grazed in the Mojave Desert in winter and were moved over into the southern San Joaquin Valley when the alfalfa stubble was available in spring. The lambs were born there, then the sheep were moved on west over to San Luis Obispo County. They arrived there in spring, and in the Cuyama Valley too, and spent several months there before herders moved them back east. Condor movements seemed to be more or less adjusted to those sheep movements.

During World War II, somewhere between 1941 and '45, larger numbers started to appear in the southern Sierra Nevada, where people had lived all their lives and never seen one. And there was a great increase in San Luis Obispo County and southern Monterey County. The McMillan brothers, for example, had been raised in San Luis Obispo County, near Shandon; their father had homesteaded there. Three, four, or five condors were the most anybody ever saw there during their lifetimes. But then, starting in the 1940s, people began to see 20 or 30 at a time. So there was a movement northward on both the east and the west sides of the San Joaquin Valley in the early 1940s. We don't know exactly what the reason for that was either—whether it was a decrease of food in one place or an increase in another. But that was the last time there was a big shift in range. Of course, there has been a shift since then out of the condor sanctuary over to Tejon Ranch.

There were still good numbers of condors in the condor sanctuary in 1966 and '67. Then suddenly, in 1968, they only found one nest there—where they'd found something like 13 nests in '66 and '67, when the Fish and Wildlife Service started to do some condor work there. It was obvious by the early 1970s that the condors were roosting over in Tejon Ranch. The numbers have just never gone back to the condor sanctuary area.

The history of the birds, as I've been telling it to you, shows that they've moved around from place to place. In the southern Sierra Nevada, for example, there were practically no records in the early days, in the 1800s. I think there was only one record, by John Audubon—or Audubon's brother, I think— somewhere up in the Tule River area, when condors moved in and started to use those areas in this century. I suspect it's all correlated with the food supply, but we just haven't ever known enough about the food supply—what the condors are eating at what time of year.

Another thing that happened, back in the 1940s, was that they started to use the compound 1080 to poison ground squirrels in the southern Sierra Nevada, north of Bakersfield. It started, I think, in 1945. In 1946 I was there watching the condors, and I relate in my book a lot of observations of condors there. I talked to a Fish and Wildlife man, Joseph Keyes, who had been observing them and had also observed large numbers of rabbits and other things killed by 1080. I think maybe that squirrel poisoning had something to do with the fact that condors started to work up farther in the Sierra Nevada—clear up to the area of Friant Dam, east of Madera.

Now, what's happened in more recent years? They say the first Fish and Wildlife Service man on the condor job in 1966 who stayed for three years, Fred Sibley, was quite an aggressive field man. He tramped around the hills a lot and did find quite a few condor nests. He thought that the population was doing very well. On the basis of the counts—the attempted simultaneous counts made on a few days in the fall—they came up with numbers in the high fifties. And they were telling us that this was a minimum number of condors—whereas the Miller-McMillan Report, which is based on data for 1963 and '64, had estimated a total of only 40. And I had estimated 60 in 1950. So either something very drastic happened about 1968, or the Fish and Wildlife reports were very much exaggerated during the late '60s. Except for those fall "census counts" there was really no hard evidence that there ever were more than 50 condors, or even more than 40, at any time since 1965. So there has been a considerable decline from 1950, when I finished my observations, to 1970. They've gone down, down.

The extent of the condor range, too, has pulled in. For example, there were many records of condors in San Luis Obispo County almost every year until the middle 1960s, and condors were seen feeding there. There was even a nesting in San Luis Obispo County in 1966-7-8. The nest, discovered by Fred Sibley, was in the same place for three successive years. So there were condors there. But now, during the last few years, there have been entire years when there have never been more than one or two condors reported in Santa Barbara or San Luis Obispo counties. This year there have been some rather vague reports for San Luis Obispo and Monterey counties, but I don't know that any of them are reliable. So it may be that the only condors using that western part of the range is one adult pair that nested in Santa Barbara County—the first time we know of in 1972, then again in 1976 and '77. That pair was slated to be watched by a group from the Santa Barbara Natural History Museum this year, and they did a lot of observation. The condors were there once in awhile, one pair, but as far as they know, there was no nesting there. It's not that they may not be nesting somewhere else—the same pair—but there seem to be only two adult condors in Santa Barbara County. Last year there was one immature seen at two different locations at about the same time in May. They seemed to be different birds, because one had very beat-up plumage and the other didn't. That could have been an offspring of that one pair. So essentially, Santa Barbara County is used practically not at all, and the western range is essentially lost to the condors.

Questioner: When you first began your study, what got you involved with the condor?

Koford: Well, it was all a mistake. My interest was in mammals. I graduated in forestry; there was no ecology or range management or wildlife management in 1937, when I graduated. The only wildlife management course in the country was at Wisconsin. Ecology? We didn't even know the word; if there was any, it had to do with plants. So I took forestry at the University of Washington. But I lived in California and took my last year at Berkeley. I went to work in the summer down at

Hastings Reservation in Carmel Valley, which is run by the Museum of Vertebrate Zoology. It's a ranch that was donated to the University. I went down there and studied ground squirrels, mainly by sitting up in a tree. I sat up in a tree all day for 42 consecutive days, watching ground squirrels and what they did. This reservation was in the charge of Gene Linsdale, one of the Museum of Vertebrate Zoology professors. Well, the National Audubon Society raised some money at that time for what they called Audubon Fellowships. The first one was on the ivory-billed woodpecker; that was done by James Tanner of the University of Tennessee. He never saw any ivory-billed woodpeckers, but he did write a book about them. They had another fellowship for condors, because they wanted an endangered. . . . a rare species, as it was called in those days. They asked Joseph Grinnell, of the Museum of Vertebrate Zoology, to have a study of the California condor conducted. Grinnell was very much interested, because he had lived in the Pasadena area as a boy, had visited most of the condor sites, and had contributed a lot to condor records. He'd seen them, grown up with them. Grinnell needed someone to do the job. I was there at the museum as a graduate student identifying bones from Indian caves, and I was recommended by Dr. Linsdale as being able to do good field work. So they gave me the fellowship. It was the grand amount of $1,500 a year for three years. In those days that was pretty good—about an assistant professor's salary.

I didn't have a car or anything; all I had was a notebook, a pair of binoculars, and a rucksack. I went down to the Los Angeles area—just took the bus down there—and got in touch with a man named Bill Pemberton who was an amateur photographer and had been taking 16 millimeter movies of condors. He had photographed them in the Sisquoc Canyon area in 1937 and '38 when there were about 20 or more condors in there, and he had pictures of them, too, feeding on sheep down in the Cuyama Valley. He was the first person to successfully photograph condors feeding. Pemberton was a well-known man because he had a job called "oil umpire." Under the Roosevelt administration they were trying to control the production of oil—hold it down and give everybody equal opportunity—and Pemberton was boss of that. Everybody knew him. He showed me his notes. He had collected birds before. He had lived in Patagonia for five years and collected Andean condors there. And many other birds for the museums. He knew his birds.

Pemberton had just recently heard about Hopper Canyon—the fact that there were a lot of condors up there, where the sanctuary is now. So he took me up there in March of 1939. There was a road right up to the top of the ridge, and anybody could go up there. There were a lot of condors, so he dumped me and a box of groceries there and went back home. I stayed up there and hiked around and found out what I could. After about two weeks of walking around and climbing down in canyons and so on, I flushed a condor out of a hole. I hid and waited about 500 yards away, and eventually the bird came back. So I was pretty sure there was a nest there. Pemberton started to come on weekends to take 16 millimeter movies of these nesting condors. We did it very gradually. We never went close to the nest; at the closest, his blind was still about 100 yards from the nest.

There are a lot of sandstone caves there; that's what they call the vaqueros formations. It's sandstone with nodules that fall out and make cavities. This is a wonderful nesting area for all hole-nesting birds: horned owls, ravens, prairie falcons, and the like. I spent all day every day watching condors at a pot-hole nest. I'd write notes all day, as many as 15 or 20 pages some days—when the birds came and when they left, whether swallows went into the nest, and whatever else I saw. We thought there was a nest pretty surely, of course, but it was still three or four weeks before we actually saw the egg. One day the condor rolled the egg with its bill out where we could see it. Pemberton had been taking movies and the condors were a little wary of that, apparently, so one condor moved from its normal position in the pot-hole right up to the entrance of the cave, and rolled the egg out there. So we got a picture of the egg.

The egg hatched 42 days after I found it, and I was there on the day it hatched. During incubation, 20 hours was a good, long sit. But the longest period I observed an incubating bird sit on the egg was 40 hours. Presumably it was the female that was sitting at the time.

Once a raven perched right at the mouth of this pot-hole, within a few inches of the adult condor, and went "caw-w-w" [here Koford made an incredibly raven-like noise] right in the face of the condor. This made me think that ravens may be dangerous to condor eggs—and any other kind of eggs.

So the egg hatched and I kept watching the young condor as much as I could. Usually I'd observe it up to five days at a time continuously. Then I'd go down for more groceries. It was about a 13-mile hike down to the town. Eventually I bought a Model T Ford for $95 and had some transportation. The bird grew and grew, and we got more pictures. We were very reluctant to touch the bird or go into the nest.

But one day, when I was away, we were invaded by a group from the Department of Fish and Game—the local game warden, Don McClain from Sacramento, and a local man who did a lot of hiking and knew where I was working. They got the local man to take them up there, and they chopped the brush. . . . I had a kind of concealed pathway, unmarked, but they chopped the brush and took their pack animals in there. They put a rope over the cliff and went down and grabbed the young bird out of the nest and held it out by the wings and photographed it. They didn't tell me anything about it, but when I got back, it was obvious that someone had been there. When we found out that we could handle that young bird without doing damage we did; I went down and put a band on the leg made out of a section of aluminum pipe slit up the side. . . .

One day I'd been down to get some groceries or something, and when I got back the bird was out of the nest. It was gone. I stood and watched for awhile, and then I found it was down in the brush below the nest. It was about a 30-foot drop, perhaps. I just watched, and the adults came and fed it down in the brush. That went on for several weeks—the adults would come every day and visit that young bird. Usually, both adults had fed the young bird in the nest. One would usually come at one time and the other at another, and they would both feed the young bird. That would take maybe ten or 12 minutes, then they'd go. One visit a day, and rarely, two. Anyway, the feeding continued after the young bird was down in the brush. I'm not sure that both adults fed it, but it was fed by one or both adults. And we eventually got a motion picture of an adult feeding the young.

Gradually the young bird moved up the cliff, and got up on top of the cliff; and it moved down, farther and farther down the canyon in this period of a couple of months when it was learning to fly. By December, it could fly—oh, maybe 100 yards. But you could still walk right up to that young bird. It had the band on its leg and I saw it as late as June of the next year in the same canyon.

But that nest has never been used again, perhaps because of all the disturbance. Then we began to look around for other nests, and eventually, we found about a dozen nests in different places, but all in that general vicinity, in Ventura County. Sometimes the young were already out of the nest, sometimes the egg was still there. So there was a pretty good rate of reproduction. But that was the only time I really followed through the whole cycle, because it took a long time to do all this.

There's one other important event I forgot to mention. About 1950 or '51, the San Diego Zoo was given a permit by Fish and Game to take two condor eggs, the only stipulation being that they not take them in the condor sanctuary. This permit expired in 1953, and then they applied to take two condors for breeding in the zoo. Lewis Wayne Walker was their capture man at the zoo. He went out and tried to catch two condors, and his main place of operating was Hopper Ranch—right on the border of the condor sanctuary. He tried different kinds of traps, and even put out steel traps around these cattle carcasses. . . .

Questioner: Steel jaw traps?

Koford: Yeah, plain old steel coyote traps; maybe he wrapped them a little, I don't know. But he didn't manage to catch a condor in two years. Not a one. As a result of his experience on Hopper Ranch, Walker wrote and mimeographed a report which said they thought the condors were disappearing because he'd been there so many months and only seen ten condors. This got to the Sierra Club. I attended a meeting of the Sierra Club Conservation Committee, chaired at the time by one of the club's big names [Harold Bradley]. Anne Brower was also at that meeting. I talked about the Walker report and told them I thought most of it was either irrelevant or wrong. Then it came up before the Fish and Game Commission, meeting in San Francisco. I was there, and Dr. Alden Miller was there, as were Dave Brower and others. At that time, my report had just been published. We gave a copy of the report to each member of the Commission, but in spite of our opposition, they gave the zoo that permit to trap condors. Mrs. Benchley, Belle Benchley at the zoo, was kind of a nervous type—a plump, middle-aged lady, very strong in her opinions. You couldn't tell her, "You shouldn't trap the condors." After all, she was doing it for conservation, and all that. But she did have a lot of political pull, and got her way on that.

But then, largely because of Ian McMillan, who went to the legislature and did a lot of lobbying, we got a law later that condors could not be taken for any purpose. That was an unrecorded but memorable episode.

Another thing you brought up was what other background I had in addition to the condor business—other things I've done. Did you want to hear about that?

Questioner: Yes, please.

Koford: After I did the condor thing, I went to South America for two years. The main result was this paper on the vicuna. It's called *The Vicuna and the Puma,* published in *Ecological Monographs,* and it's probably the most zoologically important work I've ever done. It started out as kind of a general natural history survey, but it turned out these vicunas were very territorial. At that time we knew almost zero about territoriality in mammals, except for the fur seals during mating season. So this was very far-out for its time. I was able to show a lot of little behaviorisms—things related to social behavior—so that was kind of a milestone in social biology. I believe we're still getting requests for it now, more than 20 years later.

Questioner: So you spent two years doing this one?

Koford: I did a lot of other things there; I collected mammals and birds for the museum at the same time, and also made some observations of Andean condors. In fact, one of the outstanding observations I made in my life is recounted in here: when I was watching a baby vicuna being born, and as soon as it hit the ground, a lot of shadows came over. I looked, and there were 14 condors; they all came down on the ground and surrounded this baby. The mother vicuna, plus two pregnant vicunas, drove the condors back—ran at them [with their feet] for about half an hour. By that time the baby could stand up and walk around, and the condors went away.

Questioner: Wow! That must have. . . . You were just standing there, watching this?

Koford: Well, I was sitting in my car with my telescope, rather than outside. But that was pretty good evidence to me that condors do kill young. It kind of reminds me of the condor business, when the day the chick hatched, a raven came and perched right in the nest in front of the female. In other words, in the whole lifetime of that animal, there may be just a few minutes when it's really vulnerable. That's why it's so hard to see.

Anyway, after the vicuna business I taught up here at U.C. [University of California, Berkeley] for awhile. Then I went to Colorado to work on prairie dogs, and I was there for a year. I wrote this thing called *Prairie Dogs, White Faces, and Blue Grama,* published in *Wildlife Monographs*. It's not just black-tailed prairie dogs, but uses them as an example of range rodents and their effects on grazing. That's where the white faces come in; it has to do with cattle grazing, the buffalo, blue grama grass, and the effects on plants, and so on. This has been reprinted one time. It's kind of a summary of the range-rodent problem.

Questioner: Were they actively involved in poisoning them everywhere at that time?

Koford: Oh, yes. The New York Zoological Society was worried about it.

I came back to Berkeley again then, and went from there to Panama, where I was the resident naturalist on Barro Colorado Island. I took it over from this Zetek, who had been there for practically his whole lifetime—an old guy. That was run by the Smithsonian then, but I got into furious arguments with them about how things should be done, so I only stayed a year. I came back and worked at Hopland Field Station for a year, mainly on deer. Then I went to Puerto Rico for the National Institute of Health, in the monkey business. We raised rhesus monkeys on islands off Puerto Rico. So I got into monkey management, and worked mostly on the population dynamics of those monkeys. I wrote four or five little papers about them.

One of them was called *Group Relations In an Island Colony of Rhesus Monkeys.* All the animals were marked; we caught them, tattooed them, put notches in their ears, and so on, so we knew exactly how many animals we had. When new ones were born, we knew the birthdates pretty closely and we knew the mothers. Eventually we got to know the population very well, and did a lot of behavioral research on them. There have been a succession of other people there since that have done other studies. This is another paper on the same project; the final run-down on the population dynamics is published here. We had about 23 percent new young born each year, but part of them died and we ended up with a net gain of about 17 percent a year. So the population went up, up, up, and would double in about five years.

After that, I went to Japan for a year to work on Japanese monkeys. This was in cooperation with the Japan Monkey Center. There again I was interested mostly in the birth season.

When I came back from Japan, I went to U.C. Davis. I was trying to get into the primate center in Davis, but the director there at the time, Schmidt, was not amenable to that—to have anybody around or let anybody have any authority except himself. Even though I had promised support from the National Institutes of Health, I was never able to swing that. After I'd been there about three years, I moved back down here [to Berkeley]. I started taking students out on field trips, mainly to Peru and other parts of South America, summers. I did that for several years, and did a lot more collecting.

Then, about '71, I took on the job of surveying the spotted cat situation in Latin America for World Wildlife Fund/I.U.C.N. Following that, I did the puma study—three years—in California. That more or less brings me up to 1976. Since then I've just been dabbling in everything. Kit foxes. You know, one time Fish and Game was going to take that San Joaquin kit fox off the endangered list—even though the guy who made the study did not recommend that. So I argued very hard and they changed their mind. Maybe it was and maybe it wasn't because of my argument. Anyway, they went down and saw what the situation was—habitat was just going like mad.

Questioner: The most recent stuff you've done has been on the California condor, again?

Koford: Yes. Not publishable stuff, mostly talking and writing and memos. As you get further along in your career, you get more and more bogged down in service jobs. People want you to write a report on something. It's not really work toward a scientific publication, it's to influence a legislature or a law. So that's what I've been doing. But I'm still very much interested in the mountain lion, because the moratorium is going to give out. And also the bobcat; the bobcat because there's no scientific reason for setting a limit of 6,000 exported bobcats in the state. The way the laws are, they could all be taken from one county. Or they could all be one of the rare sub-species. But Defenders of Wildlife is going to sue. They'll take it to court.

Questioner: I heard a figure of 106,000 bobcats exported, nationwide.

Koford: I think that's the total amount used in the states, not the amount exported or sold within the states. But the point is, there's nobody making any really decent studies to find out what's going on. Nobody's studying one of these hunted populations. Fish and Game has had three studies going, but they're all poor.

Questioner: There's no definitive study of bobcat populations, then?

Koford: No. No, the nearest thing to it was down in San Diego County around a reservoir where bobcats aren't hunted. It's a small area, only a couple of square miles. They did radio tracking there, and over a period of six months, they caught 15 or so. But when you plot them out—which month they caught them—you see after six months has gone by that they're not catching any again that they caught initially. The only way they can say there are any resident bobcats there at all is to redefine the word "resident" to mean any bobcat observed in their study area during a certain period. They're not there all year round. So we don't know population density, or any of the reproductive parameters, for bobcats—their survival rates or anything like that.

Questioner: You've done so much work on so many different endangered species, have you come up with any universal thoughts about the future of wildlife or what you'd like to see mankind do to help endangered species survive?

Koford: Not really, except that I think with sufficient study, all the problems would yield to scientific solutions. If you really put in the effort. When you see how much can be done by one man with very little equipment, you can see that four or five men with radios and abundant transportation—airplanes and all that—could really do a terrific job. It's the same way with the condors; I think there's no reason in the world we can't find out what's wrong and what to do about it.

Questioner: Your work foreshadows in many respects the work of many other researchers—Jane Goodall, for example, and George Schaller—who are very much into conservation as well as basic research.

Koford: Yeah. It has nearly all been done by kind of lone wolf types, which is a strange thing in a way. Since the time of Carpenter. . . . Ray Carpenter studied howler monkeys on Barro Colorado Island in the early '30s, and he was a father of modern behavioral studies of wild animals. That was typical of the way we've been doing it ever since—just one guy going out and finding out what he can.

Questioner: It's a tremendous commentary on the resources that one man can bring to bear on a problem.

Koford: Yes. It really hurts me to see these kids nowadays who don't want to do anything unless they can get substantial grant support from the very start. After I graduated, I went in the CCCs [Civilian Conservation Corps] for one term as an officer in Montana. Then I went to the Hastings Reservation down in Carmel Valley. That's really where I started, where I learned how to trap, and mark, and all that. And I was influenced a lot by Grinnell. It was on the basis of that work that I got the fellowship to work on condors, although I didn't have any interest in birds at the time.

One thing I *have* learned is that whatever I learned about birds has helped me with mammals, and whatever I learned about mammals has helped me with birds. Like this vicuna thing—unless I had known a lot about bird territoriality already, I would never have recognized what was going on there.

Questioner: That's a disincentive for overspecialization.

Koford: Oh, yes, I'm very much against overspecialization. They have this problem-oriented research now. You have a specific thing you want: "Are numbers related to food resources?" Something like that. You go out to solve that mathematically, with plenty of statistics, and so on, and only observe a small part of the life of the animal. When you get through reading such studies, you might have no idea at all what the animal looks like or how it operates. But one of the really good, landmark papers, I think, was Fraser Darling's *Herd of Red Deer*. It's hard to read because it has a lot of big Scotch names in it, but when you get through, you really have an idea how those animals live and get along with each other and with their environment.

Questioner: How does the worldwide outlook for endangered species look to you?

Koford: Very discouraging. Very. The land clearing, especially in Latin America, is terrible. I don't see how it could help but modify the climate.

Questioner: Much of the clearing is to convert forested land into grazing land, isn't it, for beef export to overdeveloped countries?

Koford: Right. When the price of sugar goes up, they take the grazing land and plant sugar on it. Then they go out and clear more forest to make room for the cattle. Mexico is an excellent bad example. Some individuals there put up a little fight once in awhile, but basically, they're destroying everything they have.

Questioner: What kinds of things can we do for endangered species internationally?

Koford: Well, it's going to depend upon the kind of species you're dealing with. Some definitely require large tracts of un-disturbed land—jaguars, for example—and they've got to have big reserves. But many others will adapt, more or less, to civilization, with little refuges or sanctuaries. I think the condor must be one like that because that's what it's been doing on its own. It doesn't have any single, big tract where it ranges.

Questioner: Once the condors are all out of an area, how can anybody decide where they should be put back? Is it anything other than a wild guess?

Koford: No, nothing more. Actually, if you look at the history of successful introductions of birds and mammals in the US, you see that the most successful ones have been exotics. Among the game birds, I think they've had some successes; but even in the game birds, once they're wiped out of some area,

it's very hard to re-establish them there. If you bring in something new, like a ring-necked pheasant, to exploit a habitat
that's been developed through agriculture, why then it breeds
like mad. Offhand, I can't think of any outstanding successes in
reintroducing a native species. Well, the buffalo. . . . Its behavior is so changed, it's not the same.

Questioner: I guess they're going to try to follow some work
they've been doing with the peregrine, and figure that between
now and the time they have any captive condors to reintroduce, they'll have learned something. It seems an awful
gamble.

Koford: I think there must be other ways of solving the peregrine problem. As you know, there's the other, the taiga sub-
species that lives up north, up toward Hudson Bay. I think one
possibility would be to study them on the periphery of the
range where they meet whatever the limiting factors are, find
out what those factors are, and then improve the habitat a little
farther south. Just make that subspecies extend farther and
farther south all the time. Whatever the limiting factor is can be
removed, and the range can be extended a little. Then we
might have to make another study to find out what the new
limiting factors are, and extend the range again.

But condors obviously fly around where there are people.
They'll feed right next to a house or an oil derrick, if there's not
too much disturbance. But I don't think they'd nest. Nesting is
extremely sensitive. I think they might be sensitive about drinking, too, because that is rarely observed. The Santa Barbara
people, Janet Hamber and that group, had a kind of a census
with about a dozen stations in that area at the end of August.
Of about 12 stations, I think at least nine of them saw one or
two adult condors. Then they went into the little condor
sanctuary, only 1,200 acres over in Sisquoc Canyon. I had
suggested to them that the brush had grown over the water
and that condors weren't watering there because they couldn't
get in. So the Santa Barbara people went in there to see if the
brush should be cleared out, and they found condor feathers in
there—a place where no condors had been observed for ten
years or more. It shows they must be landing in there, and
watering. That's slightly encouraging. But as far as I know,
there's no evidence for any more than two adult condors using

that western range—I mean Santa Barbara County, San Luis Obispo, and Monterey.

Questioner: In the environmental impact assessment, it says several times that "If the Fish and Wildlife Service doesn't take this action, the condors face extinction within 25 to 50 years." How can they make that statement?

Koford: Well, it's made on the basis of a fallacy: that condors aren't breeding. It's assuming they're not breeding at all.

Questioner: Their words were "near cessation in reproduction." But do they have enough verified biological data. . . .

Koford: No. That goes back to the contingency plan of 1976, which was submitted in July. In 1974, there were only four immature condors known in the population, and no nesting at all in 1974. So that got them started with this idea that they're not breeding. They didn't *find* any breeding and there were only four immatures. This report came out in the middle of 1976, and there had been no nesting found up until the time it was published. But later that year, they found two fledged young condors—one of them in August over in Santa Barbara County, and one in December in the condor sanctuary. It just shows how lousy their observations had been. That's where the idea came that they weren't breeding. It's obvious since then—because there are five or six or seven immatures now— that they must be breeding. Not only breeding, but surviving to fly around. For every bird that fledges successfully, that probably represents two nests that were started; with most of these big birds, there's about a 50 percent loss between the laying of the egg and the fledging.

Questioner: Do you think it's possible to protect the habitat in a way that would let condors increase their population to a sustainable level?

Koford: Yes, I think so. The question is, how you do it. The Eb McMillan way, I think—which is, the best thing that can happen to a condor nest is that nobody finds it. Because once people find it, they're going to be observing it. And they don't realize—I mean people like Borneman don't realize—the damage you can do to condor nesting even by standing up and looking at it from half a mile away. I've got another thesis over there on turkey vulture nesting in Texas; when they examined the nest during the incubation stage, quite a few were later deserted. And bald eagle nests on Vancouver Island, in British Columbia. If you just add up the statistics, and separate nests which were visited from those that weren't visited, you'll see that even one visit to the nest decreases by about 10 percent the chances of fledging a bird. Any disturbance is too much, and you can't tell by looking at the bird. You're sitting there, and the condor is sitting there; but the condor isn't going in and feeding the young, which is what it would be doing if you weren't there. There's no way you can judge how disturbed a bird is.

It seems to me there is a tremendous gap in this whole program in that there isn't a habitat plan, a habitat protection plan. We've been looking at this with respect to the biological, reproductive capacities of the condor. That is not necessarily going to give us the kind of understanding we need for the protection of habitat, which is essentially a political concern. It's our position that the politics of the situation have not been adequately addressed. There is a tremendous lack. We would feel much more confident about what is being done at the biological level if there was some concomitant plan of similar intensity for the environment. Our feeling is that this is an extraordinarily ill-balanced program.

—FRED EISSLER

3   Ian McMillan

An Objection to Feeding Condors
Poisoned Condors
Botching the Condor Program
Condors Leave Heart of California
Interview, Spring 1980

A LIFELONG resident of condor country, Ian McMillan is a rancher and naturalist from northeastern San Luis Obispo County. For more than thirty years he was involved in the observation and study of California condors. He wrote *Man and the California Condor* (Dutton, 1968), has been a frequent contributor to *Defenders of Wildlife News*, and is a Fellow of the California Academy of Sciences. "An Objection to Feeding Condors," "Poisoned Condors," and "Botching the Condor Program" appeared in *Defenders of Wildlife News* between 1965 and 1970. "Condors Leave Heart of California" first appeared in *Earth's Advocate* in 1976.

Ali Pearson

An Objection to Feeding Condors

THE INNATE HUMAN urge to tame the wild has about reached its final accomplishment—only a few remote relics remain of our wild estate and these are under direct threat by the onrushing human horde. A chronic manifestation of this urge is the proposition to feed California condors as a needed practice in condor preservation. The following is an objection to any such proposition.

Field investigations have consistently found that condors are finding a sufficient supply of food. To tamper with this normal food situation by supplementing or substituting an easily available, artificial supply would be a well-known means of upsetting a species' natural ecology and rendering it unfit for natural survival.

While the condor population has suffered loss in the last two decades, this loss cannot be attributed to lack of food but must be blamed instead mainly on inexcusable shooting. This illegal shooting and other pressing matters of condor protection might well fail to receive the needed measures of prevention if starvation should be made a scapegoat for the real trouble. If the laws and regulations now established to protect the condor were being properly administered and complied with there is good evidence that the species would be thriving and the population increasing.

The program for the protection and preservation of the condor was established to provide for the survival of the remaining population as a free-living, wilderness species under as natural conditions as may be obtained. In this program certain areas of their remote, natural habitat have been set aside to serve exclusively as refuge and sanctuary for the condors with enforced restrictions against any human activity that would disturb their normal way of living. As proved by a normal proportion of young birds found in the current population, these wilderness retreats are effectively operating as vital roosting, nesting and rearing habitat. This evidence of successful reproduction also confirms an adequate, sustained food supply. Thus, through their present mode of survival, it can be claimed with all importance and significance, that the surviving condors are still the real thing—a wild, free-living species, fending for themselves in the way of getting food. As to how long this claim may be valid, however, there is considerable question. The longer the condor prevails in the natural state the more it becomes the object of the previously mentioned human propensity to tamper with its wildness and bring it under human control.

In support of leaving the condors alone in getting their own food, three main reasons are given: (1) To feed California condors would tend to weaken and debilitate the birds for natural survival. (2) It would tend to undermine the integrity and purpose of the condor preservation program. (3) It would nullify the real human benefits that are derived through protecting and trying to preserve such things as wild condors and their wilderness habitat.

To qualify the first reason it should be pointed out that in matters of species survival available food is generally considered as the basic factor. Evolution, working through natural selection, has used this factor above all others as the implement to develop and mold different species. It may well be said that a condor is a condor by virtue of the ways in which it has had to get its food. The keen sensitivities which enable it to locate distant carrion; the marvelous adaptation for long, economical flight allowing it to cover a vast range in search of food; its nesting habits, rate of reproduction and selection of habitat, are condor characteristics that have derived mainly through adaptation to a special kind of food supply. To tamper with these natural food habits by artificial feeding might well weaken or completely nullify the forces of natural selection through which the condor has survived. It could expose this characteristically wild species to the debilitating and degenerating processes of domestication.

With regard to the second reason for this objection, it is important to point out that without firm integrity and high morale the condor preservation program could easily deteriorate into something worse than nothing at all—another farce masquerading as conservation, contributing only to the perversion and defeat of its own purpose. As understood, the purpose of the condor program has been the farthest thing from anything that would tend to beggarize or domesticate the California condor. Administrators of this program should fully assume the responsibility of upholding the integrity of this simple but vital purpose. Precedent should be firmly maintained in matters where any yielding of established restrictions or policy could lead to more of the same. Throughout their entire range the concept that condors are to be *"left alone"* has been increasingly accepted and supported. This concept should be closely adhered to in the official program of condor preservation. To be offering food to the condors is not leaving them alone. The hope, as well as the purpose, of the condor preservation program is that natural selection will be allowed to continue its infinitely accurate work of fitting the condor for natural survival. The integrity and the morale of the whole program rests on whether this purpose is conscientiously and intelligently pursued.

The third reason given against offering the condors food concerns the practical human benefits that underlie the purpose of saving condors. The real importance of saving such things as condors is not so much that we need condors, as that we need to save condors. We need to exercise and develop the human attributes required in the saving of condors; for these are the attributes so necessary in working out our own survival. The wild condor represents a remnant vestige of a recent wilderness resource out of which "man has hammered the artifact called civilization." It has become a most fitting symbol both of wilderness and of the resources derived from wilderness. In this way it also symbolizes the meaning of survival as that word continually takes on added meaning in human affairs. The wild condor, with the program for its preservation, offers a medium through which people anywhere may identify themselves in a personal way with the Conservation Movement. This program affords the average person a means of expressing a growing ecologic awareness—a feeling of respect and an attitude of acknowledgment—toward the natural principles which govern the survival of wild condors and probably the survival of the human species. The highest value of the condor preservation program is derived in the form of these stimulated and inspired human attitudes and feelings. This final value would most certainly be impaired if the California condors were no longer faced with the necessity of getting their own food.

Poisoned Condors

Kern county in central California is a main center of sheep grazing. Consequently it is also a center of Federal predator control. Much of the county lies within the present foraging range of the California condor.

In May of 1960 a disabled condor was found on a stock range in Kern County. It died and on being examined showed no injury, but had an enlarged liver. A month later another condor was found dead in the same locality with no evidence of injury. In 1963 a third condor also with no evidence of injury was found dead in the area. All three birds were found within the same ranching locality where condors commonly forage.

Although the two condor deaths in 1960 were officially known, they received no official attention except that the sick bird was first delivered to a veterinarian hospital with the carcass later taken to a museum. Poison was generally considered by local ranchers to have caused the death of the condors and this opinion was known by officials in charge of various, local poisoning operations. No attempt by any agency was made to determine the cause of the mortality.

In a survey of the California condor in 1963 and 64, special investigation was made of the condor losses in Kern County. All possible sources of information on the matter were questioned thoroughly and repeatedly. The local office of Federal predator control was given particular questioning on the possibilities of its poisoning operations being implicated in any condor mortality. All questioning received the universal response that no condors had been poisoned or could have been poisoned.

Near the end of the investigation it began to appear that although a great abundance of circumstantial evidence was available, no positive proof could be shown that any condor had ever been poisoned. Then from some deep archives came an amazing and most confirming document. From the Washington office of the Fish and Wildlife Service came a memorandum giving the details of a poisoning incident in which three condors were found in 1950 at the carcass of a poisoned coyote. This occurred in the same area where the dead condors were found in the early 1960's. The dead coyote had been partially eaten, evidently by the condors. One of the birds was dead. The other two were near death but they amazingly responded to treatment and recovered sufficiently in about a week to again be able to fly. The only persons knowing of this incident were officials and personnel of the Federal poisoning agency.

The stomach tract of the dead condor on analysis was found to contain an amount of the same poison that killed the coyote. Evidently the coyote had eaten several poisoned baits and had died with a heavy concentration of poison in its stomach. Condors commonly feed first on the viscera of dead animals. The three birds in feeding on the stomach contents of the coyote could have taken exceptional amounts of the poison.

Although this incident was of tremendous significance and importance it remained for the next fourteen years a hidden secret. During thirteen of those years the same practice in which the condors were poisoned, continued, with dead, uninjured condors continuing to be found under circumstances in which poison was the prime suspected cause of the mortality.

During the 1963-64 condor investigations when the officialdom of animal control was challenging and denying the charge that condors had been poisoned, various high officials of that officialdom knew of the yet-hidden condor poisoning incident of 1950.

Even after the confirming report was brought forth of the poison being found in the dead condor, some of the implicated officialdom, evidently through force of habit, were still denying that any condor had ever been poisoned.

This amazing propensity to evade and deny the known truth was quite dramatically exhibited in an official document issued in the summer of 1965 by the Federal Bureau of Sport Fisheries and Wildlife as its Management and Research Plan for the California Condor. Discussing the use of chemical poisonings in relation to the condor, this recent document includes the following, main statement: "There seems to be no positive proof that coyote and rodent poisoning programs in the range of the condor have contributed to its decline."

It would be interesting to know what this poisoning agency would accept as "positive proof", that any animal other than one of its "target species" has ever been poisoned or could be poisoned.

Botching the Condor Program

I N STUDIES of the California condor, one axiom has been clearly established: to survive, the great birds must have places of sanctuary and seclusion, *beyond the reach of man,* in which to nest and rear their young.

In 1947, after extensive research, the Sespe Condor Sanctuary was established as an inviolate condor nesting retreat. This 53,000 acre piece of wilderness, already a traditional center of condor nesting, was given special protection under regulations that prohibit any human disturbance of nesting condors. A patrol has been maintained to prevent illegal entry.

Although serious breakdowns have occurred in the administration of the Sespe Sanctuary, the closed area has functioned with dramatic effect as an indispensable wilderness home for the condors. In the years of intensive research which led to establishment of the refuge, Carl Koford, who carried out the study, found a maximum of four active nests in one year. In 1967, a total of six active condor nests were found in a new research project by the U.S. Fish and Wildlife Service. Five of these were in or near the Sespe Sanctuary.

This could only indicate that after twenty years in operation the refuge was functioning most effectively in accord with its purpose. It is my considered opinion that without the special protection given this vital nesting retreat, the California condor would now be extinct.

It might seem from this, that a favorable and optimistic account of the condor program can be given. Instead, an alarming and perhaps disastrous development must be reported. The new condor research, which began in 1966, is part of the much publicized Federal Endangered Species Program. Its main operation, as confirmed in the discovery of six active nests in

1967, has obviously been to find and examine condor nests. Another early result of the project was the delivery in the spring of 1967 of a strong, healthy young condor to a zoo in Los Angeles. This brings into focus an orientation toward artificial propagation that has quickly become the main aspect of the federal project. The whooping crane, like the condor, a creature of wilderness, also high on the list of endangered species, provides a parallel. Under the new Endangered Species Program artificial propagation has quickly become a conspicuous practice in the preservation of the whooping crane.

When it was first discovered that the new condor study was operating mainly as a search for and invasion of active nests, serious apprehension was registered. The activity, as it centered inside the Sespe Sanctuary, was obviously violating the specific purpose of the refuge. Despite vigorous and pointed protests, the strange operations have continued.

In the research out of which the Sespe Sanctuary was established, the effects of human disturbance on nesting condors were thoroughly studied and set forth. Carl Koford concluded a chapter of his monograph as follows: "One man can keep a pair of condors from the egg all night or prevent the feeding of a chick for an entire day merely by exposing himself within 500 yards of a nest for a few minutes at one or two critical times of the day. Loud noises can alarm condors at distances of over one mile. Individuals or groups of persons moving about must keep at least one-half mile from condor nests in order to avoid disturbance of the parent birds. If the adults soar or perch nearby when a man is close to the nest, it is because of their concern for the nest or its contents and not because of their tameness."

The occupancy and success of a condor nest can be readily determined without invading the site or even the immediate area. At a distance of a mile, nesting adults can be watched as they enter and leave the nest and a fledgling condor can be readily identified as it remains in the territory for months after leaving the nest. In view of this and the known effects of disturbance on nesting condors, it seems incredible that a concerted official project of entering and molesting condor nests would be undertaken by the authorities in charge of condor preservation.

With the annual search for active condor nests continuing unabated, opponents of this practice have hoped that the damage done to the condor population might be less than the previous research would indicate. But instead, the appeals and protests now appear to have greatly understated the potentialities of the new disturbance. Only a single occupied nest has been found in the two years following 1967 when the six active nest were examined. Since that year, no nestings have been known to occur in the Sespe Condor Sanctuary or nearby areas. The single nest that has been found to be occupied in 1968 and 1969 is remote from the Sespe Sanctuary by a distance of some 90 airline miles. Yet, even as it became obvious that the research operations might be causing a general nesting failure, this single site has been repeatedly invaded during the nesting period. Furthermore, it has been clearly noted that information gained in the repeated invasion of this lone, isolated nest could have been as readily obtained by watching the site from a convenient observation point almost a mile distant.

Nesting failure, concurrent with and evidently correlated with the new research operations, is confirmed by decreasing numbers of immature condors reported in the official annual condor surveys. Only six immature birds were identified in a total of 53 condors calculated to have been the minimum sighted in the 1969 count. This, when compared to 14 young birds noted in a total of 51 condors reported for the 1966 survey, tends to confirm a disastrous lowering of reproduction.

But here again, in this annual count, there is reason to be alarmed about the soundness and reliability of the entire new program. The first annual condor survey was conducted in 1965 as an operation headed by the California Department of Fish and Game. Since then, however, the Federal Fish and Wildlife Service has gained a dominant role in making the official determinations of the counts. And those interpretations are as scientifically questionable as the new practice of climbing into condor nests.

There is no feasible way to determine the exact number of living California condors. It is doubtful that more than about three-fourths of the population ever appear in a group or could otherwise be accurately accounted for. Except when foraging, condors generally keep to the most remote and inaccessible parts of their range. Ranging a region some 200 miles in length and almost as wide, most of which is rugged, brush-covered mountains, the great birds naturally and almost miraculously keep out of human sight. With an exact count impossible, many different criteria and methods have been employed by different authorities in reaching official population figures. As a result, contradiction and inconsistency have worked with disagreement to confuse, divide and weaken the forces of condor preservation.

The first official condor count was made by the U.S. Forest Service in the late 1930's with two observers watching for a ten-day period at two favorite condor retreats some fifty miles apart in Los Padres National Forest. From this and other information the total population in 1939 was officially estimated to number between fifty-five and sixty birds.

Carl Koford began his study in 1939 with data on condor numbers generally gathered over the following ten years. In his report published in 1953, he estimated the condor population at that time to number sixty birds. More recently, in 1964, a two-year study, sponsored by the National Audubon Society and directed by the University of California, resulted in an estimate of forty condors as the total number remaining. This indicated a decline of about a third during the decade following Koford's report.

At the time of the Koford report the confusion of official opinion regarding condor numbers was dramatically demonstrated. In 1953, a zoo in southern California was attempting to trap a pair of adult condors for purposes of propagating the species in captivity. Operating with official permission at a point on the border of the Sespe Condor Sanctuary, this project had the required approval of the California Department of Fish and Game. The trapping permit was issued on the Department's assurance that condors were far more numerous than estimated in Koford's report. One published report, based on this official information, gave the estimated number of condors in existence as "more than 150". Significantly, however, no more than twelve of the big birds were noted at one time in the year of trapping operations and the zoo failed to trap any condors.

The first condor survey of the present program was conducted in the fall of 1965 with sightings recorded at 69 observation stations located throughout the condor range. The combined sightings were interpreted to represent 38 individual birds. The next year, with the U.S. Fish and Wildlife Service becoming active in the interpretations, the number counted jumped to 51. Since that count, the annual findings have varied only slightly with a high of 53 condors calculated to have been identified in the last (1969) survey. If based on this "rock bottom" index of 53 birds, the lowest reasonable estimate of the total population would undoubtedly be at least 60 individuals. This would exceed by 20 birds, or 50 percent, the 40 condors estimated to be the total population in 1964, as determined in two years of field investigations.

Oddly, although the total number of birds counted is pointedly referred to as an "index" to the total population, there has been no official estimate of what the total number is considered to be. This evasion is clearly documented in the report of the Third California Condor Survey: "On each of the three surveys additional condor sightings, representing one or more condors unaccounted for in the survey, have been reported by nonsurvey observers. These have not been included because the final survey count is an index and not a total count. The count secondarily represents a minimum population figure, but this figure has not been projected to a total population estimate." Thus, contradiction and confusion remain the characteristic aspects of official condor information.

Having participated in the 1963-64 study, I have been concerned about how that quite extensive appraisal could have failed to account for at least a third of the condor population. Hoping to examine the concrete evidence that presumably would be the basis of the new, high figures, I have reviewed the records of the recent surveys. I have found nothing in the field data of those counts to substantiate any more condors than were indicated in the data of the 1963-64 study.

Attending different evaluation sessions of the annual count, I have observed the system used to reduce the field sightings to the number of condors reported. This method is evidently unique and was conceived as a sort of experiment by the technicians in charge. Purportedly it works to produce the "rock bottom" or "minimum" number of condors that could possibly be represented in the combined sightings. Since one condor can be sighted several times by different observers, the system of evaluation must work accurately to test whether each sighting represents a condor already listed.

To understand this system, I watched the evaluations of the fourth (1968) survey. That count produced a total of 52 condors, as reduced from a total of 174 sightings. The first 84 sightings (almost half the total), as processed in chronological order, were interpreted to represent 23 condors. This represented all sightings made prior to 1:00 P.M. The day of the count was mild and bright. This would mean that by early afternoon practically the entire condor population except nestlings would have been on the wing for hours. By one o'clock most of them would have been sighted by one or more of the 66 observation stations, which were located at strategic points throughout the condor range. It seemed obvious, therefore, that the remaining sightings would not represent as many additional condors as the 23 already listed. It also seemed inevitable that as the number of identified condors increased, the problem of evaluating the remaining sightings, so as to avoid duplication would become progressively complex and difficult.

However, instead of becoming more thorough and deliberate, the analysis of the later sightings speeded up. Criteria previously used were no longer applied with some sightings simply listed as representing new birds without reference to those already identified. Regardless of the extreme improbabilities involved, 29 new condors were counted from the sightings made after 1:00 P.M. This was six more birds than were listed for the six hours of earlier sightings. For this to have actually occurred would require an extreme deviation from normal condor foraging habits.

The general breakdown that developed late in the count was particularly noticeable in the listing of the last 10 condors. These last 10 birds were produced from the last 12 sightings. For any one of them to have been a bird not previously seen and listed in the count would be most unlikely. For 10 of the last 12 sightings to actually represent "new birds" seems beyond the realm of credibility.

Already it appears that the new high figures for population status have resulted in further confusion and contradiction. The main conclusion of an official report covering the first two years of the new research pointed out that the investigations indicated "an annual reproduction insufficient to maintain the present population." The report was issued by the U.S. Fish and Wildlife Service. Although it covered no later work than the nesting research of 1967, it failed to explain how the high number of six condor nests found that year would indicate an "insufficient" rate of reproduction. Nor did it offer any intimation of what "the present population" was considered to be. Evidently the strange conclusion was based on an estimated condor population far above even sixty inividuals. In direct contradiction to this Federal report, the official report of the 1967 Condor Survey which was issued by the California Department of Fish and Game, included this salient comment: "Based on survey information, at least 11 different young were observed. This is approximately 25 percent of the count, indicating a satisfactory proportion of young adults." Of final incredibility, the senior author of the report by the California Department of Fish and Game was the same Federal wildlife technician who did the research and prepared the contradicting report of the U.S. Fish and Wildlife Service.

For those concerned about the preservation of endangered species, and especially the California condor, it would be most heartening to have credible evidence that the condor population is considerably higher than the number reported in the previous study of 1963-64. Concrete evidence that should be required to corroborate and confirm the high figures of the new condor surveys has not been produced. Maximum groupings of condors, as noted in a growing abundance of recent field records, do not indicate a condor population of over 40 individuals. A series of baiting surveys, obviously designed to confirm the high figures of the recent official counts, has failed to produce evidence of any more condors than were indicated in the 1963-64 survey. In October of 1969, locations in 8 favorite condor foraging areas were baited and watched for 4 consecutive days. No condors came to any of the baits.

Whatever may be the objectives of the new condor program, it is obviously working to advance the argument for saving the rare birds by raising them in pens. Soon it can be expected that the nesting failures of the last two years will be projected as headline information with no word of the correlated nesting depredations. Public inquiry, as to the cause, will probably be directed to either pesticides, food shortage or urban spread. The correct number of condors when found to be less than the recent high counts, will be reported as evidence of inevitable decline. The easy, simple, and sure alternative of a caged avicultural existence for the California condor will be the final proposition, unless those who believe wildlife should remain wild will assert themselves.

Condors Leave Heart of California

I N 1911, the ornithologist, William Leon Dawson, was gathering information for his historic writings on the birds of California. Although his explorations covered practically all parts of central California, to see the California condor and an active condor nest, he made a special trip into a wild, remote canyon of the La Panza Range in eastern San Luis Obispo County.

From what he saw there Dawson wrote: "For me the heart of California lies in the condor country. And for me the heart of mystery, of wonder, and of desire lies with the California condor, that majestic and almost legendary figure that still haunts the fastnesses of our lessening wilderness."

For the several decades following Dawson's expedition, the condors here in the "heart of California" held out almost miraculously against new and increasing forms of adversity.

Even though their general population was declining from an estimated total of 60 birds in 1953 to an estimate of 40 in 1964, San Luis Obispo County condors were still appearing in fair numbers throughout the 1960s, with evidence of normal reproduction. Flocks numbering as many as 10 birds were seen at different times foraging over the open stock ranges in the eastern part of the county.

In the period 1967 to 1969 a pair of condors nested each year in one of the species' ancestral nesting haunts in the Pozo Range not far from the site of Dawson's historic visit in 1911, and not more than a dozen airline miles from the city of San Luis Obispo.

But today, the nest site sits abandoned, and the flocks of foraging condors have disappeared from San Luis Obispo County's skies.

What happened to this last nesting stronghold is typical of the travesty through which our society purports to provide for the survival of endangered species.

To survive, condors must have places of sanctuary and seclusion beyond the reach of man in which to nest and rear their young. Places of this kind have been steadily vanishing. The relic of wilderness on which the great wild bird depends for its survival is located, in dramatic paradox, practically in the midst of that area in south central California where man is doing more in less time to alter and destroy his own environment than at any other place or time in history. In the 1930s, the bulldozer appeared in condor country to begin its work of building roads for mass, motorized travel into the few remaining wilderness retreats. This brought an increase of the wanton shooting that had been a main cause of condor mortality since the first white men with guns entered the condor's range. In addition to the shooting, condors were killed from feeding on the carcasses of animals poisoned in official animal control programs.

This nesting site in San Luis Obispo County, although situated in the midst of a remnant piece of wilderness in Los Padres National Forest, was within open view and hearing distance of a new reservoir being constructed only a mile or two away in the canyon below. Urban development was sweeping over this heartland of California and the wild canyon was dammed at its lower levels to provide for the planned growth. In the spring of 1969, the new reservoir was opened as a center for water-oriented recreation.

Roads leading from the development reached into the back country near and above the condor nest. This area of public land was already becoming a national and even international center for off-road motorcycle racing and other forms of motorized, back country travel. Moreover, as if all this was not enough to destroy the area as condor habitat, the agencies responsible for protection of the condor, including the California Department of Fish and Game, the Forest Service, the Fish and Wildlife Service and the National Audubon Society, were allowing their wildlife technicians to freely invade and enter the condor nest during the nesting period, thus violating a basic precept of condor preservation.

If our society was openly and willfully working to drive the condor into extinction, the known practices by which to achieve such a result could hardly have been more thoroughly and efficiently applied and the outcome could hardly be more conclusive. Since 1969, when the new water development was opened as a recreation center, the ancestral condor nest in the canyon above has been vacant. Also, the non-nesting flocks that commonly ranged out over the outlying stockranges are absent. To my knowledge no condors were sighted in San Luis Obispo County in 1975.

Could it be that the condor is gone forever from the heart of California? If so, who would know and who would care? Almost certainly there would be the common though baseless rationale that condors and civilization are incompatible.

But an opposite view is far more realistic. The condor has been aptly compared to a canary in a coal mine: when the canary languishes, the environment has become hostile to man. It is barbarism, not civilization, that has destroyed the condor—barbarism with guns, poison, the bulldozer and ruinous economic growth.

The fact that condors were not exterminated decades ago must be attributed entirely to the program for their preservation. That program was a great human achievement and a true hallmark of civilization. Its failure can only mean that our society is losing the capacity for saving such things as condors and condor country. In this way it may be losing the key to its own survival.

Interview, Spring 1980

F RIENDS OF THE EARTH interviewed Ian McMillan in the spring of 1980. An edited version of the taped interview follows. The questioners were David Brower and David Phillips. Mr. McMillan began the interview without waiting for questions:

I think we might start back around 1953 at a hearing in San Francisco when we—just a few local individuals concerned about the condor trapping project, or the captive propagation project that was in operation—had reached a point where we felt that it had to be brought under control. It started out to be a captive breeding project on the grounds that there were plenty of condors and just taking a couple for breeding purposes in the San Diego Zoo wouldn't have an impact on the population. They went out and tried to trap them for about a year, but there weren't as many condors as they thought and they weren't so easy to trap. They changed the whole rationale around: if they didn't get them quick, well, the population was on the verge of extinction and that was the only way to save them. It appeared to become more of a publicity operation—a promotion of the captive breeding thing—than anything based on the actual concerns of the condor. We protested this at a hearing of the Fish and Game Commission, and we encountered this subterfuge that has characterized this movement from the start. They would say how careful they were being with condors, and how this trapping would be done in such a way that there would be no damage to the population—no birds injured. We knew at that time that they were using coyote traps, steel-jawed coyote traps. This was occurring right on the edge of the Sespe Condor Sanctuary at a time when the condors were nesting.

Our protest was unsuccessful because we were confronted with testimony on the other side that wasn't very sound. At that time we just happened to have a very favorable representative in the state senate, Senator Erhart. I came home and wrote a letter to Senator Erhart explaining this, and he was able to get through legislation that brought the thing to a halt. This is when I first got acquainted, well acquainted, with the general—the endemic—mood on the part of different interests to exploit the condor, this move to preserve the bird by captive propagation and zoological means. So that's when I got my first general understanding of this whole thing.

My brother and I were engaged by the National Audubon Society and the National Geographic Society to make a condor survey in 1963 and '64. Here again, when we got out we found fewer condors than we expected to find, and we found them to be suffering from all sorts of man-caused adversity that we weren't expecting to find and certainly wouldn't have found if the program had been operating right. We found dead condors. We found shot condors. We found a state of disorder in the administration of the Sespe Condor Sanctuary. We found the national forest generally to be a place where the condor wasn't getting along well. We found an amazing lack of understanding of the condor, a lack of information on the part of almost the entire administration of the national forest, including the local personnel. Above all, we found the condor—although declining—reproducing normally and demonstrating an almost incredible capacity for natural survival. Going out in the hunting grounds and the poisoning places and seeing everything the condor was up against, we were impressed with the capacity of this bird to survive. On that basis, we set up our recommendations that mainly were simply to provide the condor with opportunities to survive in its natural state—a program that was supposed to be in operation but wasn't being administered that way.

We recommended that the whole question of poison be thoroughly examined, particularly having to do with 1080. Nothing of that kind was done, and 1080 continued to be used, if anything, more extensively. And not only extensively, but with the toxicity of the bait increased. There was some improvement made in introducing the public to the condor, and some improvement made for sure in the extent to which hunters were warned about the condor. This might have been helpful. But there wasn't much done about off-road vehicles. We can still get this year, perhaps, continuing, this enduro race right out here in our own condor country—an international motorcycle race that uses to a great extent the heartland of condor country. The Forest Service literally promoted this. We couldn't see how the agency was doing that—could be doing that—and at the same time claim to be conscientiously supporting the condor program. Alden Miller, who was the advisor and head man of our survey, was the greatest orinthologist of that time in my opinion, and a very sound man in matters of integrity. A very strong person, he was really rock-ribbed in the position we were taking and was tremendously effective. After our studies were in and a new program commenced, Miller headed the advisory group that was appointed. Right as the program was getting into operation, we lost Alden Miller. He died. I am prepared to say that if this hadn't happened—if he could have lived on to see that the program we recommended was established on a firm basis—it is my firm belief that the condors would be holding their own. There would be as many condors today as we found, perhaps more.

It wasn't only that we lost Miller, but with his loss, back in moved the same captive-propagation-oriented interests that we had contested back in 1953. I replaced Alden Miller on the advisory committee, but I was quickly removed. All this pitched the condor program away from our recommendations for a natural program toward the cage-oriented program that has had, in my view, such a debilitating effect. The energy and the force and the work that is absolutely required for our kind of program wasn't there.

Questioner: There was a low priority for habitat protection?

McMillan: Right. And very vital things that took a lot of force and were unpopular but had to be done were slighted. Instead of the motorcycle races being stopped or at least confined to areas that wouldn't be too serious for the condor, they just went on. I was kind of moved out of the program. I did attend some of the counts later, because I *insisted* on it. I actually had to get my representative in the state legislature to get a seat for me so that I could witness these counts, where I found that this whole thing had shifted from what I considered sound scientific research into a subjective operation that was oriented toward producing first high figures and then the low figures that would show a drop and the futility of natural propagation.

Questioner: Do you feel that there has been a move to exclude people with a different opinion or people who have dissented on the captive breeding program, a move to exclude them from any participation in shaping the condor Recovery Plan?

McMillan: Well, in my own case, I was fired over an argument. I was removed—let's call it removed—from the advisory committee shortly after the first meeting, the very first meeting. I had learned that the new personnel in charge of the program were spending most of their time climbing into condors' nests. The new project was designed to go out and get information about nesting condors—examining, entering, invading all condor nests, any place that a bird might be. I was horrified, because if there is one thing we all agreed on—even the old egg collector that I first worked with on condors—we all agreed that when man enters and creates a disturbance, condors leave the area. This is the history of their movements. And it isn't only the condors. I've worked with other birds. The reason they go out to these remote places to nest, just as far away from man as they can get, is from an inherent defense mechanism. I asserted this very strenuously at the meeting. I very strenuously objected to this, and perhaps might have been a little harsh. But I felt I had to be. I was alone, absolutely alone, in the advisory committee.

Questioner: What year would this have been?

McMillan: This was 1967. I have a large file on this. I'm a member of the Cooper Ornithological Society, which has been one of the leading forces in condor study and condor preservation. I sent word in 1967 that I would say something at the 1967 annual meeting about the process that was being used to count the condors, which I thought was tremendously faulty. By golly, I noticed very quickly that there was going to be a rebuttal. Instead of going down to offer a little, insignificant account of this counting procedure, I was going to be confronted with a big rebuttal—the California Department of Fish and Game, the US Fish and Wildlife Service—before a group of very important people. I didn't get very far. I was quite concerned even about my colleagues of the Cooper Society, many of whom had fallen in with the opposition and were supporting their system of counting—which today, they themselves have disclaimed. My concern was that here, we have got to be careful about these counts. Because if we don't, we are going to have the first big counts. I've seen this before: the big counts; birds all over the place; no need to be concerned; everything is fine. And suddenly this changes, changes abruptly, from a high to a low that shows the condor to be absolutely beyond the point of no return—the only thing to do to save them now is to go out there and get them into cages.

Questioner: I know that Carl Koford was worried about that and said that initially, they were doing all kinds of double counting and coming up with high numbers. Now they are trying to make the numbers so low that this last-ditch method is the only thing left, captive breeding—when there have been no year-to-year changes that can be documented scientifically.

McMillan: I have a letter I want to give you that I wrote to Charlie Callison, who was then executive vice president of the National Audubon Society. I tried to tell Charlie, look here, this thing is just going headlong into a big zoo project. The young fellows they've got out in the field are inexperienced and highly susceptible to whoever's in charge of them. At that time Carl Koford was available. He had just completed some research in some other part of the world. One of the most eminent field zoologists at that time, and even now. Here he was, available for a study of the turkey vulture, which he would conduct in this area. With the turkey vulture in the same habitat and in many ways comparable to the condor, this would have provided some very good field information that we needed. Not only that, but it would have placed Carl Koford in a position to work with these inexperienced young fellows to study the whole thing and at least keep it from going completely over into this orientation for captive breeding. Here is a copy of the letter; it is just one of many futile efforts.

Questioner: What did Charlie do? Tell us.

McMillan: They [the National Audubon Society] agreed, yes, we should do this: but it would take some money. And of course, the Fish and Wildlife Service, the Forest Service, the whole bureaucracy, they liked this captive breeding proposition.

When we started our study, one of the things we noted was the attitude of the administration of the Los Padres National Forest, the higher authorities, taking the attitude that the condor was gone, that there was no use trying to save it in its natural habitat and "we can't interfere with the people's use of this forest just to save 32 birds." They were consistently trying to show that there were hardly any condors. We ran into this in our research when we made a field trip into the Sisquoc area at a time when there was a big controversy over a proposed road in the San Rafael Wilderness. The Forest Service was promoting it, conservation groups were trying to stop it. We were in a tough spot. We had to do objective research, but we were consistently confronted with the efforts of conservationists on the one side to show that this was the home of the condor and there were lots of condors, and on the other side, the Forest Service trying to pick out from our research anything that might support their argument that the condor was gone from that area.

Questioner: What do you think about some of the habitat threats now? Do you think habitat protection is still being given low priority?

McMillan: I would expect to find that if I were to go out as we did in 1963 and '64, I would find pretty much the same problems. I would still find the international enduro motorcyle races where about 500 motorcycles use a very key part of this condor area. I would just point to that as one indication of how really concerned, how really sincere, and how much the Forest Service is doing to see that this key area is protected. The program we recommended stressed the importance of getting the condors to move out and reoccupy some of their former range, which I think could still be done if they really worked at it—but you've got to work at it.

Questioner: The Sespe-Frazier Roadless Area has been proposed for wilderness designation to reduce the threats of off-road vehicles, dams, and oil exploration. But the Audubon Society, essentially through John Borneman, has back-pedaled on that. The Forest Service hasn't been willing to do much, and it doesn't look like Sespe-Frazier is going to get wilderness status. Do you have some thoughts on that?

McMillan: The Los Padres National Forest tends to know the importance of wilderness here, not just as it applies to the condor, but because of its almost weird location right here where man is doing more to destroy than any place else. But we found that the Forest Service was promoting off-road vehicle use. Incredibly, the condor warden—the man who had been placed in charge of the condor program was operating on his off days as a salesman for an off-road vehicle firm.

Questioner: One researcher, (it may have been Sibley), came up with what he considered to be a formula for how close humans could get to condors without interfering with normal roosting, nesting, and so on. John Borneman and others have now kind of adopted this. Is this sensible? Or should activity be limited even in areas where condors might potentially begin to roost and nest?

McMillan: Well, I don't know how you can overemphasize the need for seclusion, for remoteness, for isolation of the condor in its roosting retreat and its nesting retreat. Foraging grounds aren't nearly as important: condors may come right out and forage within view of a road, still wary. But when one takes its fill and rises, you can just gamble that it's heading for a retreat that is just as far as it can get from a human being or any disturbance. Until it can be said with certainty that the condor is no longer capable of viability and survival in the wild, there should be no implementation of a program for captive propagation. That's a diversion. And there are no agreed-upon criteria for determining at what point the condor can be considered no longer viable. The whooping crane population, which I think was 15 in 1921, made a remarkable recovery in the natural state. In view of this, to say that because there are only 25 to 30 condors, the condors for that reason are no longer able to survive in the wild is incredible. I am still prepared to say that if there are as many as 24 or 25 birds—let's say 18 adults, nesting adults—and if those adults are given the chance I believe they can be given, in a natural state, we will see a return to normal reproduction, a reproduction rate that not only maintains the population, but increases it. There is a tremendous difference between what you can expect from a program that has the right objective and one that hasn't.

Questioner: The captive breeding program calls for laparotomies, surgical procedures to determine the birds' sex. What is that going to do?

McMillan: Well, in other species—in cattle, for instance—this is what we call stressing. This is stressing. When you stress cattle—shipping, putting them through an auction sale, branding, and all—you cause them to be susceptible not only to all this psychological stuff, but to physical impact in the form of diseases. Knowing the condor as I do, knowing the extent to which it is inherently not an animal that is happy in captivity, to do all this we're talking about would literally render them absolutely incapable of any further hope of survival in the wild. Even if the birds were going to be used for captive propagation, it could cause a serious effect on their capacity for that.

I have studied this mainly in the hunting of quail. There is always this old question of how many quail can you harvest with a minimum of damage. First, you find out that the main damage is in all the disturbance that quite often works to alienate the birds. Quite often it works to alienate the birds to their native winter habitat. They just disappear. I have a lot of quail right out in the yard now. In my studies, I have rendered a population of quail completely dependent upon an artificial food supply, just by feeding it. I have them right now, and those quail have lost the capacity for natural survival through having this supplemental food supply at a critical time of the year. I know that they are rendered incapable of natural survival because I have shut the supplemental food supply off and seen how quickly these birds will starve. They become flightless; the dogs can catch them. And while this is going on with them, almost within hearing distance of their calls, there'll be a wild covey of birds and they're getting along well. It is a field of study that has hardly been touched. That's why I felt so strongly about the nest invasions. Members of the advisory committee felt that I was unfair when I demonstrated as strongly as I did about it. As strongly as I expressed myself, it was to no avail.

Questioner: I remember a story from Jane Goodall or someone like that about a study in a baboon area, when they were really getting along pretty well. There was some human intrusion, but there was no upset. Then one was shot, and the word just spread all around, however they transmitted the message. That destroyed the whole bunch of them, destroyed their confidence.

McMillan: Yes, they will become alienated from that area. This has never been researched much. People will go out and count birds before the season opens; then the season opens and the fellows chase them around, maybe not kill too many, and say:

"Look, we are only taking 10 percent of the population. Well, we've got to raise the bag limit. We've got to lengthen the season."

There is no measurement of the impact of this, the psychological impact, and the stress this brings on the birds.

Questioner: I am asking this here because there is no evidence of any sensitivity on the part of any of the captive-breeding proponents as to what might happen just from that business of the capture, the hooking on of the transmitter, marking, and the laparotomy.

McMillan: This is right. I thought there was going to be support for this on the advisory committee because in all the literature, this is the key thing. The purpose of the sanctuary where they were doing these nesting investigations was to protect the condor strictly from this very kind of disturbance.

Incidentally, they were finding at that time six normal nests, I think, in 1967. They were finding normal reproduction and they were *reporting* normal reproduction. They have never, to my knowledge, even tried to explain what suddenly happened about 1970. After the disturbance of normal nesting, suddenly there was none. This is an issue that I think we have to keep in mind: if you are going to try to save condors—or as far as that is concerned, any other endangered wildlife—it has got to be in the natural state. I think this idea is very damaging, that the condor can only be saved through artificial propagation. It might be carried over to the peregrine falcon and a lot of other species.

McMillan: Carleton Coon—you probably know him, the anthropologist—his proposition was that we ought to think about the survival of our own species. We better be careful about the few remaining populations of primitive hunter-gatherers, because when our civilization collapses, they are the ones who will carry on.

Questioner: One thing that came up yesterday was that Noel Snyder, one of the condor study people, had studied the

Puerto Rican parrot, the population of which had dropped to something like 12 or 13. He used none of the high-tech methods; he was just watching. He came up with the surprise result that the population was dropping because of harassment by other birds, specifically the thrasher. Which led me to comment that they would probably get as a result of their studies the surprise that condors are suffering from harassment by scientists. And I think the rescue team is the principal harassment right now.

Second questioner: They talked yesterday about how they were going to try to justify all their capture technologies and radio transmitter work on Andean condors down in South America, and I am just wondering what kinds of things we should be looking for. They seem willing to accept that if they can do it without killing the birds, that amounts to success. We are trying to redefine how you determine success. What kinds of things need to be demonstrated with Andean condors, and is experience with Andean birds even analogous?

McMillan: No. In the first place, there isn't much relationship between the Andean and the California condor. Their evolution is probably entirely different. The Andean condor is found in a very remote area, where it is still doing pretty well. I don't think it has been subjected to the impact that has occurred to the California condor, and I don't think it has suffered from handling.

There is a point to be made when this arises. I wrote a book on the condor after our study, and to do that, I had to do some homework and get into a lot of things. One of the things I had to look into was the proposition that the condor was a bird of the Pleistocene. What bird *isn't*? And a bird of the Ice Age. Well, that's not so far off. It was assumed before carbon-14 dating that the birds around the La Brea tar pits—which aren't this condor at all, they are a different condor—date back around 50,000 years. Well, here comes carbon-14 dating, and it brings this down to about 14,500 years or so, which is contemporary with the advent of man. What happened to this great Pleistocene fauna that was there at that time? There is no evidence of any really significant change. There is a little change: maybe a couple of inches of rainfall. But there wasn't any known change in the environment that could account for the vanishing of all that. What does show up—the number one correlation—is the advent of this two-legged predator with his torch and his weapons. This concept has been advanced by Paul Martin, of Arizona. Man moves into an environment where the prey doesn't understand what he can do with his torch and his weapons, so he's able to go out and make a fantastic impact on his food supply. The kind of web that seems to unwind is a different condor—*Gymnogyps amplus*, probably an ancestor—with man moving in, with the whole thing changing, with the burning, with the killing and big game vanishing, and with terrific pressure on this condor producing a whole new process of evolution. And through it all, the celebration of rituals in which condors were captured and killed. Such terrific pressures would require, for its survival, that the condor keep away from man. Here is a bird that evolved, literally evolved, to keep away from humans, even to the point that when its nesting territory is invaded, it becomes alienated and starts looking for something else.

These are all things that haven't been brought into the picture. We need a condor program that is based on a complete understanding not only of the biology of the bird, its ecology, but on the fantastic . . . you might say the fantastic philosophical significance of the bird.

Ali Pearson

4   Eben McMillan

Something Is Basically Wrong

Interview, Spring 1980

Interview, Winter 1981

A RANCHER and naturalist from Cholame, California, Eben McMillan has lived his entire life in condor country. He spent a great amount of time in the field studying condors with Dr. Carl Koford and co-authored "The Current Status and Welfare of the California Condor" with Alden Miller and Ian McMillan. He has followed the condor debate for more than forty years, and continues to lead condor-watch trips. "Something is Basically Wrong" was first presented in January 1981 at a conference on the condor sponsored by the Santa Clara Valley Audubon Society.

Something Is Basically Wrong

F OR THOSE of you who don't happen to be acquainted with me, I'm a rancher from Eastern San Luis Obispo County, born and raised in the arid grassland area of the Temblor Mountains. And I got my first experience with condors hunting their eggs with a fellow named Kelly Truesdale.

Kelly was an oologist, and condor eggs, in those days, were worth 250 bucks and that'd buy a Ford automobile at that time. So you can get an idea how much effort he put into making sure that he'd get the egg of a condor if one was available. And after several years of this, the behavior of condors became as well known to Kelly as the behavior of his next door neighbor. In other words, he watched everything that happened in order that the condor not be able to thwart him in his attempt to get a new Ford, or perhaps a winter grubstake.

With your permission, I'm not going to deal with the technological aspects of the condor problem, because they have been well covered here today. But I would like to delve into some of the philosophical matters, because I really believe that this is the crux of the problem. I think that it's a human problem: if we keep nurturing the desire of man for more and more of less and less, why, we're going to have to admit pretty soon that not only the condor, but nearly every other species is in trouble. We're going to have to watch them go out. In fact, I could name three birds in the condor range that, even if we saved the condor, would still be in trouble: the yellow-billed cuckoo, the blue grosbeak and the Swainson hawk. I saw the day in the condor range when, in the month of May, you could drive out and see 10,000 Swainson's hawks moving in migration through the Carrizo Plains in eastern San Luis Obispo County. I haven't seen one for five years. Now, this should be telling us a story. This should be telling us a very serious story, that something is basically wrong.

I'm very thankful to Santa Clara Audubon for inviting me to be one of the speakers on the platform today. The Audubon Society has sponsored many meetings in regard to the condor, but I don't know of anybody that was invited that had an opposing view. Now, to me, this is one of the real problems we face, today. The Audubon Society has involved itself with this program, this Condor Recovery Program, to the point where it can't act objectively. It is in a position where it must defend the Condor Recovery Program sponsored by Audubon and the Fish and Wildlife Service. Now, this is a sad situation. I think that private organizations such as the Audubon Society acting in concert with government bureaucracies create a situation that is very dangerous. It would be quite similar if the Sierra Club and the National Park Service were to join together in running Yosemite National Park. Once you commit yourself to a situation like that, you're never again going to be able to speak for the interests of the public in general. And that's why, from the very start, I opposed the Audubon Society's getting involved in this thing. I think the longer it goes on, the worse it is getting.

It isn't going to be the Audubon Society's representatives or the Fish and Wildlife's representatives that are going to save the condor. It is going to be the people that save the condor, because we are the only ones that will stay on the job when things get tough. We better gear ourselves up for much more of this, because if things keep going as they are now, we are going to be involved in this with many, many species. It has only been in the last half of my life, the last 35 years, that changes are taking place and you see the habitat being destroyed at a rate that was never even dreamed of before.

Another aspect I'd like to bring out is the matter of technology. We're geared towards technological development. And I don't think there's anything wrong with technology provided that it is managed. But we don't seem to realize that technology is only as responsible as the people who manage it. One thing that worries me about this whole program is that it seems to be discouraging the development of qualified field biologists. Very few young people today are developing the ability to go out and sit by themselves on a hillside and be able to analyze what is there before them. This is something that we should think about when we are charting our course for the future.

One of the main recommendations at the time that the Audubon Society and the Fish and Wildlife Service took over in 1966 was to evaluate circumstantial evidence that pointed a serious finger towards the use of 1080 in the range of the condor. In an area of less than two square miles, I found evidence of three condor carcasses. Every one of them closely associated with the squirrel poisoning program and the use of 1080 poison. The first one of these I picked up from a lady that had gotten it from her neighbor. He had thrown it underneath a piece of tin, leaning against a corral, and it had lain there for six months. She said, "I'd like to take it up and put it over my front gate, so I would have a condor as a sort of insignia." And he said, "Well, you can sure have it." She took it up, and it was sort of smelly, yet she hung it on a wire fence and she hosed this thing down. The water ran down where there were some young ducks. It killed six of those ducks in an hour.

Now this in itself should have been enough evidence to make anyone suspicious, and I was suspicious. So we sent the carcass up to the University of California Department of Vertebrate Zoology. They kept it around and looked at it for awhile, and they took the bones, and then they thought maybe this head has a few articles of meat on it yet. Let's throw that head into the dermestid beetles and let them clean it up. And this they did. The second day after they threw it in, the dermestid beetles were all dead.

One of the Condor Recovery Team mentioned that we don't have any hard evidence, well, I don't know what hard evidence is. I think you have to accept some of these things.

I think we're in a situation where the house is burning down right now, and it behooves us to grab a hose and run around there and put the fire out, if it isn't too big already. These are things we can do. I don't know about the Fish and Wildlife Service and the Audubon Society, but I'll bet you this, that I can go to pretty near any service station in this town and I can hire a fellow and take him out into the east side of San Joaquin Valley where the squirrel poison program is going on, and with a little instruction, he'll find out if condors are eating the poisoned squirrels. I don't think you have to have a degree from a college to find that out. This is what I mean when I say basic research is what is really important. What is really important right now is to find those things that are causing the de-crease in the condor population. As soon as we find this out, then we can go about all those other things. But I don't really see any purpose in spending a lot of time looking for solutions to the house on fire; by the time you come back, there will only be a pile of ashes.

I would like to leave you with this idea in mind: basically, it is the individual that is going to save our environment. And whatever saves our environment is going to save the condor and is going to save everything that can be saved.

Interview, Spring 1980

EBEN McMILLAN is one of a number of condor authorities interviewed by Friends of the Earth in the spring of 1980. David Phillips, Greg Serrurier, and Katy Schlicter were the interviewers. Excerpts from the taped and edited interview follow.

Questioner: Can we help you?

McMillan: Well, no. Actually, I've just got to lock the chickens in and gather the eggs. And I've got some wild things around here I've got to feed—a roadrunner and some quail. The roadrunner . . . if I did something wrong one night, he'd never be back. I feed him a live mouse. I let the mouse out of the trap I've got, and he catches it and runs off with it. But I've never given any indication that I'm interested in him at all; it's just to get rid of the mouse. But the quail . . . it's interesting to watch the two species, how they react. When I start to feed the quail, you walk out and kind of walk around them. I'm pretty sure they'll keep on feeding. They might flush up onto the hillside, but they'll come right back—I'm pretty sure.

But this roadrunner . . . I'll go up, and if he's there, I'll lead him down with the mouse. You can watch out the kitchen door and see me release the mouse.

Questioner: We don't want to do anything to break up your relationship with the roadrunner.

McMillan: I've had experience this way before. But if you do something wrong. . . . We had a badger here one time who'd come around and my wife would feed it every night at that door there. This went on for six months. When it first came, it was very emaciated. An automobile had run over one of its feet, and a badger that can't dig is really out of commission. It would come in the evening and beg, and my wife would give it

[139]

a couple of eggs or a little hamburger or something. I was thinking one evening, "Gee, we don't have any photographs of that badger. I'd better get my lens." So I stood back in here, and she went out to feed him. He looked in and saw me with that lens, turned around and ran off and never came back. Never showed up again. Certain animals are very sensitive. And it's usually specialized animals that are sensitive. You could take white-crowned sparrows and throw a net over the whole bunch of them and pull all their tails out, and they'd be back the next day. But if you tried to net that badger or road-runner, they'd never be back.

I'm wondering: here is the only real feeding range that the condor has left. Here's where they're going to trap them. Is there any chance that they're going to nullify this area as a feeding range of the condor? Are they going to come back and accept bait without worrying about it?

Questioner: Are they just going to flee the area?

McMillan: Well, that's what I'm wondering about. Now, I don't think they're going to research this at all. They're going to go right out and they're going to try to catch those birds, as soon as they get a permit.

I'm going to go out now and feed those quail. When you see them all gathered around and I leave, come on down and see how close they'll let you get. Now, I don't think you have to worry about the quail; tomorrow night, if you're gone, they'll all be right there sitting waiting for me.

Questioner: How serious do you consider the possibility of pesticide poisoning to be?

McMillan: My lead argument is, if they aren't taking care of that, what *are* they taking care of? If they're not digging into that, which I consider the most important facet of condor management, why aren't they? It might be that the California condor and the South American condor would react completely differently to certain poisons.

We were watching the South American condor in the zoo at San Diego when an airplane went over, and it broke the sound barrier. You know, a sonic boom? Gee, that South American condor went half crazy, there in that cage . . . banged around against the bars.

Again, my main argument opposing the captive breeding of condors is that I have no confidence in the work that has been done so far, and I am suspicious that it is a cop-out. In other words, that they have done a very poor job, and in order to cover up, they're going on. They get into this captive breeding program, with technology the average person doesn't understand. I've run a lot of crews of working men, and I don't care who they are, the average person has to have someone to tell him what to do. If you send out five fellows on a job and don't tell anyone who is boss, within 15 minutes time, one fellow will just automatically take over. He'll say, "Well, fellows, I guess we better do it this way." Well, this has been missing in the Audubon program; there has never been a boss man. There has never been anyone to advise them what to do in situations that they didn't understand at all. John Borneman has always been his own boss. And John was a performer in Fred Waring's band a year before he went to studying condors. And there's nothing wrong with that at all if there was someone to call him up every two or three days and say, "John, did you go up and do this? . . . Well, you better do it." Instead of that, John has been led to believe, and left on his own so long, that he thinks now that he is the world authority on condors.

He's a self-proclaimed expert, and Paul Howard, the fellow who hired him originally, he introduced him up at Asilomar as the person who knew more about condors than any other living man. Well, gee whiz, you can imagine how that went down. He really does believe that he is an expert.

If you hire two or three fellows and send them out to build a fence, and they're out there working a couple of days, and you go out and the braces are on backwards, and the gate doesn't open so good, and you didn't see any deadmen, you've got to say, "Fellows, I'm sorry. I can't let you keep building this fence because I'm going to wind up without any fence. So I'm going to have to fire you fellows and get somebody else and give them a chance." About the third group of guys you got, there'd be fellows who just by nature would know which side of a post to put a brace on so you could pull a wire, where to put deadmen, and stuff like this. And you'd go out on the third or fourth day and you'd see, by golly, those fellows are doing a good job. Maybe you might advise them a little, but in the main, they'd satisfy you that there were people there who could think what they were doing and go ahead and do the job.

But the Audubon Society has never had anyone going in and checking on these people. As far as I'm concerned, they could have been making mistakes from the very beginning up to the present, and nobody has ever really checked. None of us know the failure of their efforts to save condors in the wild. None of us know whether it can't be done, or whether it could have been done easy. I have always felt this: if they had turned it over to Carl Koford in the beginning, I think that they'd be sitting pretty right now. Because Carl would spend a lot of time there, and he'd be just like I am with this roadrunner. He could go in and sit on a rock, and maybe after a year or so those birds would come around and they'd light right on another rock. He'd be able to go in and move among them in such a way that they'd have no suspicion that he was an enemy. . .

Questioner: He's perceptive enough to see what kind of threats are really there?

McMillan: Oh, yes! He'd find the factors that were contributing to their decline. Now these fellows, for all the research that's been done, they don't know. They don't know whether they've made mistakes: they don't know whether there are things they should have done but didn't; and you might as well say that all this time has been wasted. It was a very, very crucial time. When we left that condor project, Eugene Percy, the guy who owned the Percy Ranch there in Hopper Canyon, he saw 17 immature birds in one group.

Questioner: What year was this?

McMillan: This would have been in '65. Now Eugene Percy was the guy who owned the place, and he knew condors about the way I know those quail. I'm just positive that he wouldn't make a mistake. But even today, everybody who is observing condors is having no trouble finding young birds.

Questioner: They say seven, six or seven immatures.

McMillan: Yeah. I've been down there half a dozen times leading groups to see condors, on Mount Pinos, and if there're four birds, there's always one bird that's an immature. Sometimes two. Sometimes there'll be seven or eight birds, and of the seven or eight, there'll be three, or maybe four. One time—it was the time when the Golden Gate Chapter of the Audubon Society was there—we saw a minimum of eight birds. And we saw five young birds. Now, there could have been eight, nine, or ten birds in all. When you're counting condors, you have to be very careful that you don't count them twice. And it's better to miss a bird than to count one twice. Particularly when the population is low, and you've got a group of people, and most of the people *want* to see condors. So they say, "Here comes another bunch! Here come five more birds—that's twelve!" Well, by the end of the day, you realize that you're seeing the same birds over and over. This is a trap that an awful lot of people get into. Five birds will disappear going in that direction, then four birds come in from this direction 30 minutes later. Now, if you've watched them very much, you find out that they leave, and circle around, and they come back. You've got feather patterns that you can follow, like tail feathers missing, wing feathers missing. . . . You're pretty near always surprised to find out that they're the same birds, because they sneak in and you wonder "How in the devil did they get around that quick?" But they do. That time, we had a maximum of eight birds, and five of those, we knew, were young birds.

Questioner: How do you distinguish between an immature and a mature?

McMillan: Well, the sub-adult—that is, the bird that's about three to five years old—can be pretty difficult, sometimes. But the immature bird has a black head. And it has spots—the white under the wings isn't pure white, it'll be mottled. There's a stage when the birds are black under the wings, the second year. Then there's a stage when they go into what they call the spot-in-the-wing, when they're going out of the dark phase into the pure white. Nobody knows how long this lasts. They watched that bird down in Los Angeles, but what happens to a bird in a zoo that's fed every day and what would happen in the wild could be entirely different. You can't depend on that at all. But the spot-in-the-wing, we figure, is between three and four. The dark phase is between two and three. The young bird when it first comes out will be mottled underneath the wing. But you can look at a young bird—a bird of the year—and you can just tell it's a young bird. They haven't perfected flight. The tail is in a kind of convex V. And the wing feathers, they're bigger than an adult bird's because the feathers haven't worn down. You'll get the impression, "There comes a big one; this has got to be an old bird, look how big he is."

Questioner: How do they wear their feathers down?

McMillan: Just flying in the air will wear them down. I had some condor feathers here. Well, you can see how that one there will wear; that's a primary feather.

Questioner: Is it possible the wear is from dragging on the ground?

McMillan: No, mostly it's vibration. When a bird flies over you, why, these primaries here are making a little hum all the time. It's like a flag in the wind: pretty soon it gets ragged out there.

Questioner: Can you tell first-few-years birds by their skillfulness in flight?

McMillan: Oh, yes. Yes. If you've been watching them for a long while, of course these things come pretty easy to you.

Basically, the adult bird is sort of slate gray on the back, and the white on the top of the wing—there's a line at the outer edge of the upper wing coverts, and they will show through white. So if he turns so you can see that, you can see this sort of slatey gray. . . .

Now a young bird is a dull black. You might almost call it a brownish black. An adult bird will shine, if the sun is reflecting off the feathers.

There are other ways to identify them, but the main thing is the pure white under the wing of the adult and the red head, the orange colored head. When you see that, you know you've got an adult. The five-year-old bird will have a yellowish head. Then there's a stage they call the ring-neck; it'll have a yellow ring all around its neck, and the head will be dark.

But these features vary quite a bit. I think probably it's like the variation among humans: one individual may mature 10 percent earlier than another. I think birds are much this way. And food: how dependable is their food supply? This is bound to be important on molt, and their well-being. But the bird with pure white under the wings and the orange head is an adult. The sub-adult would be getting the pure white, but it might have a ring neck and the orange on its head might be mottled.

The young first- and second-year birds have got a small head. It's a dull brownish-black, kind of pigskin colored. They can vary some. Lots of young birds will show white. They claim that that bird down in the Los Angeles zoo showed pretty solid white under the wings, from one to two. Maybe so, but in the wild, I've never seen a condor that I thought was an immature with pure white under the wings, with a dark head. I've never seen it. I've been watching condors for 50 years—that is, if I see one, I'll stop to observe it. And I have never, to the best of my knowledge, ever observed an immature condor with white under the wings—pure white. It's always mottled, or something, so you can tell it's an immature bird.

Questioner: They want all-purpose permits so they never have to come back for a permit again. The USFWS wants the same permit for marking as for captive breeding. A biologist's explanation to me was, "We want to mark the birds and use that to build up our data base, to collect basic information about the condor before we decide whether or not we want to do captive breeding." If they did capture those birds, and put radio transmitters on them, do you think there'd be any way to stop them from captive breeding?

McMillan: No. You know this: that their goal is captive breeding. They're going to be capturing birds for captive breeding before they find out anything, as far as a long-range study is concerned. They would have to wait five years to be able to objectively produce information about the behavior and movements of these birds. One year's data on a bird like the condor really isn't significant at all. They might do one thing one year and turn around and do completely the opposite the next. When they used to use this country here as a feeding grounds, condors would be up here commonly; you'd be seeing condors steadily. Then perhaps you'd go a year or two and never see another bird. Then they'd come back into the area again. It would take four or five years to gather the information needed to justify capturing birds, and they're not going to wait that long. They don't intend to.

What they're going to do, they're going to ask for a permit in terms that will make people think they're not really going to go in gung ho. They're going to feel their way, and if they see somebody watching them, they'll pull back a little. They will give the impression that they're really taking their time and checking on everything. Most of their data will be to satisfy *you*—to satisfy critics—not to satisfy the needs of biologists who want to manage these birds. One of the primary objectives of the research they do will be to alleviate suspicion. I don't think you're going to prevent them from working with the condor. They're going to go ahead and do a lot of things that probably will never have any meaning at all. But as long as you're there watching, they're going to be awfully careful about making mistakes.

Questioner: They say that attaching radio transmitters to the birds would get them lots of needed information: where the birds nest, roost, and feed, and so on. Koford and others indicate that the birds will be so stressed and traumatized by capture that they won't behave normally. Then they might say, "This bird isn't nesting. It isn't feeding right. Better bring it into captivity. . . ."

McMillan: Maybe a good thing to keep pounding on is the matter of the integrity of official information. Nearly all bureaucrats are suspected by the general public; you can no longer depend on what they say. Right up to the President of the United States, the public has lost faith in the integrity of official information. In your presentation of the condor question, you can ask "How reliable is this official information?"

Questioner: Just how much are their actions going to be dictated by higher-ups back in Washington?

McMillan: Yes; if he has a wife and two or three kids, it takes a pretty strong person to follow objective procedures in the face of advice from superiors. They have ways of letting these fellows know when they could get in trouble.

Questioner: We were talking to the recovery team biologists and they never once mentioned habitat. Never once mentioned the risks of their operations. They didn't know how many Andean condors had been injured or how many had died. John Ogden cited impressive statistics, that less than two per cent of African turkey vultures had been killed in huge cannon-net operations. I asked him how many had been injured. He didn't know. We were talking about habitat, and I asked John Borneman how many people were out in the field that had primary responsibility to insure that there weren't threats to the condors in essential areas by off-road vehicles, by hunters, and so on. He couldn't think of anyone. Nobody! I don't think one person is out there working on these things, that they don't want to confront the habitat, that they don't want to work on that because it's hard and you can't get a lot of publicity out of it.

McMillan: Well, that's right. Habitat isn't spectacular. They like to get into something where they can get a lot of mileage, newspaper articles, and all—releasing a condor with a red flag flying from its neck, or something like that.

I don't know, but I suspect they're going to have trouble capturing condors.

Questioner: Carl [Koford] said that; he worried about that. It could be that they're going to be able to capture birds safely.

McMillan: You know, behaviorists, working with other animals, have established that there is what is known as a delayed response to a disturbance. Photographers see this a lot. You go in to photograph a bird on a nest, and the bird will sit right there; you scare it off, and it'll come right back. You're ready to come back in two days' time, when the eggs should be hatched. You come back in two days and there's nothing there. This kind of thing happens again and again. The way the bird behaves when you're there is no indication at all of what the bird is going to do six, 24, or 48 hours later. Carl brought this out in his paper on the condor. He told about things he had seen where the birds would respond to a disturbance, or a pressure, long after it happened. The birds might be roosting in a particular tree, and a guy would drive some cattle through or a birdwatcher would come up. And the birds would sit right there while the cattle went by underneath. Maybe the guy had seen them for a week coming to that roost, but the next day, they didn't come back. Not only that, but they never came back at all; they never came to use that tree again, as a roost. Carl was one of the early observers of this phenomenon, the delayed response.

I'm wondering: maybe four adults and three young come down to a carcass; you have this big net and catch two of them—how will the birds who aren't caught behave the next time they see a carcass? Are they going to come down and eat on it? Or are they going to circle up there, and if anything looks suspicious at all, are they going to go hungry? These are things they should know, and they don't.

Questioner: What about the danger of poisoning?

McMillan: I've had information from people in the Walker Basin, a cowboy there, and he told me about watching condors after poison had been put out, after 1080 poison was put out. He told me about watching condors come in and feed where they had scattered this 1080 poison. There was a dead rat every 15 feet or so where they had scattered 1080 from a jeep or something; every ten or 15 feet, there'd be a dead rat. The condors were competing, just like chickens: you throw out food and they'll run to get ahead of each other. They were running along and picking up these rats and swallowing them whole. Well, now, Carl Koford worked on squirrels in the same area, and he found that the condors would usually leave the stomach and the head, where the pouches are. The squirrel was big enough so they could pick it apart and just eat the meat. But the kangaroo rat is small enough so they could swallow it easily, at one gulp. I didn't see this, myself. Everything I found was dead; the condor bodies I found there had been dead for quite a little while.

I was over one day after a lady had poisoned her place, and I've got a photograph where you can see eight dead rats. They always die with their stomach up, for some reason, so you'd see the white stomachs. Well, the maximum poison I took from one of the pouches was 32 grains. If there was an average of half that, of 16 grains of poison, and say a condor ingested three, so he'd get 48 or 50 grains—well, I think 50 grains of 1080 poison would probably kill an elephant, or pretty near anything. That's an awful lot . . . that's a handful of poison. This being the case, we recommended in our field notes that this be looked into very thoroughly as one of the primary factors that were endangering the condor. Because in the relatively short time that we were involved, we had evidence of four condor carcasses that could all be associated with poisoning. And later, there were three animals [condors] that were poisoned—that a Fish and Wildlife Service trapper poisoned—and one of them died. The other two, they fed; they were incapacitated, and they fed them for two or three days. The third day, they left. Well, they assumed the birds recovered. But any bird that would stay in the same place two days, and even take food, when it flew away it surely wasn't self-dependent. Whether it could find food or not is very problematical. It might not even get out of the area. There is a good chance that they died.

This evidence that I'm giving you now should have been important enough so that one of the *first* things that they did—one of the first things that the Fish and Wildlife Service and the Audubon Society did—would be to go in and look up the two factors, shooting and poisoning. And as far as I know, to this day I don't think anything has really been done. Now, they'll tell you that they did. But I've gone over a time or two, when I was working in that country . . . I was a friend of Ben Easley, who was in charge of the poison program in Kern County. He met Borneman, but the other fellows were never around, they never went out, they never talked to him about this at all.

The fellow that was running the poison program on the Tejon Ranch said they'd have about eight or ten cowboys, and they'd go along in the foothills where the squirrels were thick. They'd make perhaps four or five miles a day. They'd throw out the poison, then the fellows would make camp and leave their horses there, and the next day they'd catch their horses and move on. He said that the turkey vultures and the ravens and the condors got to anticipating where they were going to be the next day. They'd be sitting there in the trees, waiting for them. Well, you can imagine what kind of situation this would be. This is all in the notes. I'm wondering, if anybody read the notes in the Fish and Wildlife Service. I'm very suspicious of the fact that they didn't want to go in there and check on that poisoning program.

Questioner: In the Tejon Ranch?

McMillan: That's right: in the Tejon Ranch, or all along . . . wherever there are poison programs. Now, just how much the Fish and Wildlife Service could do on private property—I don't think they'd be involved. But any place there was public domain land, they were involved. And the Fish and Wildlife Service was the predatory animal consultant for the sheep industry. They'd go in on private land. If the sheepmen wanted a trapper, they'd send in their trapper. It was a Fish and Wildlife

Service employee that poisoned the sheep that poisoned the three condors, and even though he was a neighbor—he lived here in Paso Robles—and I saw him a dozen times after this happened, and he knew we were doing field work on the condor, we'd never have heard about that if it hadn't been for Starker Leopold. At a meeting he happened to be talking to a Fish and Wildlife Service fellow—I forget who it was, but anyhow, he brought it up. He said, "We had some poisoned awhile back." So apparently there was an attempt, locally, at least, to hide anything that would discredit their program.

Questioner: To your knowledge, then, has the Fish and Wildlife Service or the Audubon Society ever really embarked on a crash program to rid national forest land or other land they have access to, of pesticides?

McMillan: No. No. Not only that, but as far as I can find out, talking to people in that area, they have never gone around to landowners and tried to work out some kind of agreement with them to take care of their pests. Up until we finished our field study, the Fish and Wildlife Service was arguing that no damage could be attributed to 1080 poison except for squirrels, rodents. They did run a research project up to the east of Porterville, and they found out it just kills pretty near everything. You can get their report from the Fish and Wildlife Service. You might like to look into that, to get their report on the research that was done on the effects of 1080 poison in the general wildlife community in the area of—I think in Madera County, in the foothills of the Sierra Nevada.

The Fish and Wildlife Service did the research. They claimed it wasn't for non-target species, bobcats and things. But everything died. They are giving the information. If there had been any kind of a chance to soft-pedal this thing, they weren't going out to make it look worse than it was.

Questioner: When did you finish your field notes?

McMillan: In 1965.

Questioner: And when was Fish and Wildlife doing its research?

McMillan: Oh, that was quite a while later.

Questioner: In the later sixties?

McMillan: Yes, right. What goaded them into doing this, I

never found out, because they don't tell you anything. It's like the fellow told you, "We don't have to bring the public into this thing at all." They don't tell anything unless they are forced to. Their policy is to keep the public ignorant and release no information unless they have to. I think that's probably part of their code, the young fellows that work there. They are not talkative at all about what they do. And they know that anyone who has an interest in wildlife is not necessarily going to champion their cause, if they find out there are things like this going on.

Questioner: Do you think there are knowledgeable people who have done a lot of work on condors who are being excluded because they have different ideas about captive breeding?

McMillan: You mean professional people?

Questioner: We've heard that they ignore or dismiss or ostracize anyone—including Carl Koford and yourself—who gets in the way of the capture program. What do you think?

McMillan: Well, as I said, I think Sandy Wilbur is honest, but he's not too objective. I think Sandy has gone out of his way lots of times in his reports to make any negative information look bad. Borneman, too. A lot of the professional Fish and Wildlife Service people, and the California Division of Fish and Game people also, would feed material to Borneman and he would go out and spread it. He would argue with me, and I'd know that it didn't come from him. I think that the Fish and Wildlife Service right now would do pretty near anything to negate any information from anybody that would make their position look questionble, as if there was a good argument. You'd have to expect this. I would expect it, from pretty near anybody. The Fish and Wildlife Service is made up of people, and you have to judge people on the basis of what the average person would do. This is the course the average person would take: he'd defend his own information against anybody else's. The Audubon Society did the same thing.

The former president of the Audubon Society, Carl Buchheister, was an extremely honest fellow and just as naive as he could be. He didn't know anything about any of this, and the only thing he was searching for was what was right. He wanted to do what was right, and he would defend anybody that he thought was honest, oppose anybody he thought was dishonest. He was that kind of guy, a real man. I know that he had misgivings about the Fish and Wildlife Service because he thought perhaps they were trying to stop him a time or two.

We have a situation now, sadly, with the people who are espousing the captive breeding program where they're going ahead and they're going to defend whatever they do regardless of what happens. They are never going to admit they were wrong; you can just put that down right now in your book. Don't expect them ever to say, "Wait a minute, fellows, we're going to call this thing off." Even though [Russell] Peterson is a man who might do this himself. He did with the wildlife film program just a while back. He came right out, and he backtracked, and he admitted he was wrong [about a matter unrelated to captive breeding of condors]. We've got a situation where the public is not going to get any information that will do it any good, nothing objective. The real problem right now is, how in the world are we going to be able to get objective information? You're going to be representing Friends of the Earth, and they're not going to give you any information that would make them look bad. Now, this is what Borneman really should be doing: he should be representing the public. He should be saying to those fellows, "Listen, boys, I'm going to have to tell the members of the Audubon Society that this happened," whatever it might be. But I know that's not going to happen. Not that John wouldn't tell, if he was free. The trouble with John Borneman is he's gotten himself in a position where he pretty near *has* to believe what they tell him. He can't do anything else. John is the type of fellow who will believe that because he has to.

I wish you could have heard that guy at the last Audubon conference up at Asilomar. What was his name? He's head of the biology department at the University of Honolulu. Berger?

Questioner: Andy Berger—the nenes? I've written to him and received some of his reports.

McMillan: Have you? Well listen. They had Andy Berger there to summarize the conference. By golly, he got up there at the end and it was about as rough a summary as anybody ever gave. It wasn't on condors, so much; it was this program of going around telling people that they had preserved an endangered species when it wasn't preserved at all. The habitat was exactly the same as it was when they disappeared, and the animals they were releasing were not successful in any way. I thought it was one of the best things I ever heard from a biologist.

Questioner: Carl Koford related that he'd be someone who'd say, when all is said and done, letting the habitat slip away and holding the birds in pens for 40 years, wasn't the way to go about it. People think that the nene was brought back by reintroduction after captive breeding. Is this the case or are they putting nenes back into a deteriorating environment?

McMillan: They know every nene, what it's going to do, where it's going to stay tonight. The environment that the nene goose evolved in is difficult for it to live in right now, without the help of man. It's got to have pens where it can fly in and feed, they've got to have places where it can nest and roost away from the environmental factors that brought about its demise.

Well, now, this is the thing with the condor. My argument is that even if we had to sacrifice the condor, what we would learn by trying to save it in the wilds would help us save other species in the future. We're going to learn what it takes either to save the condor or not save it, one of the two. As it is, we're never going to know a danged thing about our environment. It's not going to tell us a thing. Sandy Wilbur is a good fellow; I like Sandy, and we're good friends. But Sandy, for some reason or other—and John Borneman—they can't see the need for looking into the future and taking the whole biological picture into perspective. Looking at it and saying, "Well, listen, how are we going to preserve this whole thing," not how are we going to preserve one little piece of it. I'm also suspicious that the notoriety that comes from saving a nene goose—they work this for every dime they can. They're using it as justification for the idea that all we have to do is leave it up to them and that's all there is to it. "We don't have to bring the public into it at all." It's dangerous.

Questioner: The [research center] biologists we talked with yesterday discussed the telemetry part of the program, but not once did they mention *any* concern for the habitat. When we brought up habitat preservation, they said "That's not our problem. We're the biologists; we're working with telemetry. The habitat isn't our concern."

McMillan: Believe me, I've known a lot of biologists, and a lot of scientists, and when you find an individual who has the capacity to hold in his mind the whole picture, they're pretty rare. They are around, but they are not on every street corner, believe me. Carl Koford was very good. One of the greatest was Aldo Leopold. Aldo Leopold had the innate ability to look at something and see all the little pieces dovetailing together. He wouldn't have to analyze them; he could just kind of project himself into it, and he'd be part of it. That's why a person shouldn't be too rough in judging a lot of these people; whether you've got to have a certain mentality or a certain background, I don't know, but not everybody is an ecologist. There are a lot of ecologists who don't really understand the field of ecology.

Questioner: One biologist says he's going to go in and look around and think a lot before he makes any decision on what he wants to do. But he also says he can't do any of that unless he puts radio transmitters on all the birds. What do you think about the implications of capturing condors?

McMillan: In the fieldwork that we did, we saw things with condors that were pretty difficult to look at without becoming anthropomorphic. In most places, if you were riding along and there was a condor half a mile away in a field and you slowed up, the condor would stop feeding and look at you. And the minute your car came to a halt, he'd be gone; he'd get out of there quick. There was a lady over in Tulare County that had a ranch. In the fall of the year, some of her heifers would have trouble. They'd lose their calves, their first calves. Lots of purebred cattle do this. Sometimes they even lose the heifer in parturition. I've watched her with her crew of people working in the corrals, the dogs barking, the people yelling, the dust coming up, gates clanging, and I've watched condors come right down 250 yards from there and feed—never pay any attention to it at all, then fly back and light and stay all afternoon, and some of them stay overnight, in a pine tree right within sight of this whole thing. And the neighbors, who were within a mile—I'd question them and they hadn't seen a condor. This would go on day after day. Those birds were coming in unseen, and they would drop right down, and they knew here was a place where they were safe. They just acted exactly like they were at home.

When you see something like this, you've got to assume that these birds are capable of understanding where they can go without being harassed or shot at, and where they can't. So I can imagine that you could set up a situation like she had, a situation where you could feed birds without their ever knowing that they were being fed. Now, on these counts—I've been on these counts ever since they started—on these counts, sitting off a mile or so with glasses, I've seen condors come down and feed, but very nervous all the time. Lots of times they'd put out bait, and the birds would come down and circle two or three times, but there'd be something about it they didn't like and they'd just leave.

I'm wondering, now. . . . Any species that survives successfully in an environment has got to be able to understand the procedures necessary for survival, and react quickly to anything that occurs to its detriment or to its advantage. You take a bird like a condor, and you throw a net over it or you trap it another way. . . . I can take a quail here and I can trap it a hundred times. They are a small bird, and they've had to accept an awful lot. There are hawks preying on them all the time; at night there are weasels down among them; there are skunks around all the time, and at night you can hear the quail roaring out of their roosts. So they are under this pressure all the time, and they've learned how to equate with this type of environment. You can go in and trap quail a hundred times, and the hundredth time you'll catch them easier than the first. Because this isn't part of their survival instinct. Their main survival factor is the ability to out-reproduce any problem that develops. If they can make it till springtime, and a female can go out and lay 40 eggs, and she can reproduce 20 times her number, then they can overcome anything unless it is a lack of food or a lack of cover, or something like that. But if the main survival factors are there, they can get by all these problems.

There are other species that behave very differently. Take a mourning dove, for instance. You can flush a mourning dove off the nest today, and go back and flush her off tomorrow, but there's no use going back the next day because she isn't there.

She will leave. There are lots of birds that are this way—that are very, very temperamental. Now, I don't know whether condors are temperamental or not, but I suspect that they are *very* temperamental. Because the factors that they have to contend with are very specialized. They have no predators. The only things they need to watch out for are a few things like food and cover.

I know this: there are people who can do *anything* with an animal, and he'll respond. Where you see it is in handling animals like horses. If you work a horse hard and turn him out in the pasture, then you go out to catch the horse, he remembers that it's going to be a hard day's work if he lets you catch him. Most people have to get the horse in a corral before they can catch him. But there are individuals who can walk right out and ride that horse for ten days until its head is hanging down, but they can walk out on the eleventh day and catch that animal. This is something we don't know anything about. There are certain people who can upset an animal just like that, with a snap of the finger. I've had dogs that would try to bite certain individuals, and other people could walk in here and steal my place, and the dog would wag his tail when they leave. This is in all animal populations; this is an ingrained instinct.

Well, now, here we come to the matter of the condor, and I don't know whether a condor is like this or not. But I'm sure of this: that the Fish and Wildlife Service doesn't know either. If the people who go in there to work with the condor don't have this sensitivity—that something that enables them to get along—they can make a real mess. They can undo everything that has been tried before.

Interview, January 1981

SHORTLY after a condor chick perished at the hands of the Recovery Team, Eben McMillan was interviewed at his ranch by David Phillips, of FOE, and Jerry Emory, executive director of the Golden Gate Audubon Society, largest of the California chapters of the National Audubon Society. Excerpts from the interview follow, Mr. McMillan speaking first:

How much can you depend on information that was given—information in regard to that condor chick that was killed? How much, really, would they incriminate themselves?

Questioner: There's a story we don't know about, I'm sure. Even though most of it's on film, the last part isn't.

McMillan: Well, they said that that guy dropped his camera to run down and help the other man. Did he? And when John Borneman called me the next day from San Diego, where he brought the chick down, I asked him point blank, "Was there any discussion about covering up?" And he didn't tell me yes or no; if there hadn't been, he would have said there wasn't any discussion.

Questioner: They did discuss it?

McMillan: Apparently there was discussion to the extent that they said, "There's no possibility. There are too many people involved."

Questioner: They were going to have a press release; Borneman was going to write it. And everybody was supposed to shut up; nobody was supposed to know about it until the press release was done. Well, somebody in the Department of Fish and Game in Sacramento found out about it and called the regional office in Portland. This was a day before they were planning to issue their press release. I got a call saying, "I just can't believe it. I've got to tell you: they just killed one of the condor chicks." So I told this to Dave Brower and other people in Friends of the Earth. They said they couldn't believe it either. They said you better not spread it; you better not tell *anybody* until you find out that's really the truth. So I got Ogden on the phone, and I said "How're things going?"

"Fine, fine."

"Even with the chick? Didn't one just die?"

"How did you find that out?"

"That doesn't matter. I just want you to confirm whether or not it died."

"I'm not going to tell you anything unless you tell me how you found out."

He would not tell me. So I said, "OK I'll tell you. I heard from John Sayer."

"Well, it did die, and you'll have to read the press release."

The press release wasn't going to be out till the next day, and I started calling around. I called Ray Dasmann on the Fish and Game Commission. I got Ray on the phone and said, "Is there anything that would lead you to believe that they might be handling the chicks?" He said:

"Absolutely not. Fullerton told them they couldn't handle the chicks."

"What would you say if I told you one of the chicks had just been killed in the handling operation?"

"Absolutely impossible, no way."

"Look, I just talked to them, it's true."

"You're kidding. I don't believe it. I'm calling Fullerton right now." And that's when he told Fullerton "You better revoke that permit right away."

McMillan: How long would a person have to be out in the field before he'd get to see a fellow who'd be stupid enough to shoot a condor if you were standing right there? I was about 100 feet from a man when he shot a bird.

Questioner: Did he kill it?

McMillan: Never found it. This was a poison crew. They had just finished and were leaving. I pulled up and I was talking to the foreman of the crew. These two fellows started walking off with a .22 rifle, and pretty soon we looked up the draw and here came two condors right down the draw, maybe 70 or 80 feet high. This foreman and I were watching and admiring how steady they were in flight. And all of a sudden, plunk! there goes the .22 and one of the legs fell down loose and dangling. The bird just kind of dropped, and then it caught itself. Well, it was on what they call the Old Sheep Trail grade, that goes up from Arvin to the top of the mountain. The bird went down and out of sight, down this canyon, and the second bird came along. It sort of crept up a ways, then pretty soon it dropped and followed behind the other bird right down one of these canyons. So Fish and Game sent an airplane down, and we flew around, but the chances of finding it. . . .

Questioner: I talked to a guy who says he's responsible for writing what he calls the law enforcement strategy plan.

McMillan: Is that so?

Questioner: He's up in Sacramento with the Fish and Wildlife Service. And he says, I know they're being shot. He said he went into Hard Luck Campground, where they were trying to get a closure for awhile. He says, I don't know how anybody could think they're not being shot. There isn't anything there that isn't shot. You put up a metal sign, it's shot full of holes. You put up a wood sign, it's full of bullets. Anybody that tells you that they're not getting shot doesn't know the facts. He says they won't fund the law enforcement plan.

They'll pay thousands—hundreds of thousands—of dollars for the captive breeding pens, but they won't pay to have a person to go out there and investigate shooting.

5   ALDEN H. MILLER *(with the McMillans)*

The Current Status and Welfare
of the California Condor

SON OF Professor Loye Miller, who studied condors for decades, Alden Miller did his undergraduate and graduate work at the University of California, Berkeley. He published more than two hundred fifty papers, including work on mammals, birds, anatomy, physiology, behavior, and various areas of environmental biology. Miller was a superb field biologist and an authority on the taxonomy of the birds of western North America. He was Director of the University of California's Museum of Vertebrate Zoology from 1940 to 1966 and President of the American Ornithologists' Union from 1953 to 1955. "The Current Status and Welfare of the California Condor" was co-authored with the McMillan brothers and appeared in the Sierra Club Bulletin, Annual Magazine, 1964.

The Current Status and Welfare of the California Condor

T HE WELFARE of the California condor has risen substantially in the conscience of the conservationists of this country and of the world through the general concern for preservation of threatened species and of natural environments. Our return to the study of condors and the watching of these great birds could not help but impress us anew with the majestic sight they present as they move in superbly controlled flight about the beautiful mountains they occupy and the great sweeps of rangeland over which they search for food. We emphatically reaffirm our purpose to preserve this natural and inspiring esthetic resource.

Our goal has been to determine gain or loss in numbers, and particularly the direction and magnitude of the trend. Our further purposes were to study reproductive success, food supply, range utilizations by condors, and the impact of changes in human occupancy of the condor country and of ranching practices. Also, unexpectedly, evidence came to hand, and obviously could not be ignored, about failures to carry out conservation practices.

Estimating of numbers was undertaken in a way to make possible a comparison of our results with Koford's carefully evaluated data of 15 years before. He used several methods, the three most direct and simple were (1) assembling high counts at single stations, (2) simultaneous counts at two stations, and (3) composite counts derived from observations only a few days apart at different stations. Where data from other observers were used, they were carefully screened for verified competence of the observer, documentation entered in written records at the time, and consistency with other records. These led to the conclusion that the population was about 60 in the late 1940's.

In our records of numbers of birds the ten best counts that we regard as reliable range from 19 to 33 whereas Koford's nine ranged from 30 to 43. Three-fourths of Koford's maximal counts fall between 30 and 33 (average 31). Four-fifths of ours fall between 19 and 24 (average 21). The trend of reduction is thus approximately 30 per cent.

Our simultaneous counts of sure totals are 17, 17, and 19, and our composite probable totals are 17, 23, 25, and 25. We will give details on only one each of these by way of example.

On September 12, 1963, Jeff Calhoun saw 9 birds at 10:55 a.m. on Frazier Mountain in Ventura County, and at 2:35 p.m. that day Eben McMillan saw 8 birds at Glennville in northern Kern County, for a total of 17.

In mid-April of 1963, approximately on the 17th, Mr. B. Strathearn counted 22 birds in southern Ventura County; these birds had been concentrating and feeding there for several days. On April 20 on Cholame Flat, at the northern edge of San Luis Obispo County, 130 miles away, 3 condors were seen by Dick Escarcia, indicating a possible total of 25.

As in the earlier study, simultaneous and combined counts do not exceed occasional large single counts. Koford had one simultaneous count of 42 and two composite counts of 34 and 43. Our 25 compared with his 43 indicates a 42 per cent lower level.

Another approach in estimating takes account, as was done 15 years ago, of late summer concentrations of adult condors in areas well removed from known nesting areas, coupled with known or assumed nest attendance by other birds. In the summer of 1963 there were 12 adult condors in the northeast section and 11 adults near Frazier Mountain, probably with little interchange, from which we may postulate a population of non-nesting adults of 20; Koford's comparable figure was 30. If we add 8 other adults that would be staying close to active nests, the total of adults rises to 28. If now, as did Koford, we estimate that immatures and otherwise undetected adults constitute an additional 50 per cent to be figured in the total (we know of 10 different immatures in existence), and thus add 14, we reach a total estimated population of 42.

Thus we have shown that maximal counts indicate a 30 per cent decrease in the condor population; composite counts indicate a 42 per cent decrease; and estimates based on breeding status and age composition of groups reflect a 30 per cent decrease. We arrive then at a general conclusion that there has been a decrease of one-third and that the total population is about 40. The downward trend and the seriousness of the loss in numbers since the 1940's is clear. We believe this loss is not in the slightest overstated.

Reproduction and Survival

We have given particular attention to verifying the presence of young birds in flocks or to those following their parents to feeding places. We have avoided inspection of nests known or suspected of being active. This is because visiting nests threatens survival of eggs and young, even if carefully done, and if a young one is found in a nest, there is no certainty it can be proved to survive the slow nest-leaving process no matter how much it is watched.

Our records of birds seen that were 12 to 15 months old, as judged from their plumage and actions, show that at least 2 young were produced in 1962. Because several observations probably did not involve the same individual, the number may have been 3 or 4. The more limited field work of the summer of 1964 brought out the fact that at least two more were produced in 1963.

We have tabulated the more satisfactory counts of immatures from one to five years old seen at one time which would indicate their abundance relative to adults. These observations suggest that such immatures comprise a third of the population near the Sespe Wildlife Area. The actual size of this age group we have determined from single maximum counts and individual marking features. It totals 10 known young birds. We must in addition suppose that we have missed a few and that the total of birds not yet at breeding age is 11 or 12. All signs are, then, that in the present total condor population of 40 almost one-third are young. This compares fairly closely with the one-quarter to possibly one-third estimated in the 1940's.

This situation and the considerable number of sightings of yearling birds indicates several important things: (1) the potential for replacement and augmentation of the population is still present in the species; (2) condors have been normally successful with their nests, primarily in the protected areas in Los Padres National Forest, in order to have produced these young; (3) the species, despite its low reproductive rate, has the capacity in its present environment to gain in total population, even though this has not resulted; (4) the reason it has lost ground rather than gained in the way that would be anticipated from reproductive success must lie in augmented mortality among free-flying adults and immatures.

In general in any species a relatively high proportion of immatures in the population indicates a balancing high mortality rate if the population total is stable. And if it is declining, as in the condor, the high proportion of immatures is a clear sign of augmentation of mortality. The evidence for production of young condors is then both encouraging and discouraging. It shows we have a degree of viability and production that can lead to success and improvement but that there have been most unfavorable factors causing mortality of free-flying birds in recent years.

Examination of life tables in detail leads us to believe that under these circumstances there is now about a 7½ per cent annual loss of post-nestling condors. This means 3 birds a year. But with a decline in the total over a number of years, we must have been losing, and doubtless still are, more than 3 birds a year.

If for the last 18 years we have lost at least 3 a year, we have lost a total of 54. Discounting about 14 that possibly were superannuated, we have lost 40 (!) condors from post-fledgling mortality other than age. We must have produced 2 a year to balance out at the present population level of 40. Actually, probably somewhat more have been produced, at least recently. If so, this again points to a greater annual loss than 3 a year.

The implications of achieving a reduction in annual loss are very clear. If losses now are 3 or 4 a year and if most of these are attributable to human interference—killing of adults—a reduction of this mortality factor so that we lose only 2 a year would set the course toward a meaningful recovery of the population. Of course, one catastrophic loss such as slaughtering of numbers at a vulnerable feeding or roosting concentration could be the turning point toward quick extinction. The population could quickly pass below some critical level necessary for successful social response, pairing, and group feeding procedures essential to the conduct of a normal nesting cycle.

In the survival and increase of any species, food supply is understood correctly to be of critical importance. While this is clearly true, the limiting factor at given periods in a species' history or at a particular level of numbers in its population may not be food resources at all. Stated simply we have found that there is an abundance of condor food at the present period in the range of the species. It is a complete misconception that artificial feeding and brush burning programs are necessary to provide food for condor survival and improvement. The dangers in such programs are not so much in what they may do that is possibly detrimental to condors but in the diversion of attention from other far more vital factors in condor decline and of facing up to the corrective practices in conservation which they call for.

In our field work we have observed condors feeding or in the immediate vicinity of food on 61 days. And we have almost continuously been surveying grazing practices, range conditions, and deer numbers in relation to the production of condor food. The carcasses of cattle and sheep, especially cattle, continue to be the principal food. Dead deer are an important secondary source and at times carcasses of small mammals are used or even preferred.

The methods of grazing and handling livestock since the 1940's and the disease trends in these herds have not diminished the numbers and availability of dead animals. Increase and spread of deer and seasonal die-off in them in the last decade has further augmented the supply. An estimated 9854 carcasses of livestock and deer are available annually in the foraging range of the condor.

Cattle are particularly available beginning in July as a result of abortions; general calving losses continue until spring. Toxic range forage, including that which causes bloat, produces major losses in both cattle and sheep from February to June. Major sheep losses occur from late winter until May. Deer mortality becomes important in April and extends through the summer and fall with the dry-period die-offs. There is no seasonal period when food is scarce.

Abundant observations show that condors have many simultaneous sources of food and move about readily among them. Great quantities of available food and partly used food are left, the birds going to forage elsewhere. This situation and the fact that condors have successfully raised young in the last five years show that there is no food shortage. The birds are not starving.

Mortality Factors

The greatest losses among condors in recent years have been from illegal shooting. The number of instances of condors shot or being shot at is alarmingly great in terms of the total condor population. We received information on nine cases of persons shooting at condors in the last four years. At least five of these events resulted in dead or injured condors. This must represent but a fraction of the total.

The shooting takes place because of extensive breakdown of law enforcement and lack of education. Condors are especially vulnerable to shooting as they fly over ridges and crests in Los Padres National Forest where thousands of hunters, uninformed and generally unsympathetic to bird preservation and firearms laws, crowd the roads and high camps. The heavy increase in human populations near the range of the condor and the great development of roads, trails, and other types of accessways have materially contributed to this serious loss from wanton shooting.

Losses connected with the use of 1080 poison in rodent control is strongly suspected and there is strong circumstantial evidence for it in some known condor deaths. This is a factor especially in the rangelands in the foothills of the southern and eastern San Joaquin Valley where condors regularly feed. Condors follow poisoning operations there, feeding on the killed rodents. Three condors have died since 1960 in a small area of northern Kern County where rodent poisoning is extensive and at a time when it was being conducted. None of them had been shot. Poisoned grain was reported to be present in at least one of the bodies.

Disturbance of the condor refuges and adjoining buffer areas has been a continual threat to successful nesting and to roosting concentrations. Fire protection systems, road and trail access, and enforcement of closures in the forest areas viewed in their relation to condor welfare have had variable attention and at times quite inadequate support.

The dangers from disturbance of condors by photographers and by low-flying aircraft in and near the refuges continue as a distinct threat.

Other mortality factors are slight at the present time.

Recommendations

The central findings of our present study are, then, that the California condor has seriously lost ground in numbers while at the same time showing a gratifying potential to reproduce itself, at its own deliberate rate. Without the refuges which were set up earlier—the consequence of concerted action by the National Audubon Society and the United States Forest Service, we would probably have seen the condor today on the very brink of extinction if not over it.

We are convinced that the condor can survive. We decry any defeatist attitudes in this regard. But make no mistake: old procedures must be greatly bolstered, new dangers warded off, and new practices vigorously pursued if we are to succeed. We outline here only the highlights of the procedures and do so in general terms.

Enforcement of the laws that protect condors and other large soaring birds with which they may be confused should have high priority. Shooting from roadways, illegal of course, is likewise in need of rigorous control. Every warden of the California Department of Fish and Game and every forest employee in or close to the range of the condor should have specific instructions to place prevention of shooting of condors and other large birds as first concern in his operations. He should attend education and briefing sessions on this matter.

We are further convinced that the National Audubon Society should finance and itself employ a full-time condor warden. His purpose should be not only to engage in law enforcement but to be able continually to move about the condor range, to anticipate and be on hand when there is threat or trouble, and to be in an independent position to detect and report breakdown in the conservation program.

With the heightened interest in the condor and with a larger mass of people in southern California than formerly, educational efforts must become positive, organized, and overt. The former proposals on education were appropriate to the times but nothing was done to implement them. The effort today requires many people. Regional Audubon offices should organize and coordinate. Fish and game and forestry officials must set up their own educational meetings and directives.

Included must be education of the general public. At the local level in communities near the points of condor concentration, effort should be directed toward enhancing local pride and responsibility as sole custodians of a national resource. Tourism and pride of civic leadership in this should be stressed. We believe that people locally can be persuaded that their civic image as well as their commercial welfare will gain significantly by being the focal point of a unique possession of national and world interest. The availability of properly controlled observation areas will need to go hand in hand with this.

On the state and national scene, education of the people of high purpose to the urgency of action and the need of firm policy is called for. As one government official has put the issue, in essence, a threatened species has absolute priority; the condor must be saved; there is no place else where you can do this than in its natural range in California. The "minority" cannot be overridden in the multiple-use approach and policy on the latter approach must give way.

The Sespe refuge has been and is crucial to the condor's survival, but as a refuge it has been barely enough. We need to hold rigorously what is now set out as protected land and we need to augment it by properly set up, permanent buffer areas and wilderness areas. The access corridors of the refuge were to have limited use; these limitations should be rigorously reaffirmed. To yield and open these corridors to water developments and to through traffic and construction would destroy the efficacy of the refuge.

The buffer and primitive areas should be permanently closed to hunting. Group camps, concessions, and mass recreational facilities in the corridors and in the Agua Blanca and Sweetwater drainages at the northern border of the Sespe refuge should be ruled out; there must be no yielding to development of a dam and a lake in that area.

Firearms closure should be instituted on forest lands in a buffer zone surrounding the refuge and the existing wild areas. This would materially help enforcement officers in checking wanton shooting along the condor flyways. Such sensitive areas exist particularly on fire roads, trails and private land access roads in and about the refuge corridors, Santa Paula Canyon, Hines Peak, the Agua Blanca and Sweetwater drainages, the Sierra Madre Ridge, and Big Pine Mountain.

Independent of the problem of roads close to the refuge is the question of the impact of road placement in other parts of the condor range. We have observed particularly the relation of roads to flyways and roosts on Sierra Madre Ridge and McChesney Mountain and their detrimental effects, potential or actual. As a consequence we recommend generally that new roads opening up sections of the national forest in the range of the condor be so located and designed as to avoid disruption to the safe use of the area by condors.

Research on the impact of 1080 poison needs to be designed and carried out by independent agencies, utilizing turkey vultures. These studies should establish the effects of dosage levels on the general health, immediate and long range, of such vultures. In view of the circumstantial evidence for death of condors by poisoning with 1080, rodent poisoning agencies should be persuaded to reduce or stop poisoning of kangaroo rats in the grazing lands in the principal range of the condor. They should be encouraged to devise different methods and timing of activities to minimize the threat to condors.

These recommendations constitute only a partial list. Many of them are difficult to achieve without dedicated effort. Law enforcement and education are the most important elements, resting critically on the existing refuge system and its enhancement. Will you make that effort?

6　Dick Smith

Excerpts from Condor Journal

B EFORE his death in 1977, Dick Smith was a condor naturalist and an untiring guardian of the Santa Barbara backcountry. He was one of several people involved in the successful effort to enlarge the San Rafael Wilderness. The following excerpt is from his book, *Condor Journal* (Capra, 1978).

Ali Pearson

Excerpts from Condor Journal

To SENSE the close passage of a traveling condor is an experience out of this world. You are riding up a trail at sunset, twenty miles from the nearest human settlement and you see racing toward you out of the sun's disc a great dark spot growing larger and larger with incredible speed. You realize it is a big dark bird. Suddenly he looms above you, peering down with age-old rather remote gaze. His eyes seem to have seen so much more than mere men that he appears only mildly interested. To feel the presence of that vast composure and to hear the rush and whistle of his feathers through the air, and to see him gone to his home in the darkening east, having passed within a rope's cast of you, is something to be forever remembered.

Despite their seeming composure, condors are insatiably curious. They like to investigate. You may see one soaring high above you. All at once he's larger and lower—just above your head, without seeming to have done anything at all to come down so quickly. This curiosity has often proved disastrous to the birds, because the temptation to shoot at anything that moves or flies is still overpowering in some people with guns. . . .

Inoffensive to mankind, this remarkable bird has suffered greatly from man's ignorance, superstition and intolerance. Even the knowledge we now have concerning the California condor has been gained at great cost to his numbers. Man has been, and continues to be, the deciding factor in the survival of this ancient species. . . .

The condor is a remarkably persistent bird. Time and again experts have predicted death of this species. Yet condors fly today as in centuries past. If man can temper concern with caution, and offer protection, space and solitude for these giant birds, they may continue to soar over wild places during our own tenure on earth. . . .

The condors flying today over Southern California's missile launching pads are but little different from the birds that circled over mammoth and mastodon, saber-toothed tiger, and Stone-age man. . . .

By 1910 experts had given up the species as lost. Only the remaining impenetrable and remote areas of the Coast Range protected the condor from immediate extinction.

Sweating up densely overgrown canyons, up nearly impassable dry waterfalls, across precarious ledges by hand and by rope, the thirsty, exhausted humans recorded the terrible, wonderful remoteness of these last hiding places. The condor had literally retreated to the heart of the wilderness. Here where remain the last vestiges of the flora of the Pleistocene era—spruce, cedar and horsetail fern—here, where there are still the silences and solitude of the earth before man, the bird too remained—for the moment.

Condors and red men had gotten along very well. Condors and white men did not. There is something unreasonable about a condor. The bird has to be comprehended, rather than analyzed. The majesty of the primitive ages is in him, as he comes winging out of the Ice Age, the majesties of the silences that were before man, and perhaps will be after him. One visualizes, too, the dignity of the slow procession of the eons of time. Since the rocks were laid down and the seas receded, and man first appeared on earth, this bird has been flying. His history may be irrevocably intermingled with that of man. The condor of mid-twentieth century that flew out from his last retreats soared over a changed and changing land.

Bulldozers had been invented. Four-wheel-drive vehicles had been perfected. Low-gear-ratio motorized vehicles designed for trail and cross-country travel were on the drawing boards. Helicopters and planes were flying. The end of World War II released these devices—and man's energy and attention and money—toward "developing" and "exploiting" what remained of our wild lands. Progress was still defined by many, even by government agencies, in terms of new roads and more gashed hillsides. Every untouched spot appeared a challenge.

Motorized vehicles came snorting up toward the last wild places, shattering the stillness. For the first time it became possible to take a machine almost anywhere, even to level the mountains if man willed. There was also an increasing feeling of "what of it?" if wilderness and condor died. "These lands belong to the people." Man's will must be served. If the Pleistocene Age was obsolete, so maybe was the condor. But at the same time there was an ever-increasing feeling among many people that something had to be done to save both condor and wilderness, that they both belonged to the people—the people for all time to come—people who ought to have a chance to know wilderness and condor as they are now and always have been.

Looking to the future, can we expect man's efforts at condor management, unsuccessful so far, will be any more successful with birds raised in captivity released into a shrinking wild environment where pollution threatens most forms of life? We know that the shells of condors' eggs show structural changes and thinning. This DDT effect is well known and has brought many bird species close to extinction. In the years since World War II millions of tons of toxic pesticides, herbicides, rodent control compounds, and agricultural chemicals have entered the food chains and the environment. Many of these have been found in the bodies of dead condors. Hormone levels affecting reproduction may be disrupted by concentrations of some of these chemical compounds. An alarming increase of mercury, lead, zinc, and other metals concentrated in condor feathers has occurred within the last ten years. Is man destroying the life around him? Isn't it time to stop and ask ourselves what we are really doing? The condor needs no more than any other living thing: clean air to breathe, freedom from molestation, room to live.

In the Condor Survey of October 1976, five flying immature birds from previous years were identified among the forty condors in the estimated count. Two fledglings were discovered later in the year. By August 1977, the parents of one of these were found to be caring for a second fledgling in the same nest. The theory that condors produce young no more often than every other year should be re-examined in the light of the documented activities of this pair, as well as the condors in the Hi Mountain area of San Luis Obispo County that are known to have successfully reared young four consecutive years in the 1960s. Historical accounts of yearly nesting should be reevaluated. Given the right circumstances, condors may be capable of greater nesting success than we have assumed. Many authorities point out that lack of information on vital aspects of condor biology and behavior raises serious questions about the wisdom of drastic measures until more is learned and understood.

There may be more condors than official records indicate. Unconfirmed sightings continue to be reported from Baja California where condors ranged as late as the 1930s. From five to twelve birds have been claimed from this area in recent years. A joint U.S.-Mexican survey, in progress during 1977 in the Sierra San Pedro Martir and Sierra Juarez, has been inconclusive, but this wild, remote region may still shelter condors following age-old survival instincts.

But we dare not become complacent. We need more than laws and government agencies. An educated public remains the most important element in any approach to the preservation of wildlife and wilderness. Traditionally, concerned individuals and citizen groups have led the way and are the ones who keep a watchful eye on the management of our wilderness heritage.

The condor symbolizes man's current troubled relationship with wild nature. In the words of one among many concerned with this problem, "If we cannot save the California condor and what he stands for, do we have the intelligence to save ourselves?"

Inadvertent capture of immatures or other nontarget birds, plus the possibility that a large number of condors would have to be taken and examined to achieve the desired sex ratio, could well place a fatal stress on a species already known for its inability to tolerate intrusion of its environment, let alone such manhandling. Nesting birds might be captured. So might birds still engaged in feeding a nestling or an immature from the previous year. Young birds apparently depend on their parents for part of their sustenance until they are almost two years old. This long associative period is also probably one of learning to forage and cope with their environment. How this vital training stage can be artificially provided for birds reared in captivity is not clear.

Assuming birds are captured, will they breed? Since the trigger mechanisms for the California condor's breeding cycle are unknown, it is by no means certain that the captives would breed successfully in their new situation, despite the fact that Andean condors have done so.

Even if young are produced, will it be possible to release them successfully into a wild environment? Topatopa, the female condor now in the Los Angeles Zoo, was about nine months old when found, fully fledged and able to fly for short distances. After she had been treated at the zoo for eleven days, she was released into a wild environment but when it became obvious that she could not survive without her parents, she was returned to the zoo. And if chicks are successfully reared and released, will they have the immunity to resist diseases and parasites present in the wild population?

It is apparent that nesting adults are keenly aware of any man in sight within 500 yards of the nest, and that they will not perform certain activities which have a very low disturbance threshold when men are near. At least they will not perform these activities with normal frequency. One cannot tell whether the normal action of a bird is being inhibited by the presence of the observer unless the normal action of that individual for that particular activity is known. As the environmental influences are many and unknown to the observer, the normal action of a free-living condor cannot be anticipated with certainty.

One man can keep a pair of condors from the egg all night or prevent the feeding of a chick for an entire day merely by exposing himself within 500 yards of a nest for a few minutes at one or two critical times of the day. Loud noises can alarm condors at distances of over one mile. Individuals or groups of persons moving about must keep at least one-half mile from condor nests in order to avoid disturbance of the parent birds. If the adults soar or perch nearby when a man is close to the nest, it is because of their concern for the nest or its contents and not because of their tameness. It is impossible to photograph nesting condors without disturbing them and causing serious deviations from their normal actions.

–Carl Koford

7   SANFORD WILBUR

Condors versus Human Activity

FORMER head research biologist for the California Condor Recovery Program, Sanford R. Wilbur is now a United States Fish and Wildlife Service biologist. The circumstances surrounding his forced departure from the program are not reassuring. Mr. Wilbur is author of a USFWS publication *The California Condor, 1966-1976: A Look at its Past and Future*, from which this segment is excerpted. Mr. Wilbur is also a frequent contributor to such journals as *Auk*, *American Birds*, and the *Wilson Bulletin*. What follows was originally published under the chapter title "Disturbance."

The fledging period of five months is perhaps as long as that of any land bird. Including the incubation period, a nest cavity may be in daily use for seven months. Allowing for six weeks variation in time each way for differences among pairs and seasons, it is apparent that nests should be protected from molestation for at least ten months of the year. This period includes neither the important season of courtship and nest selection nor the two months or more that the juvenile is out of the nest but entirely dependent on its parents for food. The last phase is especially worthy of protection because the juvenile may wander far from the nest, the parent birds are especially cautious in approaching the young, and seven months of labor on the part of the parents (and the persons who protect them) already have been "invested" in the growing bird. Obviously, then, nesting areas must be kept free from disturbance the year around if a program for conserving the California condor is to be effective.

–CARL KOFORD

Condors versus Human Activity

THE REACTION OF CONDORS to human activity varies with the duration and intensity of disturbance, whether it is noise or physical presence, and may involve flying, roosting, feeding, or nesting behavior.

Flying Condors

Flying condors show little fear of man and will often approach closely. They may even glide to a person walking along an exposed ridge, or sitting in an open area, and circle over him. Apparently the more conspicuous a person is and the more commotion he makes, the more likely a condor is to approach. Whistling and arm-waving may prolong the time the bird remains overhead (Sibley, 1969).

Condors in flight do not avoid areas of human occupancy. I have seen them regularly over the oil fields near the Sespe Condor Sanctuary, and a regularly used condor flight lane follows Interstate Highway 5 through the Tehachapi Mountains. Condors are occasionally reported flying over Bakersfield, San Jose, and other cities and towns. Although there may be a limit to the amount of ground disturbance a flying condor will tolerate, most traditional flight lanes will probably be traveled as long as related nesting, roosting, and feeding areas are usable.

Roosting Birds

Condors usually return to traditional roosting areas each afternoon. At many of these roost sites, the same trees and rock ledges have been used for at least 35 years, while nearby perches that appear identical remain unoccupied.

Roosting condors are readily disturbed by either noise or movement, and disturbances late in the day may prevent roost-

[183]

ing that night (Koford 1953). However, reaction to disturbance varies. On 31 May 1972, I walked to within 9 m (30 feet) of a year-old condor, took photographs, then entered a nearby bird blind. The young bird sat on the snag for another 30 min. departing then only because an adult condor forced it from its perch. In contrast, on 13 January 1970, movements of one person along a trail over 0.4 km (0.25 mile) from a roosting condor apparently caused it to change its perch several times and eventually leave the vicinity. Two condors roosting in a snag on 19 August 1971 showed no reaction to a sharp sonic boom, yet flew hastily from the tree when a fixed-wing aircraft passed within 1,000 feet of them. A startling sonic boom on 7 October 1971 caused three adult condors to hurriedly leave their roost area.

Occasional major disturbances will not cause condors to abandon regularly used roosts, and they may adapt to general low-level disturbance. A summer roosting area in Tulare County is less than 0.6 mile from radio towers, a fire lookout, and summer homes, yet is occupied by condors almost every night from May to September. However, noise levels are low and few people actually approach within 0.25 mile of roost trees. Some levels of noise and activity will cause condors to permanently leave an area; two roosting areas were abandoned near the Sespe Condor Sanctuary. One area, on the west side of Hopper Ridge 0.6 mile north of Hopper Mountain was regularly used by condors in 1939 and 1946. There was some disturbance in the area, including an occasional automobile being driven within 150-300 feet of the site. Now there is a battery of oil wells 1 km (0.6 mile) away in line of sight of the roost trees, and there is almost constant, but usually low-level, noise and oil-related activity. Condors no longer roost on the west side of Hopper Ridge in that area, although they continue to roost within 1.2 miles of the oil operation where roosts are shielded topographically from sight and most sound of the oil fields.

A second roost site was located in cliffs of Pole Creek, about 1.2 miles southwest of Hopper Mountain. Condors were seen there regularly in 1940 and 1941, and the regular presence of a very young condor one year suggests it may have been a nest site as well. There was a lightly-traveled farm road within 0.75 mile of the roost, and some limited oil exploration had occurred about 1 mile away. Now a major portion of the Sespe Oil Field occupies the area within 1 mile of the roost, and there are producing oil wells within 0.6 mile. It has not been used by condors for many years.

No one was systematically documenting condor observations on Hopper Mountain during 1950-65, so it is not possible to show a positive cause-and-effect relationship between oil field development and abandonment of these roosts. However, lack of use at these sites, contrasted with continued condor occupation of traditional roosts just beyond the influence of the oil fields, suggests such a relationship.

Feeding Birds

Condors normally feed in relatively isolated areas and usually leave if approached within a few hundred meters (about 1,000 feet) by vehicles or people (Koford 1953). They seldom feed on animals killed on highways or in areas of regular disturbance. Koford (1953), however, recorded them feeding within 500 yards of an occupied ranch house, and on several occasions I have observed them feeding within 1,000 feet of well-traveled roads.

Startling noises sometimes frighten condors from food: on 1 May 1969 a sonic boom caused four condors to fly up and the remaining two to run some distance from a carcass. On 2 May 1969 a sonic boom caused condors to fly from a carcass briefly, but a second boom elicited only a mild startle reaction (heads up, looking around; F. C. Sibley, unpublished field notes). One condor and six turkey vultures I observed at a carcass on 3 August 1972 showed no apparent reaction to a moderately loud sonic boom.

Condors have abandoned feeding sites once used regularly, but most such sites have a greatly diminished food supply as well as increased human disturbance. Probably the greater and more regular the disturbance, the less likely condors are to feed in the area.

Nesting Condors

Sibley (1969) plotted the location of condor nest sites in relation to roads, trails, and oil field activity. He found that, even though apparently suitable nest sites existed closer, no occupied nest sites were located nearer to various developments than the following:

1. *Lightly used dirt roads*—0.8 mile when the site was un-shielded from sight and sound of the road, occasionally closer (0.5 mile) when completely shielded.
2. *Regularly used dirt roads*—1.2 miles when unshielded, closest shielded about 0.7 mile.
3. *Paved road*—2.2 miles.
4. *Oil wells*—2.3 miles when nest was in view of the well; 1.2 miles when shielded from sight and most sound.

Both regularity and magnitude of disturbance are involved in discouraging condor nesting, as nests may be located nearer to lightly used roads than to regular travel routes or oil operations. Condors have nested very near intermittently used foot trails. It appears that the greater the disturbance, either in frequency or noise level, the less likely condors are to nest nearby. Since 1965 nests are known to have hatched successfully 0.5 mile from an infrequently used administrative road, 0.8 mile from a regularly used dirt road, 2.2 miles from a paved highway, and 2.2 miles from an operating oil well. Only 2 of the 10 nest sites used since 1966 are closer to any road than 1 mile. One of these, successful four times in a row, has not been used since 1969. Human disturbance at that site has increased appreciably in recent years, and may be the cause of current disuse, although there are other possibilities, such as death of one or both members of the resident pair.

Some nest sites used in past years now appear abandoned. Reasons for disuse are seldom obvious, but increased disturbance locally is a possible cause in some instances. As suggested for roost sites, I think that there is a maximum level of disturbance that condors will tolerate at a nest site. This undoubtedly varies with location, especially as related to topography, but it appears likely that condors usually will not nest within 1.5 miles of regularly traveled roads or similar activity (Sibley 1969).

Even if nest sites are not permanently abandoned due to disturbance, noise and human activity may effectively thwart nesting success. Peregrine falcons subjected to repeated disturbance are thought to build up "some sort of cumulative nervousness" that may eventually lead to nest failure (Herbert and Herbert 1965). Bald eagles will stay near traditional nest sites in spite of considerable disturbance, but may not breed (Broley 1947). "Fear" reactions of various types are thought to inhibit breeding in birds, perhaps by curtailing ovulation (Marshall 1952, 1961).

It has been suggested (Moll 1969; Oehme 1969) that sonic booms may addle eggs and kill embryos, but laboratory tests indicate this is unlikely (Memphis State University 1971). Sudden loud noises have been known to frighten adult birds from the nest (Ames and Mersereau 1964; Hagar 1969). Activity near nests has caused young raptors to fly prematurely, which sometimes resulted in their death or injury (Grier 1969; White 1969; Garber 1972).

Condors may not abandon nests despite repeated disturbance during the nesting cycle. Observations were made near one nest on 107 days during one nesting season, and the condors were disturbed at times by whistling, handclapping, and other human activity (Koford 1953). The young bird fledged successfully. Koford (1953) also reported instances where men actually entered the nest cave while nesting was taking place, with no apparent detrimental effects. However, broken eggs and dead chicks have been found at nests, and human disturbance has been implicated in some of these losses. For example, one nest visitor startled an incubating condor, which knocked its egg from the nest as it hurriedly departed (Sibley 1969). Two other examples that did not result in egg loss, but that show the potential, are also recorded by Sibley (1969). In the first, an incubating condor was startled by a man nearby, and in its haste to get up it kicked the egg several inches forward. On another occasion, a condor sleeping in a pothole virtually "exploded" from the cave when a sonic boom occurred, and it appeared visibly agitated for the next hour. Sibley (unpublished field notes) on two occasions was inside small nest-type caves when sonic booms occurred. He found the experience very unpleasant, and experienced considerable ringing in his ears.

Repeated disturbance of condors at nests might cause egg loss through chilling, or inadequate feeding of the young bird might result (Koford 1953). In addition, repeated disturbance during courtship might frustrate mating attempts. Sibley (1969) watched a courting pair of condors obviously disturbed by airplane traffic overhead. Each time a plane was heard, the displaying bird would fold its wings and look toward the sound, then begin again. If such interruptions were repeated regularly, courtship and subsequent reproduction might be inhibited.

Ali Pearson

8   RECOVERY TEAM JOURNAL

Death of a Condor, Illustrated

From the preliminary draft of their journal, we have taken a continuous excerpt of the observations by Noel Snyder and John Ogden, of the Condor Research Center, pertaining to the death of the older of the two condor chicks known to exist in 1980. The younger chick, found to be of about one-third the age and one-half the weight of the older, survived. It had been handled by the two biologists, whose work with the chick was photographed by Jeff Foott and Tupper Ansel Blake. Access to the second chick's nest proved to be so difficult a climbing problem that the biologists remained above, and William Lehman, who had climbing experience but no training in handling raptors, handled the chick alone. We believe it possible that the impact of the nest visit upon the chick and its parents may be of importance and is not likely to be measureable. We believe that this preliminary draft, which was presented to the California Fish and Game Commission, has a value of immediacy that would be lacking in any revision. The photographs are blown up from individual frames of the 16mm color motion picture made by Mr. Foott, an experienced wildlife photographer. It is our understanding that as the chick began showing evidence of trauma from the handling procedures, he put his camera down and moved in to give assistance, and thus did not photograph the actual expiration.

Autopsy revealed that death was caused by the stress of handling. Prolonged struggling in confinement and release of adrenalin owing to fear caused too great a strain on the heart. Otherwise the chick was entirely healthy; no parasites, no pesticide load, no weight deficiency.

Death of a Condor, Illustrated

T HIS San Rafael Wilderness condor nest was visited on 30 June, 1980, with a plan to repeat the procedures and collection of information conducted at the first site. Age of the chick was unknown, but had been estimated to be approximately the same or slightly older than the first chick. This nest had been under observation for several consecutive days prior to the 30th by Hank Hamber and Chris Kogan, who were joined on the morning of the 30th at the observation station by Ogden, Snyder, Lehman, Gary Falxa of the CRC, Jan Hamber of the Santa Barbara Natural History Museum, Judy Tartaglia of the Los Padres National Forest and J. Foott. The chick had not been fed on the 29th but had been briefly fed by one adult between 10:00 and 11:00 on the 30th, after which the adult left the nest area.

1100 We first view the chick from Hamber's observation station and estimate it to be approximately similar to the first chick in size though to be somewhat more advanced in feather development.

1230 Snyder, Ogden, Lehman, Falxa, and Foott start the hike toward the nest site; everyone else remaining at the observation station but in radio contact.

1315 We reach the top of the escarpment above the nest ledge and estimate the nest to be approximately 75' below the top. The site is determined to be unreachable except by rope descent. Lehman and Foott prepare to make the descent. Hamber reports from the observation station that when the first rope is thrown down the cliff past the nest site the chick responds by backing into the corner of the nest cavity.

1330 Foott lowers himself to a position approximately 12 to 15
     feet off to one side of the nest ledge and does some filming
     of the chick from that distance.
1345 Lehman lowers himself to the nest ledge between Foott
     and the chick. Snyder and Falxa are stationed on top of the   .
     escarpment; Ogden is about one half way down to the nest
     ledge but about 40' off to one side. Lehman reports to
     Ogden, Snyder, and Falxa (who cannot see the chick from
     their positions) that the chick is larger than the first chick
     and shows more feather development.
1350-1425 Lehman weighs and measures the chick. The initial
     responses of the chick to Lehman are similar to those of the
     first chick in that the bird backs into a corner, faces him,

repeatedly hisses and vigorously jabs at him with opened bill when approached. The chick does not regurgitate as did the first chick. Lehman catches the chick in the same manner as before with a quick grab of the head with one hand followed by pulling the bird forward with both hands. Lehman reports that the chick struggles more vigorously and bites harder than the first chick, and that the processing will likely take longer than with the first chick. During the processing Lehman first attempts to weigh the chick in the horse feed bag used on the first chick, but when he finds that the bag is not large enough to accommodate the chick he soon switches to a back pack. At one point during the weighing and again after taking wing

measurements the bird is released and it walks quickly back to its nest cave where it resumes a defensive stance for periods of approximately 1 to 3 minutes before being recaptured for further measurements. During the processing of the chick Lehman considers that the bird behaves similarly to the first chick except for the more vigorous squirming and biting which he assumes to be a function of the bird's greater size. He notes that the bird's respiration rate appears to be reasonably stable until the end of measuring. Although the bird is heard to hiss through much of the processing and has the bill open with tongue partially extended, through essentially all of the processing Bill did not hear gasping or other signs of respiratory dis-

tress. The last measurements taken are of the bill, during which the bird is still resistive, necessitating a firm but gentle grip on the back of its head.

1425 Immediately following the completion of the bill measurements the bird's head is released and Bill notes that it begins to wobble in a few seconds. He releases the bird immediately and calls for advice. Within about 30 seconds of the time he notes the first signs of unsteadiness of the bird's head, the head falls to the ground and the bird appears to have lost consciousness. No signs of pulse or breath are detected from this point onward.

1426-1435 The chick is closely examined by Lehman. At about 1428 some drops of water are sprinkled on the bird's head on the guess that the bird might have been suffering heat stress, but the bird is believed to have been already dead at this point.

1435-1440 The chick is transported to the top of the cliff in a pack.

1440-1445 Falxa and Snyder find no sign of life in the chick. Ambient air temperature checked and found to be 24° C, sky mostly overcast.

1445-1630 The chick is transported back to the observation station and a discussion of the events is carried on with personnel at the observation station. No probable causes of mortality became evident from this discussion.

1620-2130 Chick is transported to Santa Barbara where it is packed in ice, then driven to Ojai where it is kept refrigerated overnight. Snyder contacts Art Risser of the San Diego Zoo for advice on how chick should best be maintained prior to autopsy.

On July 1, after contacting state and federal officials about the loss of the chick and securing clearance to have the bird autopsied, Snyder and Borneman fly the chick, still packed in ice, to San Diego where first examination begins about 1430. Gross autopsy is completed at 22:30 with no clear causes of death evident. A final determination awaits the histo-pathological examination of internal tissues and analyses of various tissues for environmental contaminants.

RESULTS OF NEST VISITATION
weight—5710 gms
culmen—not recorded
bill tip to nostril—5.24 cm
third primary—11.57 cm

wing span—62.2 cm
No. adult feathers collected—10
No. eggshell fragments collected—
   10 (maximum diameter 1.7 cm)

No adult condors seen in nest area during visitation. One adult returns in late afternoon.

9   DAVID DESANTE

To the Fish and Game Commission

So Gentle a Ghoul

Another View

LANDBIRD BIOLOGIST for the Point Reyes Bird Observatory, David
DeSante is author of numerous studies on bird biology and behavior. He
received his PhD in biological sciences from Stanford University in 1973. He
wrote a letter to the California Fish and Game Commission in May 1980
that is reproduced here. "So Gentle a Ghoul" and "Another View" were written after the death of the condor chick and appeared in the *Point Reyes Bird
Observatory Newsletter*, September 1980 and June 1981, respectively.

The prevention of the death of a single condor or of the failure of a single nest may mean that the population will show an increase rather than a decrease for that year. Persons in a position to influence the welfare of individual condors, and especially of their nests, should keep in mind that the precarious natural balance of the population can be easily upset in the direction leading to extinction of the species.

—CARL KOFORD

To the Fish and Game Commission

I T IS AFTER careful scrutiny of the "Justification Statement-Permit Application to Capture California Condors" and the "California Condor Recovery Plan, Dated January, 1980," that I *strongly urge you to deny* the permit requested of you by the Patuxent Wildlife Research Center of the U.S. Fish and Wildlife Service to capture selected individuals of the endangered California Condor in order to fit them with radio-transmitters or take them into captivity for the purpose of captive propagation. In addition, I request that copies of this letter be distributed to the five Commissioners.

My reasons for this recommendation are fourfold. First, I believe that certain of the specific plans and methods to be implemented by the U.S. Fish and Wildlife Service have a very real probability of causing serious irrevocable harm to the existing population of condors. Second, I believe that the proposed activities are not adequately justified at this time. Third, I believe that the tone of the permit application displays an underlying abandonment of the present condor habitat. Fourth, I believe that a blanket permit for manipulating an endangered species over a thirty-five-year period should not be given to any agency without some built-in means of public review of the results of that manipulation every few years.

I must point out at this time that I am not categorically opposed to all "hands-on" attempts to increase the California Condor population through manipulation or captive propagation. However, I feel strongly that the proposed activities and the time-frame in which they are to be implemented will *increase, rather than lessen* the probability of extinction of wild California Condors.

1. *Opposition based upon the extreme danger of certain specific plans and methods proposed in the permit application.*

[199]

a. *The use of patagial tag markers on which to mount transmitter units.*

George Jonkel, the Chief of the U.S. Fish and Wildlife Services's Bird Banding Laboratory in Laurel, Maryland, has recently informed me of work by Mike Lockhart, also of the U.S. Fish and Wildlife Service, in Sheridan, Wyoming, that indicates that patagial tags seriously interfere with courtship in adult Golden Eagles. This interference produced greatly aberrant behavior in these eagles to the extent that the breeding success was severely impaired. This impairment was serious enough that Jonkel was considering denying permission to use patagial markers on adult Golden Eagles. No mention of Lockhart's work is contained in the Justification Statement for the Permit Application which only discusses the use of patagial tag markers on Turkey and Black Vultures. One cannot assume, since California Condors are cathartid vultures, that their behavior will always be analogous to the smaller vultures. The Permit Application states that attempts will be made to capture and radio-tag two condors during September 1980. The results of this initial radioing effort will be monitored for one month, and "if no unresolveable problems have arisen," eight additional birds will be radioed prior to February 1, 1981. This means that ten condors, *fully one-third to one-half of the entire world's population,* will be radioed before it is possible to ascertain any detrimental effects of patagial tags or radio transmitters on the breeding behavior of these birds. *This is totally irresponsible!* If some detrimental effect does occur, and the work on the Golden Eagles indicates that it is a real possibility, extinction of the wild population of California Condors may become a certainty. It is imperative, therefore, that the use of patagial tag-mounted radio transmitters be tested on a *maximum of only two* California Condors for a complete breeding cycle, and that no additional radio tags be used until the absence of detrimental effects of patagial tags and radio transmitters on the breeding success of these birds *is proven.*

b) *The techniques of re-introduction of captive-bred California Condors into the wild that assures their future breeding success in the wild have not yet been tried, let alone proven.* There seems to be little question that captive California Condors will successfully breed in captivity. However, whether captive-bred condors can be successfully re-introduced into the wild, and whether these captive-bred individuals will successfully breed in the wild remain problematical. This is the ultimate test that must be established before substantial numbers of California Condors are taken from the wild! This may seem to be self-evident, but proponents for captive breeding argue that given enough trials, we are bound to discover how to successfully re-introduce these birds. However, we need only to look at the Peregrine Falcon situation to realize the dangers involved. Despite large numbers of Peregrines raised in captivity, successful breeding in the wild of captive-bred Peregrines has been virtually nil.

The situation, therefore, is as follows. Taking nine condors out of the wild for captive breeding will necessarily severely hurt the chance for recovery of the wild population. This is especially so if any immatures are taken. The only way that this can be justified is if the taking of these condors will ultimately increase the chance for recovery of the wild population. This necessitates the successful breeding in the wild of re-introduced captive-bred birds. Since the probability of this is completely unknown (and perhaps is quite low), rational justification can only be obtained if the present population has virtually no chance for survival by itself. I will show below that this is not necessarily the case (despite a statement to the contrary in the Permit Application). Thus, there is a distinct possibility (one, I believe, that is quite high) that the captive breeding program will actually increase the probability of extinction of the wild population of the California Condor. Thus, it must not be permitted.

2. *Opposition based upon insufficient justification for the proposed activities.*

The ultimate justification for all of the high-risk activities proposed by the U.S. Fish and Wildlife Service is stated on page one of the Permit Application, "Despite long-standing research and management efforts on behalf of the California Condor, the species has shown a continuing decline and is now so reduced in numbers that it is virtually certain to become extinct unless fundamentally new approaches are initiated." I do not believe that this statement has been satisfactorily documented and proven.

a. *Magnitude of the recent decline and prognosis for the future.* The

Permit application cites three references that supposedly document the magnitude of the recent decline. (J. Verner, California Condors: Status of the Recovery Effort, U.S. Forest Service General Technical Report PSW-28, 1978; R. E. Ricklefs (editor), Report of the Advisory Panel on the California Condor, Audubon Conservation Report 6, 1978; and D. B. Clark (chairman), Report of the Sierra Club Condor Advisory Committee, Sierra Club, 1979). Ricklefs states (page 8), "The size of the population is a controversial issue. . . . The confidence limits on estimates of the population are unknown but must certainly be very wide." Clearly, we do not know how many condors still exist. Ricklefs then states (page 12), ". . . . we cannot estimate reliably such critical population parameters as population size, age structure, sex ratio, age of first breeding, frequency of breeding longevity, and age-specific mortality rates. Accurate estimates of these parameters would be required to construct predictive models of the population, and significant errors in some parameters would profoundly affect the accuracy of simulations and management decisions based on such models. . . . Results from previous research on population models of long-lived species . . . " suggest that the data presently available for the California Condor will not permit the construction of an accurate prediction model for this population, although some inferences might be drawn from the comparisons with other species having apparently similar population characteristics." Thus the virtual certainty of extinction that is used to justify the proposed activities is clearly based on only inferential evidence.

And just what is that inference? Ricklefs clearly states it on page 13: "Because protection similar to that provided for the Whooping Crane, which recovered from a low of fifteen individuals in 1941 to seventy in 1977, has not led to a similar recovery of the California Condor—the condor population has continued to decline rather than increase—other measures clearly are necessary." First, does the Whooping Crane have "similar population characteristics" to those of the condor? It does not! And second, consider the "protection" supplied during this time to the condor. Between 1946 and 1969, over *four million pounds of DDT* were sprayed on the foothills and plains of the southern San Joaquin Valley for the control of beet leafhoppers (S. G. Herman, from a paper presented at the Vulture Symposium in Santa Barbara, 1979). . . . And this, the U.S. Fish and Wildlife Service proudly claims, is "protection"! One is, therefore, forced to the conclusion that the virtual certainty of extinction used to justify this Permit Application is based not only on inferential evidence, but on evidence that is actually inaccurate and apparently intentionally misleading.

b. *Causes of the decline.* The Permit Application is very vague as to the causes of the recent decline and uses this vagueness to justify the risky biotechnical methods of radiotelemetry and captive propagation that it recommends. But are the causes of recent decline so "speculative"? Ricklefs states (page 11) that, "Recent analyses have shown that California Condors and their eggs have very high concentrations of DDE and smaller concentrations of other chlorinated hydrocarbons. A condor killed accidentally in 1965 had 30 ppm DDE in its fat. . . . An individual found dead in 1974 had 200 ppm DDE (dry weight) in its leg muscle (equivalent to 2,700 ppm in fat). . . . Another condor shot in 1976 had 105 ppm DDE. . . . DDE has also been detected, at concentrations between 43 and 200 ppm, in lipids extracted from the membranes of eggshell fragments collected from three nests between 1967 and 1977. . . . These concentration of DDE are among the *highest ever reported in terrestrial birds and indicate a significant threat to condors.* The level of 200 ppm DDE in the muscle of the 1974 condor is equal to levels that proved fatal to American kestrels *(Falco sparverius)* when residues were mobilized during a period of stress. . . . *This condor may have died of DDE poisoning.* The concentrations of between 43 and 200 ppm DDE in egg lipids of condors are in the range associated with eggshell thinning and reproductive failure in other species. . . . The average thickness of shells from condor eggs laid between 1964 and 1977 was *thirty-two percent less* than that of eggshells collected prior to 1944. . . . This degree of eggshell thinning is associated with total hatching failure in other species." (Emphasis mine.) All of these figures are fully referenced in the Ricklefs report.

In view of this evidence, how can the Permit Application state (page 3): "Causes of the apparent low production of young in recent years are for the most part speculative; it is not even known with certainty whether the problems lie with frequent nesting failure or with frequent failure of adults to attempt breeding"? The Application continues (page 3): ". . . use of DDT has been banned in the region since 1971 and it is questionable that this pesticide might still be causing significant difficulties." What about the 1974 and 1976 birds mentioned above? What seems amazing is that this information was available (reference the 1965 bird) when the DDT problem was brought to the public attention with regard to Brown Pelicans, Ospreys, and Peregrine Falcons. But was any mention made at the time of DDT's possible connection to the decline of the condor? No! Apparently the U.S. Fish and Wildlife Service chose to suppress this information and, as evidenced by the vague nature of the Permit Application, is still supressing this information.

Of additional importance is the fact that the 1976 bird was found shot. Ricklefs (page 10) states, "Considering the odds against discovery of a shot condor and the fact that the population decline has been on the order of one or two individuals per year, hunting may be an important factor." Still another potential cause of the condor's decline has been the aerial application of Compound 1080 to the condor's feeding range to kill ground squirrels. Ricklefs states (page 11), "Although the U.S. Department of the Interior has claimed that 1080 is noncumulative and poses little hazard of secondary poisoning to birds . . . we know of no long-term studies investigating the effects, lethal and sublethal, of repeated exposure."

In summary, the available evidence very strongly suggests that the causes for the recent decline of the condor include impairment of reproduction through pesticide contamination and direct mortality through shooting and poisoning. In other words, the cause is the failure of the U.S. Fish and Wildlife Service to provide adequate protection to the birds and to their habitat. The Permit Application, however, states (page 1), "The basic causes of decline are not known with certainty, and there is an urgent need for expanded research to elucidate the problems and an urgent need to initiate captive breeding efforts as a safeguard against total loss of the species." This is totally misleading when, in fact, there is an urgent need to provide total protection to the condor population and its habitat!

c. Inadequacy of traditional research methods. Just as the U.S. Fish and Wildlife Service has been remiss in providing adequate protection to the condors, they have also been remiss in providing adequate research of the remaining condors. Ricklefs clearly states (page 8) that ". . . the condor census program has *varied annually in design and effort*" and includes "the annual count in October . . . *casual* surveys of known nesting sites and condor range throughout the year, and an *informal* network of spotters whose observations are tabulated and interpreted by the Recovery Team" (emphasis mine). Furthermore, "The number of observer-days in the field has not been uniform since the present monitoring program was initiated. . . ." The scientific community cannot and does not accept such effort as valid research. Thus, the statement in the Permit Application that traditional research methods have been inadequate is categorically false. Traditional research methods have not even been tried! Furthermore, the approved California Condor Recovery Plan (date January, 1980) includes no mention of the initiation of scientifically valid traditional research methods. It merely proposes to continue the casual, unscientific censuses and surveys as a supplement (presumably) to its radio telemetry program.

The serious dangers of the telemetry program have aleady been discussed. Any positive value accrued from the telemetry program can only be obtained if individual condors can be continuously followed throughout their lives. The determination of the exact location of any bird will depend upon its being simultaneously picked-up by at least two receiving stations. No mention is made in the Permit Application of the schedule of establishment of such receiving stations. However, I have been informed by John Ogden and John Borneman of the Condor Research Center that only three stations will have been established by the time that up to ten condors have been fitted with transmitters. This, again, is totally irresponsible! The U.S. Fish and Wildlife Service apparently intends to seriously endanger a substantial portion of the remaining condors by affixing radio transmitters to them without assuring that the telemetry program will even work. If the radioed condors move to a different part of their range, away from the receiving stations (as seems entirely possible due to the trauma of capture), their locations will not even be determinable. You must not permit such irresponsible action to proceed!

3. *Opposition based upon an implied abandonment of the present condor habitat.*

The Permit Application has two major sections: I. Justification for the Proposed Activities, and II. Details of Proposed Activities. This second section contains three parts: A. Trapping and Handling Procedures. B. The Radio-Telemetry Program, and C. Formation of a Captive Population. Isn't something missing here? What about the reintroduction of captive-bred condors into the wild? Isn't that what the whole captive propagation program is about? Without the inclusion of this section, the Permit Application must be found incomplete and deficient and must be straightforwardly rejected!

In all fairness, there is a third, very brief, major section called, "III. Duration of the Project and Final Disposition of Condors." I will now quote *all* the details about the reintroduction of condors to the wild (page 20 of the Permit Application): "Some progeny from the program will be used to form additional breeding pairs, and the rest will be released to the wild." How many will be released to the wild? As to where they will be reintroduced, we find one sentence, "Habitats to be utilized during the California Condor reintroduction program *will be* identified from information gained during the telemetry studies in California, and *future* habitat analyses within the present and historical range of the condor." (Emphasis mine.) There is no positive indication that *any* condors will be reintroduced into their present range! The U.S. Fish and Wildlife Service, therefore, is requesting permission (if they so decide) to extirpate the California Condor from its present range and to reintroduce captive-bred individuals is some other, as yet unknown, area. This is not only totally irresponsible, it is completely illogical and, I believe, legally and morally wrong.

One of the basic principles of Ecological Science is that the habitats and ranges of species and populations have evolved through natural selection to be those areas where survivorship and reproductive success are maximized. It is ill-conceived to think that California Condors could fare better in areas outside their present range than within their present range, provided that their present range is protected from pesticide contamination, shooting, poisoning, human disturbance, and development. Herein lies my strongest objection to the Permit Application. By admitting to the possibility that captive-bred condors will not be reintroduced into the present condor range, the U.S. Fish and Wildlife Service admits that it cannot, or will not, provide maximum protection to the habitat and range of the California Condor.

Proponents of captive propagation may argue that it will be difficult to save the condor habitat. But can they think that the task will be made easier if the condors are absent rather than if they are, and have always been, present? I believe that the underlying tone of the Permit Application speaks of the abandonment of the present habitat and range of the California Condor. And in the end it must be stressed that there can be no hope of saving the California Condor if we do not save its habitat and its range.

4. *Opposition based upon the inadvisability of granting permission to manipulate an endangered species for 35 years without some provision for public review of the results of that manipulation.*

I would be extremely reluctant to give blanket permission for such a length of time to any agency dealing with an endangered species. Furthermore, considering the failure of the U.S. Fish and Wildlife Service to provide adequate protection to the California Condor and to initiate adequate research by traditional methods on the present population of condors, such a long-term permit should not even be considered.

In summary, I believe that the California Condor can be saved—in its present range and habitat and without high-risk biotechnical research methods and/or captive propagation. What is needed is a total commitment to the immediate protection of the condor's present habitat and range, and a total commitment to the initiation of a sound research program to be carried out virtually entirely by traditional methods. I believe that the proposed activities requested in the Permit Application will only increase the probability of extinction of wild California Condors. I most strongly urge you to deny this permit.

But for me the heart of California lies in the condor country. And for me the heart of mystery, of wonder, and of desire lies with the California Condor, that majestic and almost legendary figure, which still haunts the fastnesses of our lessening wilderness.

—WILLIAM LEON DAWSON

So Gentle a Ghoul

O N 30 JUNE 1980, a 2-month-old California condor chick died in its nest cavity while being weighed, measured, and photographed. The final autopsy, released 1 August 1980, revealed that the death was due to shock and acute heart failure caused by the stress of handling. It was a sad day in the history of this species, for it came at a home of increasing optimism over the discovery that California condors were reproducing in the wild. The death of a single bird, especially one of the only two known chicks, from a world population thought not to exceed thirty individuals, is of extreme importance. It serves as a grim and sorrowful reminder than everyone who shares any concern for the fate of this species— certainly one of the most magnificent birds on our planet— must consider the actions that should be taken to save it from the extinction to which it has just moved one step closer.

Several points must be emphasized in connection with the condor death. First, the death was directly attributable to the Condor Recovery Program, a joint operation of the U.S. Fish and Wildlife Service (USFWS) and the National Audubon Society (NAS). Second, the entire incident was filmed by a cinematographer on contract from the USFWS. The film is a lucid account of a badly mis-managed operation. Third, this work was apparently done illegally in terms of the legislation cited to support the Recovery Program: the Endangered Species Act. The California Department of Fish and Game (DFG) has now acknowledged that it did not have authorization to grant permission for handling chicks. And finally, the work was attempted in secrecy, without notification to the public. As pointed out by Dr. Steve Herman of Evergreen State College, this action "demonstrates a kind of unprofessionalism and bad faith that has no place in the wildlife profession or the business of endangered species research."

DFG revokes permits

The result of the June 30th tragedy was that Charles Fullerton, Director of the Department of Fish and Game, revoked all state permits that allow any capture, handling or captive breeding of California Condors. He stated that any re-authorization will not be considered until after the USFWS requests a hearing before the Fish and Game Commission and shows why studies involving the capture and handling of condors should proceed. Huey Johnson, Secretary of the California Resources Agency, has called for a complete investigation of the incident.

Weighing, measuring, and photographing nestling birds is not a particuarly dangerous (to the bird) or untested procedure. The fact that it ended in tragedy for a California Condor only serves to underline the necessity of considering all manipulative measures of "saving" condors to be extremely high risk operations to be resorted to only when all else fails. And the point is, all else hadn't failed, nor even been given a fair chance.

We can only hope that the tragic death of the young condor will cause the Recovery Team to heed the warnings and counsel of three generations of condor researchers concerning the dangers of manipulative techniques of all kinds.

Perhaps the saddest part of the current crisis is the split that has developed within the conservation community over the Condor Research Program. The Friends of the Earth and the Golden Gate Chapter of the Audubon Society have both opposed the Recovery Plan endorsed and partly run by the NAS. It is imperative that this split be mended as quickly as possible, for we cannot hope to save the condor if we are not in agreement on how to do it. The recent condor tragedy must provide the necessary impetus for drafting a new Recovery Plan that can be enthusiastically supported by all individuals and agencies committed to saving the condor.

Sufficient habitat

Two points must be emphasized in any truly effective Condor Recovery Plan. The first is that we cannot hope to save the condor without saving its habitat. Even the most wildly successful captive breeding program would be for naught if there is not sufficient suitable habitat to support the birds after their release into the wild. However the Recovery Plan statement indicating that captive-propagated condors might be reintroduced in areas other than their present range displays a willingness to abandon the present-day condor habitat.

Furthermore, as pointed out by Dr. Paul Ehrlich in a letter to Secretary of the Interior Cecil Andrus, many other species and genetically distinct populations are also endangered within the condors' range, including, for example, populations of *Euphydryas* butterflies. "Public attention is easily drawn to the state of prominent endangered species like the condor, but not to populations of insignificant 'bugs'. That the 'bugs' are quite likely more important components of the ecological systems that provide crucial (and free) services to humanity is unrecognized by almost all decision makers. The condor, therefore, should be preserved not just out of intrinsic interest, compassion, and for its own ecological role, but most importantly because it can serve as a rallying symbol for protecting large areas of habitat and thus many other endangered organisms."

Grim prediction

A second requirement for an effective Condor Recovery Program must be the de-emphasis of manipulative, high technology, "hands-on" techniques and a return to traditional "hands-off" methods of studying this majestic species. In his 12 February 1980 letter to Secretary Andrus, Ehrlich stated, "The notion that something could be learned from such studies (i.e. manipulative, 'hands-on' studies) that would contribute to the specific question of how to preserve condors is naive at best—unless it would be that harassment leads to behavioral changes and injuries that drive down population size." On 30 June 1980 the prediction, sadly, came true.

The difficulties of studying such a wide-ranging species with such a low population size by traditional methods were recognized and well stated by David Clark in these pages one year ago. (Sierra Club Blue Ribbon Report) But those problems do not mean we must give up. What is needed is a well-coordinated effort involving the full-time energies of a large number of trained and conscientious field researchers. This is not the approach that is typically championed by government agencies. They generally choose high technology, equipment-intensive methods over personnel-intensive efforts.

Still, there is something you can do if you, like William Leon Dawson, are "not ashamed to have fallen in love with so gentle a ghoul." Write to the Secretary of the Interior, Washington, D.C. 20242, to E. C. Fullerton, Director, California Department of Fish and Game, 1416 Ninth Street, Sacramento, CA 95814, and to Russell Peterson, President, National Audubon Society, 950 Third Avenue, New York, N.Y. 10022, and urge them to adopt a new Recovery Plan that emphasizes habitat protection and a "hands-off" research program.

If any animal can command the massive public sentiment and support necessary to save it and its habitat, the condor can. *Gymnogyps calfornianus* sailing free and majestically over the rugged terrain of southern California mountains represents, more than any other sight in North America, the splendor and freedom of the natural world. We will not have many more chances to preserve that sight.

Another View

I N A PREVIOUS article, I criticized certain aspects of the Condor Recovery Program as it was then constituted, particularly its emphasis on manipulative techniques and its program of nest entry. Those elements of the program were suspended following the death of the nestling condor last summer. I would now like to present the basic elements of a Condor Recovery Program that I believe will maximize the species' chances for persisting in the wild.

1. The Recovery Program should have a precisely defined objective, one against which progress and success can be accurately measured, and one that can be overwhelmingly acceptable to all groups and agencies committed to saving the condor. As such, I believe that there can be only one valid objective: to allow and to aid the increase in numbers of California Condors within their natural range to, say, fifty individuals by taking those actions that minimize the probability of extinction of the wild population. This is basically a conservative approach, that is, one that minimizes the risk of total loss (extinction) rather than one that maximizes the rate at which the increase could take place. The objective, then, is to roughly double the wild population.

It should be noted that this objective does *not* preclude the use of manipulative techniques such as radio-telemetry or captive propagation. It does, however, constrain the use of those techniques to comply with a minimum-risk decision-making strategy.

2. The Recovery Program should emphasize the immediate implementation of solutions to the problem of a decreased condor population.

It is often stated that we cannot effectively implement solutions at this time because we do not know the exact causes of the condor's decline. This attitude is both misleading and counterproductive. The weight of available evidence does not imply that some unknown factor has caused the condor population to decrease. Rather, it strongly implies that a combination of several straightforward human-caused factors such as impairment of reproduction by pesticides, and direct mortality by shooting and secondary poisoning have been responsible for the condor's decrease. While we may not be able to state exactly to what extent each of these causes has contributed to the decline, we can be assured that if we take steps to rectify all of these potential causes, we will maximize the chances of the condor's survival. It is true that this may not be the most *energy* effective approach to the problem—we may expend some energy that will not directly aid the condor. However, it is the most *time* effective approach. And time, I believe, is of the essence in implementing these solutions. We cannot afford to wait for manipulative techniques to be tested and to produce results. For instance, radio-telemetry has been proposed in part to provide information on mortality by allowing the recovery of condor corpses. But we should not wait for radio-telemetry to reveal a pattern of mortality in condors before we take steps to prevent those mortalities.

Time is so important because virtually all of the factors potentially causing the decrease in the condor population depend on current (or recent) human practices. Effective solutions, therefore, necessitate changes in those practices. Such changes typically do not come about overnight, nor can they generally be simply legislated and enforced. Rather, such changes only come about by the slow, painstaking process of education. We must realize that we cannot hope to buy or set aside huge portions of southern California for exclusive use of condors. The solutions to condor survival problems must work in the context of some degree of coexistence of humans and condors.

Of course the potential solutions to problems faced by the condor will be difficult to implement. How do we force hunters to retrieve their game (especially if it is vermin such as ground squirrels or rabbits) in order to protect condors against possible lead poisoning? How do we save crucial areas from development? Here is where the Recovery Program needs the unified, wholehearted support of all conservation organizations. Here is where the National Audubon Society, Sierra Club, Friends of the Earth, and others must joint forces and commit their energy and resources.

3. The Recovery Program should continue and even increase traditional non-manipulative field work on the California Condor. Only two years ago, there was no positive evidence that condors were reproducing at all in the wild. Recovery Team personnel suggested that it was entirely possible that very little successful reproduction had occurred over the past several years and that radio-telemetry was the only means of providing answers to such questions. Since then, however, the highly commendable and extremely successful efforts of the Recovery Team resulted in the discovery of two active nests during the spring of 1980. And five apparently mated pairs of condors (four of which were seemingly engaged in courtship) had been identified and located by mid-December 1980. More good information concerning the condor and its reproductive behavior has been accumulated during the past year than had been gathered in all the years since Koford's work. More could be accomplished with more personnel.

I am not advocating placing hundreds of observers on mountain tops throughout the condor's range. I am advocating increasing the average number of people in the field on any given day from about five to about twenty. In view of the recent successes of the Recovery Team, I believe that a nearly complete monitoring of the reproductive effort and success of the current condor population could be achieved with a team of this size by entirely non-manipulative techniques.

4. The Recovery Program should continue field and laboratory testing on appropriate surrogate species of all manipulative techniques proposed for the California Condor. Specifically, four studies should be continued or initiated with all possible effort and speed.

The first study is the continuation and expansion of the large-scale program of capturing and radio tagging wild Andean Condors to: a) thoroughly test the use of cannon and/or rocket nets under every conceivable circumstance (it appears that the Recovery Team is becoming committed to such capture methods since they have shown that the risk of injury is high with clap traps and they feel that efficiency is unacceptably low

with walk-in traps); b) thoroughly test methods for sexing individuals by using growing contour feathers (earlier plans for
laparoscopy should be discontinued if this new method proves
successful); c) thoroughly test materials and designs for patagial tags and radio transmitters; and d) ascertain that wild captured Andean Condors, equipped with patagial tag-mounted
radio transmitters, will breed successfully in the wild.

The second study is the continuation and expansion of the
large-scale program for the captive breeding of Andean Condors in order to determine: a) the protocol for achieving successful breeding in captivity; b) the protocol for achieving the
successful release into the wild of captive-bred birds; and c)
whether captive-bred and released individuals will successfully
reproduce in the wild.

The third study is the establishment of a radio-telemetry
program on Turkey Vultures within the current range of the
California Condor in order to develop and test all technical
details of a radio-telemetry program that might subsequently
be employed with condors.

The fourth study is the establishment and/or continuation of
an intensive program of laboratory testing of the effects of ingestion of pesticides, poisons and heavy metals (particularly
lead) on both Turkey Vultures and Andean Condors.

5. The Recovery Program should establish a review process
for all proposed manipulative actions, since the applicability
and timeliness of such actions must necessarily depend upon
the current state of the condor population. I suggest that a
program of specific, pre-tested manipulative actions should be
formulated each year, for a period of only one year, and should
be based upon the reproductive success of that year and the
population estimates and mortality estimates of the previous
year. The proposed actions for each year should be subject to
review and public comment, but the time frame of such review
and comment should be limited (to about one month) so that
the program is not jeopardized. Late summer may be an opti-
mal time for such formulation and review, since reproductive
success should be quite accurately known by then even though
fledging does not actually occur until fall.

Based upon the current status of the California Condor population, including the existence of five potential breeding pairs, I

will make the following recommendations regarding the use of manipulative actions:

a) Under no circumstances should nest entry be considered during the 1981 breeding season. I see no indication that any information that could greatly aid the recovery of wild California Condors would be obtained from such intrusions. The available historical data and that from 1980 indicate that the growth rates of condor chicks may show such high variability that the detailed monitoring of one or even several chicks over one or more seasons would provide very little real information as to reproductive difficulties that condors in general may be facing. Information collected on a single nest intrusion would be virtually useless in this regard. Thus, nest intrusions could only serve as a potentially dangerous and unnecessary harassment of wild condors.

In late November 1980, the AOU Condor Advisory Committee issued a preliminary recommendation supporting nest intrusions in which patagial tag-mounted radio transmitters would be placed on California Condor chicks. I know of no precedent in placing patagial markers on nestling birds. I know of no preliminary work like this being done on either Andean Condors or Turkey Vultures. This would be an entirely untested manipulation which could only serve to widen the controversy among groups and individuals committed to saving the condor and might ultimately hinder the Recovery Program.

b) Radio-telemetry studies of wild California Condors should not be initiated until 1) it is established that wild-captured radio-tagged Andean Condors successfully breed in the wild, and 2) all technical details and equipment necessary for the California Condor radio-telemetry study have been established and tested on Turkey Vultures in the condor's range. The first requirement could be met very soon, since a patagial-tagged bird was observed defending a nest site in the Andes in October 1980 and several breeding-aged adults now carry radio transmitters there. It is also conceivable that the second requirement could be established within eight months so that radio-telemetry studies of California Condors could be initiated as early as the fall of 1981.

Whenever radio-telemetry studies begin, I recommend that only *three* California Condors be captured and radio-tagged the first fall. The first should be an adult that is strongly expected to breed in the following year. This will provide a test for continuing the radio-telemetry program: that wild-captured radio-tagged California Condors will successfully breed in the wild. The other two birds should (if possible) be an adult expected not to breed in the following year (so that the behavior of a nonbreeder can be monitored) and an immature or sub-adult. No other condor should be captured and radio-tagged for a period of about one year, that is until a review of the results of this first attempt is completed.

This recommendation contrasts with previous recovery program plans to capture and radio-tag up to ten condors during the first fall and winter of the radio telemetry program. I believe that one-third to nearly one-half of the entire population of California Condors is too much to risk on the first attempt at radio-telemetry with this species, even when details have been worked out on the closely-related Andean Condor. A great deal will be learned from the first three radio-tagged birds just as a great deal is now being learned from Andean Condors.

c) *One* sub-adult female California Condor should be taken from the wild as a potential mate for Topa Topa in order to attempt to establish a captive breeding population. *No* other breeding or potentially breeding California Condors should be taken from the wild as long as successful reproduction is occurring in the wild (especially at the rate at which they may now be reproducing). No other California Condors should be taken from the wild until it is demonstrated that captive-bred and released Andean Condors successfully produce young in the wild. This demonstration is probably at least four or five years away.

The possibility of creating a captive breeding population by taking freshly-laid eggs of wild California Condors, and thus inducing the birds to "double-clutch," should be considered extremely tentative at this time. Work should be initiated immediately on induced "double-clutching" in wild Andean Condors and on incubation procedures for Andean Condor eggs (a great many Peregrine eggs were lost in the early days of that manipulative recovery program). However, no California Condor eggs should be taken until the above research programs are completed and until it is demonstrated that captive-bred and released Andean Condors successfully produce young in the wild.

A successful captive breeding program does provide a possible means of augmenting a successfully breeding wild population. It does not, however, provide a means of saving the condor (other than as a zoological curiosity or a caged gene pool). This is because the success of a captive breeding program aimed at reintroducing birds to the wild is ultimately dependent upon the maintenance of the wild population. Recent evidence on Andean Condors emphasizes that the successful release of captive-bred birds depends upon the existence of a wild population into which the captive-bred birds can be integrated. Thus, the development of a captive breeding population must be considered secondary to the maintenance of the wild breeding population.

In summary, I hope that this proposed Condor Recovery Program will be viewed as an active but balanced plan aimed at maintaining and increasing the wild condor population. It is one that recognizes both the benefits and dangers of manipulative techniques and one that urges careful reviews of procedures and alternatives, and a cooperative attitude among groups and individuals dedicated to saving the condor.

Wild or Caged?
A Call for Reappraisal

(with Richard J. Vogl)

N INE YEARS after Professor Loye Miller began writing about the condor-like vultures of the La Brea tar pits (that was in 1910), Roland Ross started working on condor bones himself. He was twenty-three then, and that was the beginning of his own studies of condor form and function. As paleontologists would, he extrapolated how the extraordinary design worked, eons ago, in life. In the years that followed—and there have been six decades of years—he reconstructed skeletons and skins, wrote, led classes and field trips, founded organizations, worked for the protection of the habitats of endangered species of plants and animals, taught living ornithology, then escaped to pseudo-retirement to make the most of his training in ecology, botany, geology, and meteorology. The California Institute of Technology named the Ornithological Collection of Living Birds after him; he built it. He is emeritus professor of Nature Study and Ornithology at California State University, Los Angeles, and is now working on the ecology of Lake Mathews, a forty-two-year-old Los Angeles reservoir, and on restoring part of Arroyo Seco Park to the wild, but has no designs on the Rose Bowl. If Roland Ross were a reincarnationist and elected to be a California condor, fellow condors would admire his expertise and understanding.

Richard J. Vogl is professor of Biology at California State University, Los Angeles. Author of more than forty-five scientific papers on plant ecology and wildlife management, Dr. Vogl was Vice-Chairman of the Applied Ecology Section of the Ecological Society of America.

To soar, you have to have muscles. You have to *use* the muscles. So in a cage, no matter how glorified it is, there isn't any way you can get a condor to do two things: either to build up his muscles. . . . See, the young one builds up his muscles because his folks are up there, they're coming in and he's skittering around. Every meal that he gets comes out of the sky. Everything in his life is downhill; everything in his life is jumping into space and then coming back to be safe, to get home. Well, for Christ's sake, all this has to do with experience. You don't have those incentives, you have no *reason* to jump off, you have no reason to soar, and you have not developed these long, tendinous muscles that have to do with the intricate art of soaring. If you haven't developed the muscles, you aren't going to soar. You've got the wings, but you haven't got the muscles.

Second, you haven't got anybody who knows how. There isn't anybody up there doing it, bringing you warm food. Nobody; nobody is coming in on the air, borne by it. If the condor is a pig grown in a cage with garbage all his life, he's a feathered pig. When you get three generations of feathered pigs, pigs is all they know how to be.

The habitat itself is far more important than the condor. As a symbol, the habitat involves everyone and all forms of life within it. So that the habitat, in a sense, should be preserved irrespective of whether the condor is still there to fly about it.

—S. DILLON RIPLEY

A Call for Reappraisal

I N THIS DAY of the specialist and expert, we often fail to recognize that "what we see depends upon what we look for." We tend to overlook those things that we are unaware of, or in which we have not received training. Our indifference to, and acceptance or rejection of facts and ideas relates to certain experiences we have had, basic assumptions we have made, and correct or incorrect information that we have obtained. As a result, we come to perceive the world around us in certain ways that influence how we attempt to solve problems.

In the following pages we question the direction of the current condor management and some of the assumptions on which it is based, and urge, with Paul Sears, that the ecologist's task is not only to see what is there, but to see what is going on.

We believe that habitat changes induced by modern man are the major cause of the current decline of California condors. This conclusion can be supported with the following evidence:

1. The California condor is not a naturally declining relict bird but a highly plastic species that has continued to survive until now because of its ability to adapt to natural changes through time. Among the Pleistocene avifauna, the California condor is one of three members of the Cathartid family to survive, while six out of nine species perished. Instead of becoming extinct the condor survived the last Ice Age and is extant, though reduced to an island called California. During the interregnum of dryness since Pleistocene, the condor survived by shrinking territory, reducing numbers, but feeding as usual in grasslands, savannas, and openings.

All was well until about 1850, when the condors began to encounter problems—man problems, not bird problems in essence. Since then the condor has had to win against hardship, loss, and opposition created by implacable, aggressive, and irresponsible man. If the species can outlast modern man the returning Ice Age will proliferate the condor to dominate the skies throughout the Far West again,—and to be cherished by future man. We must erase conceptions of senescence, relict, and failure.

2. The condor is largely a *grassland animal* because grasslands, oak or pine savannas, potreros, and openings are key ecosystems necessary for condor survival. Chaparral and forest are not essential for condors—condors live above them, not in them. Only freshly burned chaparral can be briefly utilized by condors for feeding, while fire-ravaged forests are largely unusable. Mature chaparral and forests lack food quantity and diversity and are impenetrable. In contrast, native grasslands, savannas, and openings are highly productive ecosystems capable of providing sufficient carrion for the successful reproduction of condors. Bush rabbits and deer in chaparral are sparse and fewer by far than the cottontails and deer of edges, and the antelope, elk, deer, and jack rabbits of the grasslands and savannas that formerly occupied the open valley floors. These more open vegetation types facilitated the detection of carcasses (they were subject to frequent fire) and permitted easy and safe ingress and egress of condors for feeding.

Man-induced degradation of these essential condor habitats has occurred in numerous ways. One of the most pronounced has been the *relentless heavy grazing* by Spanish and American ranchers. This has produced soil compaction, sheet and gully erosion with a loss of topsoil, and a degrading replacement of native plants with weedy aliens. Overgrazing eliminated the recurring natural fires that maintained and stimulated grassland plants and animals. These fires also created diversified and productive edges along chaparral and forest fronts.

Rangeland degradation leads to a number of imbalances or secondary effects including reduction in stream flow and springs, and irruptions of rodents and rabbits that produce plant "eat outs" resulting in range depletions even beyond the reach of livestock. The end result of these changes has been a severe reduction in the kinds and numbers of grassland animals available as condor food. Much of the degraded rangeland has also gone from reduced use to no condor use with conversion to farmland or urbanization.

Purposeful fire exclusion has resulted in the transformation of some oak and pine savannas to less productive forests. The original fireproof savannas are now sometimes destroyed or converted to brushfields by crown fires. Fire control, along with sanitation tree removal and logging, has led to a reduction in the number of condor perch trees.

Some areas currently dominated by the relatively useless coastal sage scrub may have formerly supported grasslands. Recognition of coastal sage scrub as a natural vegetation type may lead us to a misconception that this association is entirely natural in its occurrence, when, in fact, it may often be a product of grazing degradation, unnatural fire frequencies and times, and fire control.

3. The first significant losses of secure, undisturbed condor feeding grounds since 1850 were the California coastal strand and tidelands. The seashore with its flotsam of carcasses was a condor resource, but rarely since 1910. The condor capitalized on these graveyards of the Pacific with their continuous supplies of beached seals, sea lions, whales, and fishes. Man's omnipresence on the coast has largely eliminated condors from strand feeding. Estuaries, lagoons, and tidal marshes were also rich in life, with inviting mud flats that were undoubtedly used by condors. These marshlands are now reduced to a fraction of their former extent and are off-limits to condors because they are now unproductive or are encircled by development.

Rivers with flood-scoured shorelines, open bars, spits, and secondary channels must have provided carcasses for condors, including large numbers of flood fatalities periodically. Many of these rivers have been tamed, channelized, dammed, inhabited by humans, or in some other way rendered useless to condors.

Playa lakes and ephemeral ponds such as Buena Vista and Tulare Lakes drew vast numbers of kinds of waterfowl, including geese, white pelicans, and cranes. These waterfowl were sometimes subject to massive die-offs due to botulism and avian cholera. These and areas like the delta of the Sacramento and San Joaquin Rivers were accessible to condors during drought periods and when opened by fires. These wetlands also attracted and concentrated large and small mammals, particularly during droughts.

4. Condors have suffered further by displacement from soaring areas, travel lanes, and perches by intruding people and their attendant loud noises. Intrusions range from hikers, hunters, offroad motorcyclists, bulldozers, and mining operations to aircraft. One human intruder on a ridge, for example (fuelbreaks often facilitate such intrusion), can throw a condor off course, perhaps for an entire day which might mean that the bird will not find food that day. The standing air waves that exist above ridges are corridors of traveling power to condors, and displacement puts the condor at the mercy of the ambient wind without the sharp structural uplift of the ridge wave. Unfortunately, most of the areas that are utilized by condors for feeding are also open to access and use by people.

It appears that some of the thinking, research efforts, and plans for condor management are misdirected or likely to be unsuccessful because of certain assumptions, educational deficiencies, and management hangups. A widespread problem in wildlife management is the overemphasis on the study of an animal's anatomy, physiology, reproduction, and the like while neglecting its habitat. The principle that appears to be commonly ignored states that if a species is provided a proper habitat, it can maintain itself and even increase its numbers.

Attitudes and the direction of management are definitely skewed if the assumptions are made that the condor is a poorly adapted species that has been on a natural decline before modern man's arrival; that there is not much man can do to stop this inevitable descent to oblivion; that man-caused habitat changes have little to do with the condor decline; and that species that do not respond immediately to protection must be ill-adapted. Wildlife managers often assume that species that fail to make an immediate comeback after legal protection are poorly adapted, but perhaps they have not responded because of the generally unrecognized phenomenon of degradation overrun. In the semi-arid Southwest, for example, degradation and negative changes continue and compound in a network of spreading and devious successions long after the removal of the disturbance agent or factor. Such overruns must be arrested before natural recovery of systems and organisms can begin.

Wildlife biologists do not spend enough time attempting to understand such things as succession, retrogression, shock stagnation, ecosystem dynamics, limiting factors, perturbations, and restoration. Learning to raise an animal in captivity is lately considered by lab technicians to be a more viable solution for a declining species than understanding and correcting the adverse changes to its environment. Without first correcting or restoring feeding habitat, biologists are likely to discover that released condors will become merely delayed failures—more candidates for the statistics of oblivion.

Conclusions and recommendations

1) We recommend that those concerned with condors critically re-examine their thinking, basic assumptions and approaches.

2) Logic, common sense, and holistic thinking should prevail. Facts about condors are stupid things until they are related to general principles.

3) We think the recovery team should stop all handling, capture, and disturbance of condors. A captive breeding program is premature and detracts from more important issues that should be addressed first. Radio telemetry and tracking of daily movements are deterrents to privacy. They monitor abnormality and provide statistics on morbidity, both of which are off-target.

4) Present activities should be replaced with *habitat restoration and management of* ecosystems that provide food and feeding sites for condors. Enough is presently known about the degradation of California habitats to begin management and restoration without waiting for more studies to be completed.

5) The sanctuary of mountain forested and brushland country must be extended to condor feeding areas. Insecurity and frustration currently plague the condor at the feeding place. This is the fatal flaw. Condor requirements at the feeding site go beyond actual feeding to include an uninterrupted digestion period and close social interactions for an otherwise largely solitary bird.

6) Human and vehicle (land and air) intrusions must be eliminated to provide condors with privacy. Condor patrol officers should become a nuisance to intruding people, not to condors. At present, time would be better spent watching people rather than watching condors.

We set our course towards an area that we had studied through binoculars the day before. All agreed that it was a likely spot to find Turkey Vultures and because of similar vulture habits, therefore a possible roost for condors. By following the sandstone grooves, creek beds, and cliff edges, we were able to avoid direct opposition of the dense underbrush most of the time. After several hours, our circuitous route brought us to a gully that seemingly opened out onto the edge of the world. The suddenness of our escape from the maze surprised us almost as much as the sight we beheld directly before us. Less than a hundred yards away, standing on the edge of the abyss, were seven tremendous black birds absorbing the sunlight and its reflections from the warm sandstone.

This sudden meeting took both us and the condors by such complete surprise that we stood eyeing each other for the better part of a minute before they pitched off the edge of the cliff and took to the air. Once on the wing, the gigantic birds were much more at ease and the seven of them wheeled about apparently unafraid and extremely curious as we made our way to the edge of the cliff.

. . .

11. Lowell Sumner and Joseph S. Dixon

The Condor in the Sierra Nevada Wildlife and Human Use

EXTENSIVE field investigation of the Kings Canyon area of the Sierra Nevada was begun in 1916 by the Museum of Vertebrate Zoology, University of California, Berkeley. Similar cross-sectional surveys were conducted later. That of Yosemite, by Joseph Grinnell, and Tracy Storer, was published in 1924. The Lassen survey, by Grinnell, Joseph Dixon, and Jean M. Linsdale, was published in 1930. In 1953 the Kings Canyon study was published as *Birds and Mammals of the Sierra Nevada, with Records from Sequoia and Kings Canyon National Parks*, by Dixon and Lowell Sumner.

Joseph Dixon had previously published studies on the Allen and rufous hummingbirds in the Sierra Nevada, on the swift and California mule deer in Sequoia National Park, and on the birds of Kings Canyon National Park.

Lowell Sumner, senior author of *Birds and Mammals*, helped bring it to completion. Among his other duties, he has served as Regional Biologist for the National Park Service. In that role he had given extremely valuable advice on ameliorating various impacts—of the Sierra Club's high-mountain trips, of administrators on the national parks, and of public apathy concerning Alaska wilderness and wildlife. He was stepfather of Terry and Renny Russell, whose book *On the Loose* is one of the great statements on the value of wilderness to civilization. He is also the man to whom I owe, more than to anyone else, such ecological sense as I have.

From *Birds and Mammals* we have selected most of the section on the condor and excerpts on wildlife and human use, written to tell what the national parks could do to protect both uses, but all related as well as to the future of the condor and its endangered relatives. —DRB

[229]

. . .

The gracefulness, the strength, the magnificence of their flight is difficult to describe. The very steadiness of their movement as they soared through constantly changing air currents seemed uncanny. There was none of the unsteady rocking of the Turkey Vulture whose flight we had often admired. As a flyer, the turkey buzzard seemed but a novice in comparison to this giant of the sky. Awe inspired, we stood and watched as some swooped within fifteen or twenty feet of our position. Closer observation revealed the controlling mechanism of their flying. There were eight or nine long individual feathers extending from the end of each wing to form a slotted wing tip. The twenty to twenty-five pound weight of the airborne bird caused the nine to ten feet of wingspread to bow decidedly, with the "finger feathers" almost curling at the ends. Each feather was an individually controlled aileron which efficiently subjugated changing air currents to the will of the bird. While steadiness of flight depended upon the manipulation of the wing tips and support by the vast wing area, direction of flight was ruled by the fan-tailed rudder which was in constant motion up and down and from side to side.

As if it were a gondola suspended from a lighter-than-air craft, the condor's bare head moved with little regard to the flight operation of the rest of the unique structure. As the bird passed by us, the bare neck would extend as if it were made of rubber and the bald head would swing under a wing or around its legs as the rest of the craft went blindly on, controlled and avoiding collision with the other birds by some unconscious mechanism.

We watched this group of birds for more than an hour as they played follow-the-leader and gyrated in circles, parabolas, and figure eights, before they soared out over the canyon and returned for one last sweep before disappearing beyond the hills. This was the last curtain call and the show was over.

—TELFORD WORK

The Condor in the Sierra Nevada

T HOUSANDS of years ago, in the prehistoric days when camels, elephants, and saber-toothed tigers in countless numbers roamed California's wide valleys, condors apparently were numerous and widespread. Their fossil remains are abundant in the Pleistocene asphalt beds of Rancho La Brea in Los Angeles; they have also been found as far away as Florida (Wetmore, in Bent, 1932). Even as late as the 1830's, the California condor was reported feeding on dead salmon along the lower Columbia River, and apparently it persisted in southern Oregon until 1904. Its southern range limit seems to have been the wild, rugged mountains of northern lower California, where there still may be a few individuals, though this is doubtful.

The California condor is the lingering symbol of a vanished era. This era disappeared when the white man greatly reduced or exterminated the tule elk, antelope, grizzly bear, and numerous lesser animals that once were abundant enough to assure the great bird a large and continuous source of food. A few condors persist in their last California stronghold—the wild, rough mountains of Kern, Ventura, and Santa Barbara counties.

In a changing world where the smaller, more agile, adaptable, and elusive forms of wildlife have been better able to survive an expanding civilization than large, specialized, conspicuous forms, size has been the condor's undoing. The bird is so large that, like an airplane, it needs 50 or 60 feet of clear space for its take-off if there is no headwind. It is helpless if it inadvertently lands in dense brush or forest land. Hence it seldom benefits from deer kills made by mountain lions or hunters, because these are usually in forest or brushland.

Now that the salmon runs are a fraction of their original size, and irrigated farm lands occupy the green valleys in which millions of prairie game animals once roamed, the gaint vulture is chiefly dependent on occasional carcasses of horses, sheep, and cattle on the large foothill grazing ranges. The future food supply of the bird is dubious, for under modern livestock-raising methods, domestic animals are marketed before they reach old age, and few die from disease, since diseases have been greatly reduced by vaccination and other preventive measures. Only on a few old-fashioned ranches that still use the methods current in Spanish times are livestock losses large enough to support even a single pair of condors.

The condor's digestive system appears to resist, to some extent, the poisons placed in carcasses of livestock for the purpose of killing coyotes. However, there seems to be some ground for the belief that over the years such poisons have killed many condors. Walter Fry writes:

". . . while I was stopping at Huron, Fresno County, California, during January, 1890, Mr. Mánuel Cadoza, a sheep herder, brought in two beautiful dead Condors. . . . Coyotes had killed two of his sheep and he had poisoned the carcasses with the hope of killing the coyotes; but instead of getting the animals he got the two big birds that had been feeding on the dead sheep. Cadoza . . . noticed several of the Condors around the poisoned sheep the . . . day before, and upon going out in the evening found the dead ones a few yards from the bait.

"Those were the first Condors that I had seen, and such was their size and curious appearance they seemed to me rather the birds of some fabulous tale than ones that lived in these modern days."

Condors bathe frequently in shallow pools hidden in the recesses of certain wild canyons of the California Coast Ranges.

A single egg is laid, almost invariably on the bare ground in some rugged and inaccessible mountain area, preferably in a cave or large rock crevice. Apparently, a given pair does not nest every year, and the young require several years to reach full maturity.

[The condor was] formerly a regular resident in the parks, [and is] now a rare visitor. Walter Fry observed condors in the early days of Sequoia, as follows:

"On September 15, 1899, I saw two Condors near Castle Rocks, elevation 6,800 feet. The birds were feeding on a dead horse, and I got within 50 yards of them before they flew. They glided off from the top of the carcass. On November 10, 1905, I saw one Condor with five buzzards feeding on dead elk at Salt Springs, elevation 1,600 feet. Ranger C. W. Blossom and I, under cover of bushes, approached within 100 feet of these birds and watched them for almost an hour . . . When we stepped from under cover, the buzzards were first to fly, but the Condor ran on the ground with wings partly spread for a distance of fifty feet before taking wing. On September 30, 1907, I found one large Condor feeding on a dead sheep near Twin Peaks, elevation 10,550 feet. I rode on horseback to within 40 yards of this bird before it flew; and it ran about 20 feet to the edge of a cliff, then pitched off down the canyon. On September 27, 1919, I saw one Condor and two ravens feeding on a dead cow at Wet Meadows, elevation 9,200 feet. I approached within 100 feet on horseback in plain sight and watched them for a few moments before they took flight. The ravens were first to go, and the Condor remained for some time after. When taking flight the Condor ran across the meadow about 60 feet at a rapid pace, and with wings partly unfolded, before leaving the ground."

On Sept. 18, 1934, Bob Roberts, fire lookout at Paradise [Milk Ranch], saw a California condor circling 500 ft. above his lookout station. Through a pair of binoculars he plainly saw the bare head, the ruff of feathers on the neck, and the white patch under the wing.

In 1924, Superintendent Guy Hopping of General Grant National Park (now the Grant Grove Section of the Kings) saw a California condor feeding on a dead burro about ¾ mi. below Ash Mtn. Hdqrs. on the Kaweah River. Oberhansley reports that nine condors were watched and photographed in Yokol Valley, July 15, 1942, about 13 mi. southwest of the Sequoia National Park boundary, as they fed on a dead cow; park residents saw a few stragglers soaring over the western part of the park late in July and in August.

On Oct. 2, 1949, Park Naturalist Howard Stagner saw two condors flying over Moro Rock. The Fresno *Bee*, Sept. 14, 1949, reported that Game Warden Ross Welch had observed from close up a flock of twelve feeding on a dead calf along the Tule River, "south of the old Orange school house" (10 or 15 mi. south of Sequoia). On Oct. 2, the *Bee* reported that state and federal forestry officials had observed five condors in the vicinity of Squaw Valley, 15 mi. west of the Grant Grove Section of the Kings.

In the summer of 1950, the *Bee* announced that Welch had found a condor nest in a hollow high up in a giant sequoia on the Tule Indian Reservation, a short distance south of Sequoia National Park. In September, Carl B. Koford and other ornithologists saw a young condor standing at the entrance to the natural cavity, 100 ft. up in the massive tree's unscalable trunk. From a tall pine growing near by, photographs were taken of the young bird. ("First Condor Nest in Tree Discovered," Los Angeles *Times*, Sept. 24, 1950.)

It seems likely that from time to time condors from the mountains of Kern, Ventura, and Santa Barbara counties fly to the Sierra foothills and wander as far north as the Sequoia–Kings Canyon area in search of food, a distance of less than 150 mi.

Wildlife and Human Use

S CARS ON ancient trees show that the wilderness has recovered many times from forest fires. Seldom or never has it recovered from the effects of a paved highway. Because the automobile road has destroyed more primeval areas than any other single development, the National Park Service tries to hold road construction to a minimum.

Fifty years ago, when most wilderness areas were so remote that it took days of travel just to reach them, roads were built to make such places "accessible." But times have changed, and the entrances to remaining primeval areas now can be reached by automobile in a few hours. The building of a road in order to make the wilderness "accessible" defeats its own purpose: as soon as the road permits the motorist to see "unspoiled nature" without getting out of his car, the wilderness, together with various wildlife species, vanishes.

The secondary effects of a road are often more detrimental than the primary effect. Initial construction tends to be only the first step in a gradual process of "development," for it invites new gas stations, cabins, stores, ski lifts, trailer camps, fire-protection roads, telephone and power lines, water-storage systems, and sewage-disposal systems. Eventually, the area may require residences and garages for administrative personnel, overnight accommodations, a post office, hospital, and sometimes even a school.

When the new buildings come, the safety standards of a residential area begin to enter the picture. The rules say that snags, inflammable undergrowth, and dead wood must be removed within a thousand-foot radius of such buildings. When these are removed the wildlife must go elsewhere.

Go elsewhere? It is not that simple, for wild creatures that are thrown out of their homes cannot easily move to some new place. In accordance with a fundamental law of animal populations, suitable near-by territory usually is occupied already by other individuals of the same species. Hence the refugees are even worse off than most human displaced persons, for no one is willing or able to take them in, and there is no charitable organization to feed them. Some wildlife DP's, by hard fighting, may be able to seize living space from their competitors; but this only lowers the margin of survival for all. Therefore, every area developed for human visitors means deprivation or death for many wild creatures originally found there.

Development of an area for the convenience of large crowds and preservation of natural features and wildlife turn out, then, to be very nearly opposites. At least they can be reconciled only by a compromise of some kind. This means real compromise: wildlife must be sacrificed in some areas, but man must exercise some restraint in order to preserve for the future not only the wildlife but the underlying beauty and harmony of natural forces that exist in wilderness areas.

A new development plan cannot be justified merely by statistics showing that the acreage already under intensive development is small compared to the total park area. Such statistics would be particularly misleading in the Sequoia and Kings Canyon National Parks, because most of that region is deficient in livable habitat for large numbers of wild creatures, although it is replete with beautiful scenery. As has been already pointed out, neither wildlife nor human beings can live on scenery alone. Therefore, preservation of a reasonable amount of accessible, fertile, really desirable areas free from human development requires special care in the Sequoia and Kings Canyon National Parks.

In weighing the arguments for further development, the National Park Service feels that human developments in vital areas must be justified by considerations other than that of making it possible for a great many people to have "a great deal of fun." It is the duty of custodians of national treasures to pass them on to posterity, unimpaired. The enjoyment of national treasures by the public has to be limited by the degree of perishability of the treasures.

Like the park lands themselves, National Park Service wildlife policies are unique because they are based on the obligation to preserve natural conditions. Therefore, the techniques of wildlife management used in the parks differ somewhat from those used elsewhere.

Outside the parks, the objective of most wildlife management is to produce a crop of animals for sportsmen to shoot. These animals must be nursed along like any other crop that is harvested. Since vast changes in the original habitat have upset the natural order, the wildlife manager has to protect these animals by suppressing their enemies and competitors, just as the farmer destroys native wildflowers when they compete with his beans. Thus, the wildlife manager outside the parks usually persecutes the predators because they eat the birds and mammals that he wishes to kill for his own recreation.

Inside the national parks and monuments, where there is no hunting, all the native animals are given equal protection. This policy preserves the original natural balance. It also gives camera enthusiasts, and others who do not want to shoot the animals, special opportunities to enjoy at close range many wild creatures that are usually hunted, and to observe various rare and vanishing species which, because they eat game animals or other "crops" of man, have been nearly exterminated elsewhere.

From this experience, the following National Park Service policies have evolved:

1. Every species, for its greatest ultimate good, shall be left to carry on its struggle for existence unaided, unless there is real reason for believing that it will perish if it is unassisted.

2. Where artificial feeding, control of natural enemies, or other protective measures are necessary to save a species that is unable to cope with civilization's influences, every effort shall be made to place that species on a self-sustaining basis once more, so that these artificial aids, which themselves have harmful consequences, will no longer be needed.

3. The rare predators shall be considered special charges of the national parks and shall be given protection in the parks in proportion to their persecution elsewhere.

4. No native predator shall be destroyed to protect another park animal on which it normally preys, unless that animal is in

immediate danger of extermination, and then the predator shall be killed only if it is not also a vanishing form.

5. Species predatory upon fish shall be allowed to continue in normal numbers and share normally in the benefits of fish culture.

More permanent and more difficult to correct is the biological upset that results when some native species, particularly a predator, has been exterminated. Disappearance of mountain lions, for example, has been in part the cause of severely destructive increases in the number of deer in many western states. Some national parks and monuments that are too small to preserve lions within their boundaries have suffered from this type of biological unbalance, particularly Zion, Grand Canyon, and Glacier national parks and the Lava Beds National Monument. In a few places where the predators have been destroyed, the resulting hordes of deer have virtually exterminated shrubs, wildflowers, and young trees essential to forest reproduction.

Giant Forest provides a small-scale example of unbalance resulting from the partial retreat of mountain lions from an area that has become thickly occupied by human beings (see section on California Mule Deer).

When shrub- and tree-eating animals become too numerous because their controlling natural enemies cannot be restored, the general policy of the national parks provides that:

6. The numbers of hoofed animals (deer, elk, buffalo, moose) on a deteriorated range shall not be allowed to exceed its reduced carrying capacity, and, if possible, shall be kept below the carrying capacity until the range can be brought back to its original productiveness.

7. No management measure or other interference with biotic relationships shall be undertaken unless a properly conducted investigation has shown that it would be beneficial.

8. Any native species which has been exterminated from the park shall be brought back, if possible; but if this species has become extinct, no related form shall be reintroduced in its place.

"If possible" recognizes the practical limitations. The Park Service could not consider restoring either the wolf or the grizzly to the Sequoia-Kings, because near-by livestock might be endangered. Any grizzly introduction also would be contrary to policy on scientific grounds, for the native California grizzly is extinct. To a sportsman, this distinction might seem trivial, but many scientists feel that substitution of some other nonnative species, even though closely related, would seriously distort the history of each local race, obscuring its origin and making difficult the study of its adaptations to its particular environment.

9. Any nonnative species that has already become established in a park shall be either eliminated or held to a minimum if complete eradication is not feasible.

At one time, in order to provide a spectacle for visitors, animals were lured to special feeding areas. However, this proved even more harmful to the animals than caging them. Bears fed at garbage pits lost their natural feeding habits and became dependent upon easily obtained but unhealthful swill. The young bears suffered most of all, because, dependent from infancy, they never learned to live entirely on natural food obtained by their own efforts. Each fall when the garbage supplies were curtailed abruptly at the end of the tourist season, dozens of malnourished bears, their fear of human beings reduced through summer-long familiarity, broke into cabins, storehouses, tents, and cars. As their hunger increased, the boldest offenders became so dangerous that it was necessary to shoot them. Among the bird population, some young blue jays, no longer able to obtain food from campers, actually starved·

When the feeding of garbage to bears in Sequoia National Park was discontinued, in 1940, bear depredations diminished appreciably. In Kings Canyon National Park, bears never have been deliberately fed, although at Cedar Grove, where garbage disposal has been inadequate owing to lack of funds, some bears have acquired perverted appetites and have learned to steal from human beings.

In the past, the Park Service has at times fed buffalo, elk, deer, and bighorn; but even when this was done primarily to help the animals to survive winter storms, more harm than good resulted. Like the garbage-fed bears, the hoofed animals preferred to eat the inferior food provided for them, such as hay, rather than search for more suitable natural forage. Overcrowding on the feeding grounds caused contagious diseases to spread rapidly through entire herds. At Glacier National Park, one band of bighorn was almost exterminated by a lung disease before biologists discovered that the only way to save the remnant of the herd was to stop the artificial feeding. When this was done, the bighorn recovered.

Thus, in relations between visitors and animals in the national park system, the policy provides that:

10. Presentation of the animal life of the parks to the public shall be a wholly natural one.

11. No animal shall be encouraged to become dependent upon man for its support.

12. Problems of injury to visitors, to their property, or to other special interests of man in the park shall be solved, if possible, by methods other than killing the animals or interfering with their normal way of life.

Since national park wildlife is relatively unafraid, and year by year becomes more trustful, the visitor may wonder why it is not more abundant—the old-time stories tell of flocks that darkened the skies and herds that took days to pass a given point. The answer is that the high mountain country of most national parks, though often majestic, is by comparison to the lowlands a cold and barren world. Wildlife, like man, cannot live on scenery alone. However, this fundamental fact is often overlooked when the designation "wildlife sanctuary" or "park" is conferred upon some snowy crest or desert canyon.

In marked contrast to the cold, still, mountaintop areas, it is the foothills and lower valleys, with their abundant moisture, warmth, and deep soil, that swarm with life. The tall grass of lowland fields and valleys nourishes the billions of insects that furnish food for the hordes of insect-eating songbirds and rodents. These in turn must be abundant if there are to be appreciable numbers of badgers, foxes, and other fur bearers, and of eagles and large hawks.

In lowland forests and chaparral, bark bettles and leaf-eating insects are abundant enough to feed the forest's big defense army of flycatchers, chickadees, and woodpeckers. Squirrels, grouse, deer, moose, and elk thrive in these lowlands because their food grows more luxuriantly there than at higher, colder elevations. Coyotes, raccoons, and bears also are more numerous because of the greater abundance of their natural food supplies. In lowland marshes, ponds, and rivers, the warmer waters and more fertile bottoms give to pondweeds and rushes a luxuriance unknown in higher places. The swarms of crustacea and insect larvae that live on this vegetation provide food for far more frogs, marsh wrens, curlews, blackbirds, rails, and bitterns than ever inhabited our mountains even in the earliest days. Fish in lowland waters grow more rapidly than those that live in icy alpine streams, and the abundance of food supports them in vastly greater numbers.

Because the idea of setting aside land for national parks did not develop until after the more fertile lands had already been put to other uses, the tendency has been to create parks chiefly out of remote, unproductive lands. Therefore, in spite of the fact that the national parks and monuments are dedicated to wildlife conservation, proportionately more barren rocks and alpine wastes are included in the national park system than in the lands of any other wildlife conservation agency. Boundaries of national parks almost never have been drawn to meet wildlife protection needs, and very few parks areas are so situated as to provide satisfactory year-round living conditions for all their native species.

Creation of Kings Canyon National Park adjoining previously established Sequoia resulted in a better than average wilderness sanctuary for the protection of endangered California species. The combined area of the two parks would probably be sufficient to give adequate protection if all the boundaries coincided with the biological barriers. Boundary troubles are particularly acute on the east side of these parks, where the line follows the crest of the Sierra and thus permits a formidable leak in the wildlife reservoir. Since these mountaintop boundaries cut right through the heart of the natural alpine habitat, a marten, fisher, wolverine, mountain lion, band-tailed pigeon, or bighorn that cannot read the boundary signs does not know when it is outside the park and its protection. If the boundaries followed natural barriers such as deep canyons or low-elevation contour lines, thousands of animals would not have to lose their lives because of their inability to read.

On the west slope of the Sierra, the biological boundaries of Kings Canyon National Park are less effective than those of

Sequoia. Relatively little chaparral was included in the Kings, and, as will be repeatedly brought out in the species descriptions that follow, this is the reason that the Kings lacks many of the species that are quite common in Sequoia.

Smaller parks can never hope to restore the vanishing members of their original wildlife communities, although usually these are the species that most need protection in the country as a whole. Particularly inadequate are such mountaintop parks as Lassen, Mount Rainier, and Crater Lake, which are little islands of wilderness surrounded by an ocean of logged-over, burned, overgrazed, and plowed-up land, where the wildlife has been destroyed by trapping, poisoning, or shooting.

Although economic obstacles may prevent all efforts to remedy such boundary deficiencies; wherever possible, as in minor boundary realignments, the National Park Service policy provides that:

13. Each park shall contain the year-round habitats of all native resident species.

14. Each park shall include a sufficient amount of all these required habitats to maintain at least the minimum population of each species necessary to insure its perpetuation.

15. Park boundaries shall be drafted to follow natural biological barriers where possible, particularly life-zone or similar habitat boundaries.

To the Condor Advisory Committee
Excerpts from the Leopold Report

PRESIDENT THEODORE ROOSEVELT designated Pelican Island in Florida as a federal refuge in 1903. Its purpose was to protect nesting pelicans, herons, and egrets from molestation by plume hunters and fishermen. Sixty-five years later the National Wildlife Refuge System comprised 317 major units, with a combined area of nearly 29 million acres. At that time Secretary of the Interior Stewart Udall appointed an Advisory Committee to consider how the system should be managed. On it were some of the most notable names in wildlife conservation of the time—Clarence Cottam, Ian McTaggart Cowan, Ira N. Gabrielson, and Thomas L. Kimball. A. Starker Leopold was chairman.

The Committee's report to the Secretary was published in the Transactions of the Thirty-Third North American Wildlife and Natural Resources Conference held March 11-13, 1968. The report attempted to appraise the significance of the national refuges, to comment on management practices, to envision the ultimate pattern of the system, and to broaden the view of what each refuge might mean to the public.

Below are a few excerpts from the report that have relevance to the protection of condors. It was not thought necessary fourteen years ago to warn against the possibility of molestation not only by plume hunters and fishermen, but also by the broader public, including biologists.

Professor Leopold was then director of the Museum of Vertebrate Zoology, University of California, Berkeley. Author, researcher, teacher, and perpetual student of what is going on in the world's ecosystems, he has traveled and advised widely. Among his achievements is winning the Aldo Leopold Medal, named for an illustrious father, and awarded to a no less illustrious son.   —DRB

[243]

To The Condor Advisory Committee

IN A LONG discussion with Starker Leopold and Professor Frank Pitelka about the condor controversy, a group of us from Friends of the Earth and the Golden Gate Audubon Society were reminded of the Leopold Committee report, and also learned of a letter from Professor Leopold to the Condor Advisory Committee several years ago. He agreed to search for it. It went, he said, either to Doug Leitz or Sandy Wilbur, "elaborating my doubts about the condor propagation program." His search failed, but was followed on August 26, 1981, by his letter from the University of California, Berkeley:

"Mr. David Brower, Friends of the Earth, San Francisco.

"The general idea about condors that I expressed to the Condor Advisory Committee was this:

"The wild population of condors appears to be failing. Reproduction apparently is less than attrition. What could be the reason or reasons for reproductive inadequacy?

1. Some or more of the surviving adults are senile.
2. The adult breeders are obtaining toxic materials in their food that precludes mating or production of viable eggs.
3. Nesting pairs are being disturbed enough to disrupt effective reproduction. Disturbance could be from oil rigs, hunters, hikers, photographers or airplanes.
4. Available food in proximity of nests is inadequate (unlikely).
5. Deaths by shooting or by accidents continue to exceed number of young fledged.

"There may be other reasons that I cannot think of now.

"Unless the causes of reproductive failure are understood *and corrected* there is nothing to be gained by pen-raising birds and putting them back in an unreceptive environment. None of the above listed deficiencies is corrected by propagation.

A. Starker Leopold"

Excerpts from the Leopold Report

IN ESSENCE, we are proposing to add a "natural ecosystem" component to the program of refuge management. Wherever a fragment of some native biota remains on a refuge it should be retained or expanded and restored insofar as this is practicable and in conformance with the primary function of the refuge. Native plants would be as much a part of this concept as native animals, and should where possible be used in landscaping and in development of wildlife coverts.

* * *

Unfortunately, the proximity of urban masses leads inevitably to pressure for larger picnic grounds, camping facilities, improved swimming beaches, motorboat marinas, water skiing, baseball fields, bridle paths, target ranges, and other assorted forms of play which are only obliquely related to refuge purposes. Once any of these forms of public use becomes established, it is difficult to terminate. Therefore the master plan for each refuge should have a firm and definite program of development for recreational programs and facilities favoring those activities appropriate to the refuge area and excluding or firmly limiting those that are inappropriate.

* * *

However carefully refuge sites may be selected, the lands are forever subject to invasion by government agencies with higher rights of eminent domain, such as military services, Atomic Energy Commission, Corps of Engineers, Bureau of Reclamation, and the Bureau of Public Roads. After a refuge is acquired and developed, it often has to be defended.

* * *

In 1964 the Department of Defense and the Atomic Energy Commission arranged to fire an undergound atomic shot on

Amchitka Island, one of the central islands in the Aleutian Islands National Wildlife Refuge and the stronghold of the northern sea otter herd. "Project Longshot" led to detonation in 1965, but instead of terminating the project the agencies followed with plans for five more atomic blasts, some possibly powerful enough to blow the side out of the island and endanger life in the adjoining seas. Amchitka has been converted from a wildlife refuge to an atomic testing ground without benefit of democratic process and over the objections of Governor Hickel of Alaska, filed in September of 1967.

*   *   *

Hunting and fishing are appropriate uses for portions of many refuges. Keeping in mind the primary objectives of the refuges, both hunting and fishing along with other public activities should be managed to prevent undue disturbance of birds and mammals or interference with their welfare.

13. David R. Brower

An Exchange with Russell Peterson
The Condor and a Sense of Place

EDITING BOOKS, writing articles, and speaking about mountains and conservation has kept David Brower busy since 1933. He was designer and general editor of thirty volumes published in exhibit format by the Sierra Club and Friends of the Earth, some of the early volumes bringing him the Carey-Thomas Award for outstanding achievement in creative publishing; one volume *"In Wilderness Is the Preservation of the World,"* was judged one of the ten most beautiful books in the world at the Leipzig International Book Fair, 1963. He served as executive director of the Sierra Club from 1952 to 1969, when he founded Friends of the Earth and became its first president. He was also a founder of the Sierra Club Foundation, the League of Conservation Voters, Friends of the Earth Foundation, and Friends of the Earth organizations in several countries. He was the principal biographee in John McPhee's *Encounters with the Archdruid*, serves as Chairman of the Board of Friends of the Earth, and is the father of Kenneth Brower. He holds six honorary degrees, received the Sierra Club's John Muir Award, and was twice nominated for the Nobel Peace Prize.

RUSSELL PETERSON, before becoming president of the National Audubon Society in 1979, served four years as Governor of Delaware, three as Chairman of the Council on Environmental Quality, two as president of New Directions, one as Director of the Office of Technology Assessment, and also served on the President's Committee on the Accident at Three Mile Island. He received his PhD at the University of Wisconsin in 1938 and has received many awards, including the Audubon Medal and four honorary doctorates. He was with the DuPont Company from 1942 to 1969 in research and development. He shares a column in *Who's Who* with Roger Tory Peterson, and between the two of them, there is little room left for anyone else.

An Exchange with Russell Peterson

ARGEST of the California chapters of the National Audubon Society, the Golden Gate Audubon Society opposed the national society's approach to a condor recovery program, opposition expressed in a letter to the national president, Russell Peterson, from Jerry Emory, the Golden Gate Society's young executive director. On August 15 Dr. Peterson replied, and the reply was apparently given wide circulation. David Brower, Chairman of Friends of the Earth and founder of that organization, was one of the people who responded to Dr. Peterson. The letter to Mr. Emory appears first, its paragraphs numbered in brackets as an aid to references to it in Mr. Brower's letter, which follows Dr. Peterson's.

National Audubon Society
950 Third Avenue
New York, N.Y. 10022
August 15, 1980

Dear Mr. Emory:

[1] I am writing in response to your letter to Glenn Paulson with regard to the tragic death of the young condor on June 30, an occurrence that all of us on the staff of the National Audubon Society deeply regret. I also want to take this opportunity to discuss the Golden Gate Audubon Society's present opposition to our condor program.

[2] After personally reviewing all of the facts in this matter, I can only conclude that the death of this condor chick, however unfortunate, is no cause to abandon the three-part program of greatly intensified research, expanded habitat protection, and captive propagation for the purpose of returning captive-bred

progeny to the wild that the National Audubon Society itself proposed to the U.S. Fish and Wildlife Service almost two years ago.

[3] Our goal in advocating this program and in approving captive propagation for this desperately endangered species, was *and is* that of attempting to do everything possible to ensure the perpetuation of a wild, free-flying population of the condor. This was an explicit provision of the resolution adopted by our Board of Directors when it first approved of captive propagation for the California Condor, *in principle*, at its meeting in San Francisco in January 1977. You may recall that at that time, indeed in that same resolution, the Board of Directors also directed our staff to arrange for an objective review of the entire condor situation by an independent panel of distinguished scientists. With the welcome assistance of the American Ornithologists' Union, that panel was appointed in the fall of 1977 and delivered its report in May 1978.

[4] I am personally convinced that the death of this young condor does not change any of the reasons that led National Audubon, again with the concurrence of our Board of Directors, to propose to the U.S. Fish and Wildlife Service the long-term, three-part program envisioned in the *Report of the Advisory Panel on the California Condor*. It also does not change any of the basic arguments that we presented to the Congress of the United States last year, when we went to the Congress and convinced that body that it should authorize a 30-40 year program for the condor.

[5] At the same time, however, it is evident to me that, in hindsight, we did make mistakes in the conduct of the examination of the condor chick that died on June 30. I want to assure you that at our own initiative we are reviewing all of our research and handling procedures so that we can propose, in cooperation with the U.S. Fish and Wildlife Service, a series of additional safeguards designed to reduce the risk of any recurrence of this tragic event. This would have been required, as you know, by one of the conditions of the permit that was in the process of being issued by the California Fish and Game Commission which reads in part: "If a condor is killed or injured during trapping or handling, the Department shall be immediately informed, and trapping operations shall im-

mediately cease until a full evaluation of causes has been made, and necessary modifications of equipment or procedures developed."

[6] I would like to draw an analogy to another similar, very tragic occurrence in the early stages of another national scientific program. I refer to the death of the three astronauts in the capsule fire on the launching pad at Cape Canaveral, at an early stage in the moon rocket program. This was also a terrible and tragic event, and it was enormously regretted, but it did not halt the NASA program. Instead, we did learn from that tragic loss of life, the technology was improved, and the Nation did succeed in placing men on the moon.

[7] I should also emphasize that the National Audubon Society and the Fish and Wildlife Service are not trying to hide anything. The very fact that the tragic death of this young condor is recorded on film is a direct result of the fact that the team that planned the entire condor program insisted, on their own volition, that all handling operations be filmed as a *safeguard*, so that one could extract the maximum possible amount of information from each handling of a condor, so that any unusual or unexpected condor behavior could be documented, and so that, in case something did go wrong with one of the handling procedures, it could be studied so as to help avoid later problems. Thus the provision that all handling of condors be filmed was added to the handling protocol as a safeguard. I think that this was a wise safeguard, for without that film we would not have been able to see and to analyze what went wrong as well as we now can.

[8] Although the death of this condor chick is terribly unfortunate and very much regretted by the National Audubon Society and by all of the other cooperating agencies in the California Condor research program, it is hoped that the resulting damage to the Condor population will be somewhat alleviated by a successful breeding next year by the parents of the lost chick rather than in two years, the normal interval for a breeding pair that successfully fledges an offspring.

[9] In view of the above factors I cannot accept your argument that the entire California Condor program, so long discussed and debated, should now be abandoned because of the tragic death of this single condor chick.

[10] Like the members of the Advisory Panel on the California Condor, I am convinced that, without man's conscientious intervention on many fronts at once, there is simply no way that the present condor population can grow from its present low numbers, probably on the order of 20 to 30 individuals, to a more healthy and safe level sufficient to ensure the pepetuation of the species, *i.e.,* to the level of 50 individuals that was the goal of the original Recovery Plan adopted in 1975 or to the expanded goal of at least 100 individuals, well distributed within the former breeding range, that is the goal of the newly revised Recovery Plan.

[11] In addition to the research directed toward identifying and understanding the forces causing the decline in the number of condors and the captive breeding to ensure a viable population, we must, as I pointed out at the start of my letter, continue efforts to ensure that adequate habitat is available for the condor. The condor now ranges over 32 million acres. Of that vast area of mountains, foothills, valleys, croplands and dry rangelands, approximately 50% is in private ownership. Less than 1% of the remainder is closed to human entry in order to protect known condor nest sites and roosting areas. Even after the addition of the proposed Sespe-Frazier Wilderness closure, which we strongly support, over 98% of the condor's current range will still be open to human intervention. In addition, outside the immense range of today's few condors there are huge adjoining wilderness areas. Why aren't these areas used? Does the condor have enough range without them? These are critical questions that we must try to answer with facts, not with unfounded speculation.

[12] In conclusion, I urge the Golden Gate Audubon Society to reconsider its present opposition to our California Condor program, to carefully review the recommendations contained in the *Report of the Advisory Panel on the California Condor,* and to help National Audubon to implement, with every feasible safeguard that we can devise to protect condors against injury or death, the long-term, 30-40 year program that we believe gives us the best possible chance to ensure the perpetuation of a wild, free-flying population of this magnificent species.

[13] As my predecessor, Elvis J. Stahr, pointed out in his testimony before the Congress last year, it has taken more than

40 years and many kinds of human intervention to restore the Whooping Crane from its 1938 low of only 14 or possibly 15 individuals wintering at Aransas National Wildlife Refuge in Texas to its present numbers, now well in excess of 100 individuals. What we now propose to do for the California Condor involves no less an effort, no less a time period. It may be that, over the next three to four decades, we will face other setbacks such as the tragic death of this young condor. But we—and I am here speaking for the National Audubon Society—are determined to do whatever can be done, on the basis of the best available scientific advice, to give the California Condor the best possible chance for survival, and we are equally determined that this unfortunate incident of June 30 shall not be used as a pretext to halt this imaginative, far-ranging program.

[14] In short, we do not intend to stand idly by and watch this magnificent bird disappear forever. It is undoubtedly in trouble because of man's intervention. We are convinced that it can be saved only by man's intervention. Thus, this is a moral issue to us. We believe it better to try and fail than never to try at all.

Sincerely,

Russell W. Peterson
President

Friends of the Earth
124 Spear Street
San Francisco, California 94105
September 11, 1980

Dr. Russell W. Peterson, President
National Audubon Society
950 Third Avenue
New York, N.Y. 10022

Dear Russ:

Several of our members have seen and forwarded copies of your letter of August 15 to Jerry Emory (of the Golden Gate Audubon Society to which I have long belonged) about the condor and your deep concern.

My own concern goes back a long way and quite a bit of it is relevant. In 1941, when John Baker was organizing the National Audubon Society, I applied to him for a job but lost out to Bert Harwell, whose work with birds I had known well from my years in Yosemite. Instead, I became an editor at the University of California Press, which enabled me to work on many monographs from the Life Sciences Building, most of them from the Museum of Vertebrate Zoology. Some of my work was with Loye Miller, but much more was with his son Alden, then Director of MVZ and for some time Chairman of the university's Editorial Committee. I also worked with Frank Pitelka and Robert C. Stebbins.

It was this UC connection that enabled me to publish condor material in the *Sierra Club Bulletin*, the editing of which I was deeply involved in from 1935 to 1969. I was also deeply involved in the Sierra Club Conservation Committee, which I helped organize in 1940. I rarely missed a meeting, stimulated as I was by the success of the club's effort in the battle to establish Kings Canyon National Park. Carl Koford used to attend those meetings. My interest in the condor began at about the same time he began his Audubon/University of California study.

Carl's work still informs me, and I wish it informed all who are concerned with saving the condor. The hapless chick would still be alive. On page 1 of the book he did for Audubon—*The California Condor*—Carl warned, "Because of the danger of injury, it is inadvisable to trap and mark condors." On the next to last page: "Therefore, the only way of completely protecting condors from molestation is through the cooperation of people throughout the range of the condors. Sensational publicity is harmful in that it causes persons who otherwise would have no direct influence upon condors to seek the birds and to disturb them." Such an admonition led me long ago to decide that I would rather hear about condors than see them if the seeing might in any way disturb and endanger them.

My other concerns with wildlife grew as I worked with Lowell Sumner, George Collins, and Victor Cahalane of the National Park Service, with E. Raymond Hall, with Starker Leopold and his students, including Lee Talbot, and with Olaus and Mardy Murie. I first began to like birds a great deal in 1937, when my most frequent climbing companion was Morgan Harris, an amateur birder who would become chairman of the Department of Zoology at Berkeley and is still active. He, along with many others, is not at all happy about the hands-on part of the condor recovery plan. Some of us are beginning to call it the Condor Disposal Program. It worried Dave Phillips, Ray Dasmann, and me when we first had a chance to discuss it together in the course of Ray's receiving the Aldo Leopold Medal in Toronto.

This long prelude was stimulated by your writing of "personally reviewing all the facts in this matter." Your subsequent remarks show that you have missed a substantial body of vital information, including, we think, that which we have been quite assiduous in digging up. I think it worth while to go point by point over the matters where we think you are wrong.

Your paragraph two implies that those who disagree with you wish to abandon the three-part program. They don't. They merely want the dangerous third part dropped—its danger is something we predicted and the recovery team has proved. By all means more research, but research on the natural behavior of the condor, not the behavior of a molested one. By all means expanded habitat protection—the kind advocated by Alden Miller, Carl Koford, and a long list of people who know a great deal about the bird's natural habitat, as much as is left of it. I have been close enough to behaviorists to know the importance of the observer's melting into the natural background. That melting does not accommodate harassment, capture, marking, surgery, or captive breeding.

The essential point your third paragraph speaks of is "to ensure the perpetuation of a wild, free-flying population of the condor." We wish you would carefully read Carl Koford's and Dick Smith's books so that you would no longer misconstrue what "wild and free-flying" consists of. San Diego is not wild, and whatever its virtues, it cannot inform a condor the way its wild range can, or its free-flying parents. Condor competence did not evolve by virtue of human help, nor can that competence be expected to survive an obsession with management. That is not the way genes get to know what they must if they are to keep a creature alive in the wild.

To miss that essential point is to miss one of the most important warnings in The Global 2000 Report to the President: If people go on doing what they are doing, then by the year 2000 between 500,000 and two million species of plants and animals that are now here won't be here any more. No species has the right to do that to other species and to expect or deserve, to survive them. What leads to this dire projection is humanity's messing up habitat and wildness. The present Condor "Recovery" Plan exacerbates the problem instead of providing the best possible example of ways in which humanity can reform, and spare the extinctions that Joseph Wood Krutch said would make our voyage on this planet a lonely one. The present plan's research stresses gadgetry instead of wildness, its contribution to habitat protection has lamentably been negligible, and 'captive' by definition is the opposite of 'free.' I cannot see how to consider a panel of ornithologists to have been either objective or expert if they have not seriously addressed the problem The Global 2000 Report presents. They ought to have participated in the three-year study the report required; indeed, they should have anticipated its relation to the condor. Surely the world needs a better idea than spending twenty or thirty million dollars each to take species off the endangered species list. The better idea, we think, is to save the ecosystem that enables an endangered species to remain natural, not to become an artifact.

Your paragraph four, in short, states that the death of the chick does not change anything. We hope that it will lead to some contrition, to the admission of possible fallibility, to a willingness to reexamine the most controversial step National Audubon has taken on in all its years. I do not see how you can remain confident that you are right when so many good people believe Carl Koford was right. His recommendations remain the sound ones. The program National Audubon supports, moreover, ignored the warnings of many members of the public and the scientific community, and deceived the Fish and Game Commission and the Director of the Department of Fish and Game in California.

There are times when it is wise to return to Square One. I think the condors would like you to. Technology assessment has had its inning. I think it is time for behaviorists' biological assessment to have its time at bat. A thirty-to-forty-year program for the condor is an excellent idea. But it ought to be for the condor, not for a managed facsimile of the original—provided captive breeding succeeds.

Paragraph five speaks of perceiving mistakes in hindsight. It troubles us that people around the recovery team were foreseeing these mistakes, but warnings were lost in the deafness that overconfidence brings. What the condor needs now is not a modification of equipment or procedures involved in trapping, but a reformation of human concept and performance.

The reference to the Cape Canaveral tragedy in paragraph six has bothered a lot of people. If there were only twenty-nine humans left, and through bad luck or stupidity the technology for sending them off the planet incinerated three of them, then surely the remedy would not be merely to improve the technology, but to reassess the goal. Will a distant, untried environment be safer? Or, instead of seeking escape, should we concentrate on fixing the place we are in, and have been adapted to and shaped by? Incidentally, Wes Jackson observes that we did not place men on the moon. They did not even touch it. What did touch it was the sophisticated bit of earth environment that they were encapsulated with. That's not the way for condors to go!

Paragraph seven, about filming the episode so as not to hide anything, misses several critical points. First, though the handling of condors' chicks was acknowledged to have risks, the action was never brought before the Fish and Game Commission or the public. John Ogden, National Audubon Society's condor research biologist, subsequently commented that he could not conduct his research in the "public arena." Earlier, in 1967, there had been severe criticism of the National Wildlife Federation's disturbing condors by the very act of filming them for a special issue of *National Wildlife*. Koford, the McMillans, and others repeatedly warned of the immediate and delayed threat to condors resulting from disturbance, and that ought to be seen to include disturbance caused by photographers. Dick Smith, in *Condor Journal*, told of some of the disturbance caused by photographers who were well concealed in blinds. Jeff Foott and Tupper Blake were not concealed at all—certainly not from the chicks being photographed, and conceivably not from the parents. The condor's ability to discern disturbance from afar ought to be assumed. Observers assigned to give radio warning of the parents' return should not presume they could see distant condors as well as distant condors could observe what was going on in their most critical environment of all—their nests.

As a further point, please look carefully at the footage taken by Jeff Foott, and estimate how much the fatally traumatized chick was handled in order to get close-ups as well as medium shots of the various actions—capture, pulling, stuffing into the horse-feed bag, stuffing into the knapsack, weighing, measuring wing length, straddling, and measuring beak length. After all that, Jeff Foott reportedly became alarmed, put the camera down, and tried to help, thus missing the final death throes.

We are not happy that photographers were permitted to accompany the team, but not the promised veterinarian or the independent observers we had urged to be present. It is easy to conclude that the photography related more to public relations than to an effort to document good and bad moves. Except in an Andy Warhol film that omits nothing, the camera will get only what the photographer is ready to shoot—provided it comes out. Photography helps, but the expert observer's eye is what counts. When the chick was killed, no experts were watching, either to advise or to remember, and the shots dwelling on the Audubon arm patch are a bit embarrassing. Without the film, for all the other errors, there might well now be two chicks, not one, both less traumatized. Far from its being a safeguard, the filming added a hazard. We are forced to infer that the USFWS and National Audubon Society researchers knew that if they had brought their plan for close-range photography and handling before the Commission, it would not have been allowed. With condor-recovery priorities where we urged that they should be, there would have been no trauma. New initiatives for habitat protection would be under way, not stalled.

While your eighth paragraph regrets the unfortunate death, in the Cronkite segment on the tragedy your field crew said the handling of the chick was normal. That should have alarmed the Society as it does us. Nor should there be comfort in the hope that the death might persuade the parents to breed again sooner. If "normal handling" loses one chick out of two, the condors won't gain appreciably.

Paragraph nine restates your misconception in paragraph two. We have heard no one, including Jerry Emory, argue that the entire California condor program be abandoned. Your many opponents argue that the program should be strengthened by placing a moratorium on trapping, handling, capture, marking, surgery, and caged breeding until, after a major effort in habitat protection, it is proved necessary and it has been proved successful on surrogate species. We are still duly concerned that even if captive breeding were to "succeed," it would more likely ensure a dependent population than one able to survive on its own.

Conscientious human intervention on many fronts, such as called for in your paragraph ten, should begin with intervention against the human intervenors. If, given a chance because we all work to assure that chance, the condor begins to recover by virtue of its own proved fecundity on its own ground, then we will have some of the information essential for recovering for the condor some of the former breeding range you speak of. For now, we need to hang on hard to the known nest areas, present and recent.

Your eleventh paragraph discusses the amount of range a condor needs. Carl Koford, in 1952, narrowed the nesting sites essentially to the terrain between 1500 and 4500 feet within a gross area of some two million acres. Condors ranged beyond that, of course, but ranged back. Nesting, roosting, and watering sites, suitably isolated, seem to have been the critical requirement then, and must still be now. We need to know much more, and Carl Koford, Dick Smith, the McMillans, and others have shown us how to find out. Eyes on! Surely much of the essential range must be wild. Thus we would like very much to see Audubon's strong support for the proposed Sespe-Frazier Wilderness, but it has by no means materialized. Our check, and the Sierra Club's, has turned up only the one letter from John Borneman to Congressman Lagomarsino and a brief one to the California Fish and Game Commission, both of which are welcome, but much more is needed. Faint heart will not win fair maiden. And Mr. Borneman, after the chick's death, reverted to his old argument against wilderness: it is a "people magnet." It is true that more people use wilderness now than when Aldo Leopold got us the Gila Wilderness. It is also true that California's population has quintupled since then. We believe that the most dangerous magnet now is the resource magnet. Without wilderness protection, this area will attract the people who care least about condors, the people who want to bring in all the encumbrances of resource exploitation. Their marks would be of far more lasting impact on condors than trail walkers' footprints.

We grant that there is excitement, challenge, and romance in the enthusiasm for captive breeding. There have manifestly been some short-term successes, and there may well be more. But beware how one manipulative step leads to another: intervene, protect, mollycoddle, spoil, and destroy.

It is worth thinking hard about Carl Koford's warning to the Fish and Wildlife Service on November 27, 1967. Concerning Topa Topa, presumably before the bird was captured, he wrote: "I recommend feeding it on the spot without capturing it and later, if necessary, moving it to a higher point away from human habitation. In addition, I specifically recommended keeping it out of the zoo, especially the Los Angeles one." He then noted that after the bird had been captive for more than a month, it had been exposed to zoo diseases and was otherwise "spoiled for potential release to the wild." There was then a consensus that "the captive was not to be used for public display or zoo publicity, but apparently it is now being used for both."

It still is used for both and so, we fear, is the ill-fated Condor Recovery Plan National Audubon so ardently espouses. We could wish Topa Topa better luck, considering its narrow escape from death when John Borneman tried to release it, with a leash still attached, in the vicinity of wild birds that were now hostile to it.

For all the people expert in wildlife matters that I have worked with and learned from, Robinson Jeffers (whom I never met) taught me most with the fewest words:

> What but the wolf's tooth whittled so fine
>   The fleet limbs of the antelope?
> What but fear winged the birds, and hunger
>   Jewelled with such eyes the great goshawk's head?

This truth has escaped the captive breeders, and should escape them no longer. They must learn what the force of creation consists of, how long it has been successful, and how little they know about it. While wilderness, to John Borneman, and to others who support it timidly, may be a people magnet, it was understood far better by Nancy Newhall: "Wilderness holds answers," she wrote, "to questions we have not yet learned how to ask." The captive-breeding approach speeds and excuses its demise.

We dare not let the last wilderness on earth go by our own hand, and hope that technology will somehow get us to a new wilderness on some remote planet. Or that somehow we can save little samples of genes in bottles or on ice, isolated and manageable, or reduce the great vistas to longlasting videotape, destroying the originals to sustain the balance of trade and of egos.

Back to Jeffers again, and his powerful poem, The Answer:

> *. . . However ugly the parts appear the whole remains beautiful.*
> *A severed hand Is an ugly thing, and man dissevered*
> *   from the earth and stars and his history . . .*
> *   Often appears atrociously ugly.*
> *   Integrity is wholeness,*
> *   the greatest beauty is organic wholeness,*
> *   the wholeness of life and things,*
> *   the divine beauty of the universe.*
> *   Love that, not man apart from that,*
> *   or else you will share man's pitiful confusions,*
> *   or drown in despair when his days darken.*

The Global 2000 Report to the President has certainly projected dark days on the screen. I think we must surely agree that the prospect, for the year 2000, of five billion new acres of desert, and of two million missing species of plants and animals, is an entirely unacceptable prospect. It will not do to settle for dioramas of tropical forest—or of the Sespe-Frazier and environs—in some hall of the American Museum of Natural History. It will not do to be so presumptuous as to think we can quick-freeze the flow of wildness through two million species, to dispose of if it loses its integrity or to release when convenient into a habitat that neither knows these species nor is known by them. It will not do to continue the illusion that a condor and zoo are compatible. A condor severed from the wild is an ugly thing; the whole is beautiful, and William Dawson knew it. In *Birds of California,* he wrote:

"But for me the heart of California lies in the condor country. And for me the heart of mystery, of wonder, and of desire lies with the California Condor, that majestic and almost legendary figure, which still haunts that fastnesses of our lessening wilderness."

A condor in a zoo, however elaborate the enclosure, is to be pitied. The National Audubon Society should play no further role in such sad incarceration. We pray that the Society and you, in the words of Maurice Strong, can adjust your thinking. There is vital work to be done to save the condor. The present condor Recovery Plan is not doing it. Let us join forces and get about it!

Sincerely,
David R. Brower
Chairman

The Condor and a Sense of Place

USE IT TOO OFTEN and the word *habitat* begins to shed its meaning. The word *environment* already suffers, and but feebly connotes the entity that makes it possible for us to be. *Ecosystem* and *ecosphere* vaunt themselves too much. *Niche* has a good ecological spot in the book but is too small for a condor. So how about *place*?

In 1971 Alan Gussow, in his book, *A Sense of Place: The Artist and the American Land*, wrote about "the qualities in certain natural places which certain men and women have responded to with love. . . . For all of us have our loved places; all of us have laid claim to parts of the earth; and all of us, whether we know it or not, are in some measure the products of our sense of place."

Like most of us, Mr. Gussow was conscious of man as a violator of the earth's lovely places. "There is a great deal of talk these days," he said, "about saving the environment. We must, for the environment sustains our bodies. But as humans we also require support for our spirits, and this is what certain kinds of places provide." He saw the earth as a collection of places that sustain our humanity. "We are homesick for places, we are reminded of places, and it is the sounds and smells and sights of places which haunt us." Against them we measure our past and present. My own prefatorial remark in the book agreed with John Muir about places: Throughout the course of life on earth, wildness has flowed from form to form, each more beautiful than what went before. But, I added, "suddenly, with a speed of attack there is no precedent for, man undertook to simplify that wildness, foreclose on diversity, dry up springs, and praise himself."

What condors need most right now is our sense of their place. To attain that insight, according to former Audubon screen-tour lecturer John Taft, we might try to think like a condor, and realize how superior to ours is a condor's visual grasp of its place. Roland Ross, who wrote an earlier chapter in this book, goes further. Recently he was demonstrating condor aerodynamics before the California Fish and Game Commission, and was so realistic in his gestures that he might well have become airborne had the room been bigger. A room was no place to be a condor in.

It should help us to wonder what kinds of places are necessary to let condors' spirit fly. What sustains their condorness? What sounds, smells, and sights, what flow of wildness? What tradition or social custom? It must surely be tradition, for example, that persuades condors to use the same roosting tree on the Tejon Ranch for thirty-five years. They find that ranch part of their social custom, a keystone, more aptly, in the mountain arc they range, and they could collapse without it. A huge keystone it is, a ranch occupying nearly two hundred eighty thousand acres where the San Joaquin Valley yields to the Tehachapis. It harbors a large roosting and foraging area for the condors. How important is it to them?

"The Tejon Ranch is absolutely vital to the population for its winter survival," said the Advisory Panel on the California Condor in its report of May 28, 1978, to the National Audubon Society and the American Ornithologists' Union. "The loss of the ranch to development or to a marked change in ranching practices would be disastrous."

Thirty months later they were saying, "There is presently no way to know what constitutes critical habitat for the condor." In that interim there had arisen a need to rationalize radio-tagging of condors. They were right in May. What could have caused the switch?

The Rancho El Tejon Draft Environmental Impact Report of May 21, 1981, suggests an answer. It proposes a monumental development and quite substantial change in ranching practices. For a ranch on which as much as two-thirds of the condor population spends half the year, the proposal calls for "2500 permanent dwelling units, 7,554 second homes ranging from cabins to rural estates, and 2460 campsites that would convert approximately 17,143 acres of extensive agricultural lands to a variety of residential, recreational, and agricultural uses." Contemplating the general proposal in October 1980, Kern County officials said that a preliminary analysis indicated that "existing water supplies would not be adequate and that only the Peripheral Canal or a comparable water-importation system would make the project feasible." Thus the Canal would become a major threat to the condors by leading to incompatible development of their favorite ranch.

El Tejon, incidentally, means *the badger*. It is an unhappy coincidence that the Badger Ranch seems destined to be the place where condors may be most effectively badgered. Permission to trap condors there has apparently been arranged with the ranch management, and it is not difficult to infer that conversion of the 17,143 acres would be easier if the condors were frightened away, trapped, or shipped away to pens in Los Angeles and San Diego. The pen or the zoo thus becomes the easy way out, captive breeding the 'safety net' for disappearing species. The combination provides a guilt-assuaging way of saving the gorilla, for example, from destruction of its habitat by primitive people. Or the wild condor's from sophisticated developers. Thus could good civilized intentions come to threaten a wild creature as thoroughly as primitive hunger. One wonders how much good intentions should be influenced by bad schemes.

One of the hard questions confronting people who care about the condor or other endangered species is the question of growth in California. The proposed Tejon development is but a step, although a major one, toward a California future in which a traveler would have to contend with freeway signs reading:

LOS ANGELES—NEXT 250 EXITS.

Must Paul Bunyan move to California, go into real estate, and ride a giant leaping frog, racing north from Los Angeles in twenty-mile leapfrog hops, leaving colossal subdivision plans at each landing? If so, the destruction of California that Raymond Dasmann wrote a book about in 1965 will remain on schedule. No one in leadership dares to say *STOP!* So count on Japan's present population as the model for California's Year 2080, and China's for the United States as a whole; after all, we are talking about roughly the same respective areas. Such a

LAND USE CONCEPT
YEAR 2000

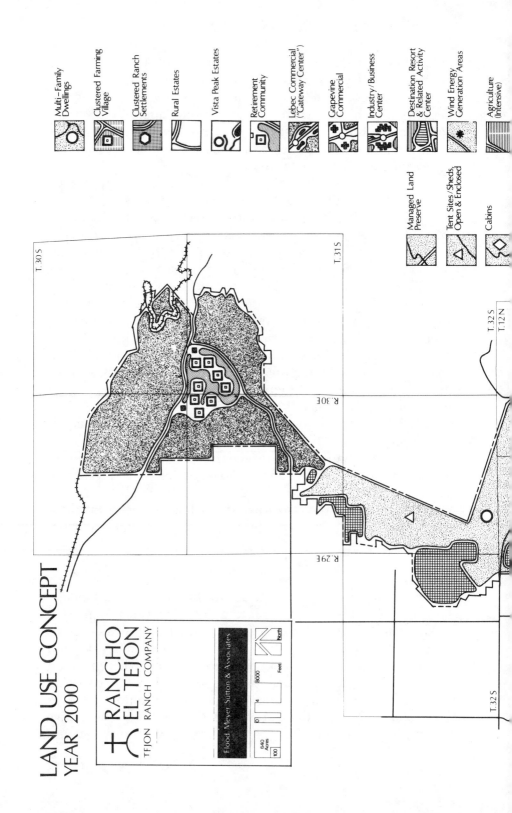

RANCHO EL TEJON
TEJON RANCH COMPANY

Flood Meyer Sutton & Associates

640 Acres
100

0 4 8000
Feet

North

Multi-Family Dwellings

Clustered Farming Village

Clustered Ranch Settlements

Rural Estates

Vista Peak Estates

Retirement Community

Lebec Commercial ("Gateway Center")

Grapevine Commercial

Industry/Business Center

Destination Resort & Related Activity Center

Wind Energy Generation Areas

Agriculture (Intensive)

Managed Land Preserve

Tent Sites/Sheds, Open & Enclosed

Cabins

T. 30 S
T. 31 S
T. 32 S
T. 12 N
R. 29 E
R. 30 E

Agriculture
(Extensive)

Mining
& Extraction

Land Use Concept for the Tejon Ranch for the Year 2000
(from the Environmental Impact Report, May 1981)

grim future, with its coalescing cities and suburbs, will have far too little room for people and no room at all for condors.

We believe that there is a better future for people and condors. It is implicit in the long-range objective of the California Condor Recovery Plan—"to establish a secure and self-sustaining wild population of the California Condor." A secure condor would symbolize a new maturity in our thinking: we would be back in reasonable balance, thanks to self-restraint, willingness to live and let live, and living better for it.

That noble long-range objective, however, is immediately aborted in the very program thereupon presented to achieve it. (See Appendix.) A wild population requires wildness, and the program speeds the demise of wildness for condors and everyone else as well. It has already cost the life of one condor chick, possibly another, and the lives of various living things in the hundred acres a program-initiated forest fire burned over. Such losses, and the concomitant disturbing of adults, will not speed condor recovery.

A disturbing event that took place some forty years ago was related to me by Roland Ross. A naturalist, then like Ross a Cooper Club member and avid condor student, set up a blind under a cliff in which condors were nesting. He came out for exercise only after dark, and in various ways kept himself out of the condors' ken well enough that the pair was not upset by his presence. One day one of the condors became extraordinarily agitated, moved up and down the cliff, then into the nest and broke the egg. The nest was thereupon deserted. The naturalist had looked at his watch and later noted that the agitation coincided with the arrival, ten miles away, of a steer carcass brought in by horse and sled as supplementary food for the condors, a supplement the naturalist had arranged for. Carl Koford told David Phillips in a 1979 interview of the same incident or a similar one at which Dr. Koford was there with the naturalist—who later denied the happening to Dr. Koford, refused ten years ago to discuss it with Professor Ross, and recently said it was someone else.

Forty years can blur details, of course, but some events are etched clearly and don't blur easily. The egg might well have been destroyed for another reason. There remains the chance, however, that its breaking was more than coincident with the arrival of the carcass. And had the nest not been discovered and the food not brought in, a condor might have been spared to be a parent for ten or fifteen more condors. One can further wonder what condors caught in cannon nets, variously explored, radio-tagged, and released, might do upon return to their nests.

In any event, the 1980 condor chick died of shock caused by the trauma of handling. The death of the 1981 chick could be due to overzealousness of the Condor Research Center observers. Details are hard to uncover, but from what we have been able to piece together, the parents of the first chick killed were soon nesting again about a mile away. Perhaps because of the apprehension about the Research-Center observers near by, they next moved five miles away from their first disaster and there produced and incubated an egg. Observers moved close. Unprecedented condor behavior resulted. The male was disturbed enough to destroy the egg or the newly hatched chick—the observers were not quite close enough to be sure. Chances are, however, they were close enough to cause aberant behavior. This account may be wrong too. It is nevertheless a fair indication of what could reasonably be expected. We do know the research-center members, in trying out their cannon nets, created a new problem, described in identical editorials. The *Ventura County Star–Free Press* headed its editorial of August 14, 1981:

Strike two on the condor-savers

The *Tulare Advance-Register* editorial five days later was headlined:

Protecting the California condors
—even if it kills all of them

It continued:

"It's starting to sound like the scenario for an old-time movie script: 'Laurel and Hardy Save the Condor.' But so far, the scenes aren't very funny.

"First, the condor-savers killed a baby condor. Then they started a brush fire that burned 100 acres and nearly burned some homes. . . ." As part of the condor-saving program, a baby condor chick died while being handled in the wilds by an Audubon Society biologist last year. One official explanation was that the condor chick may have been 'predisposed to die,' which would make it mere coincidence that the chick happened to die while it was being handled.

"Obviously, the only reason to believe that is to want to believe it. The only impartial conclusion is, the condor-savers killed a baby condor.

"That put the condor-saving program on 'hold' for months, while the wisdom of trapping was debated some more. But those who pushed trapping were undeterred by the death of the condor chick.

"Grown condors are harder to trap than chicks, since they know how to fly, so grabbing them by hand doesn't work. (Lucky for them.) The technique to be used to trap adult condors is a net shot from a cannon. (How's that for preserving their natural habitat?)

"Some members of the Audubon Society were practicing with the cannon last Wednesday in Southern California, trying to trap buzzards as a tune-up for trapping condors. The cannon started a brush fire that quickly burned more than 100 acres before firemen got it under control. It took 150 firefighters, 18 engines, 3 water tenders, 3 helicopters, 2 planes and 2 bulldozers to knock down the fire and save half-a-dozen homes.

"Nobody doubts the sincerity of the naturalists who believe that aggressive tactics are needed to save the condor, such as trapping and handling and measuring and tagging those released, and trying to breed others in captivity. Neither should anyone doubt the sincerity of the naturalists who believe the way to save the condor is naturally—by keeping people away from the condor refuge and keeping hands off the condors.

"It's not a debate that's easily resolved, but one thing is clear at this point: The 'hands-off' naturalists haven't killed any condors or started any fires."

There was a report that some buzzards escaped and some were burned. This was denied, and the denial is probably correct. But birds could easily have been burned and were certainly traumatized.

The hands-on people seem clearly to lack the sensitivity epitomized by Carl Koford in his last interview. In the fall of 1979, just a week before he died, he was asked a last question by David Phillips: "Do you think it's possible to protect the habitat in a way that would let condors increase their population to a sustainable level?"

Koford replied: "Yes, I think so. The question is, how do you do it? The Eb McMillan way, I think—which is, the best thing that can happen to a condor nest is that nobody finds it. Because once people find it, they're going to be observing it. And they don't realize . . . the damage you can do to condor nesting even by standing up and looking at it from half a mile away. . . . If you just add up the statistics, and separate nests which were visited from those that weren't visited, you'll see that even one visit to the nest decreases by about 10 per cent the chances of fledging a bird. Any disturbance is too much, and you can't tell by looking at the bird. You're sitting there, and the condor is sitting there, but the condor isn't going in and feeding the young, which is what it would be doing if you weren't there. There's no way you can judge how disturbed a bird is."

There will surely be less disturbance if one recognizes, as Les Reid of the Sierra Club does, that condors have rights. That includes the right to their own dignity. We can grant them their rights, or we can preempt them all. One particular right the condor once had was freedom of the sky. From the Coast Ranges, eastward along the Tehachapis, and north to the old sequoias of the Sierra Nevada, an array of thermals and condors' knowing the wind kept the huge birds aloft and made that vast mountain arc their home. Then the different flood came, as humanity reached its second billion in the late 'twenties and its most recent billion since the assassination of John F. Kennedy. This new flood, as it surges ever higher, extinguishes old freedoms. What replaces them is not new freedom but license, an arrogant assumption that no title to a place is valid unless we write it in our newly invented language and insist, as one of the most recent arrivals on the planet, that we must second-guess the Creator and manage it all.

If we remove condors from the wild and, with convenient rationalization, move ourselves in, we lose. As Professor Starker Leopold has pointed out, "Unless the causes of reproductive failure are understood *and corrected* there is nothing to be gained by pen-raising birds and putting them back in an unreceptive environment."

If we cannot save a receptive environment for the condor, symbol of the global threat to endangered species, what can we save? California and the condor deserve better than the present high-technology condor-disaster plan. It is high time for the federal government to obey its own requirements in the National Environmental Protection Act. By providing the essential Environmental Impact Statement conservationists have been asking for, the NEPA approach can search out alternatives and find the dynamic one. Our choice would be a spacious international condor reserve with congenial development on the edges, not in dead center.

Americans can save the condor's place from ourselves. There are twenty-four steps that ought to precede any further molestation of the condor, and will probably preclude molestation. The steps are summarized in the Appendix and augmented in the Introduction by David Phillips. Steps like these can be followed elsewhere for other species, to slow the reckless attack on the earth's diversity and save its organic wholeness.

"What's the use of a house," Thoreau asked, "if you haven't got a tolerable planet to put it on?" He knew what losses in his time had made the place less and less tolerable. In his journal for March 23, 1856, he regretted that "the nobler animals have been exterminated here—the cougar, panther, lynx, wolverine, wolf, bear, moose, deer, the beaver, the turkey," leaving him a tamed and emasculated country, a maimed and imperfect nature like "a tribe of Indians that had lost all its warriors."

What he wanted instead was not attainable then, much less now: but can still give us pause:

"I seek acquaintance with Nature, to know her moods and manners," he explained. "I take infinite pains to know all the phenomena of the spring, for instance, thinking that I have here the entire poem, and then, to my chagrin, I hear that it is but an imperfect copy that I possess and have read, that my ancestors have torn out many of the first leaves and grandest passages, and mutilated it in many places. I should not like to think that some demigod had come before me and picked out some of the best of the stars. I wish to know an entire heaven and an entire earth."

Thoreau's ancestors were novices at mutilation. We can mutilate at breakneck speed. We seem determined in our own time to elbow two million species of plants and animals into oblivion in the next two decades, and will succeed if we insist on flooding the earth with our own numbers and draining it of unreplenishable resources. Sparing us from this latter-day flood will require a good many more Noahs than are now at work. They can succeed where today's few institutions for the future have faltered. There can be a new Ark, and it is not too late for the splendid creature the condor is—and for many lesser ones we have yet to learn about. The miraculous flow of information in their wild genes, their unique chemistries, and their love of life can be passed on. We need not be wanton and banish them. They can survive and hold onto their freedom.

The Condor Question, we hope, will enhance the opportunity for the rest of us to keep intact the wildness and wild living things that remain in the sea, on the land, and in the air, to prevent a wake for them and their not-so-distant relatives, ourselves. We and they need our places, our islands of sanctuary.

Let it speed the California condor's recovery to measure the bird arbitrarily about like this: A condor is five per cent feathers, flesh, blood, and bone. All the rest is *place*. Condors are soaring manifestations of the place that built them and coded their genes. That place requires space to nest in, to teach fledglings, to roost in unmolested, to bathe and drink in, to find other condors in and not too many biologists, and to fly over wild and free. If it is to be worthy at all, our sense of ethics about other living things requires our being able to grant that their place transcends our urge to satisfy our curiosity, to probe, to draw blood, to insult, to incarcerate. We can respect the dignity of a creature that has done our species no wrong—except, perhaps, to prefer us at a distance.

Tim Bowles

The National Park Idea, 1865

The first point to be kept in mind then is the preservation and maintenance as exactly as is possible of the natural scenery; the restriction, that is to say, within the narrowest limits consistent with the necessary accommodation of visitors, of all artificial constructions and the prevention of all constructions markedly inharmonious with the scenery or which would unnecessarily obscure, distort or detract from the dignity of the scenery.

In addition to the more immediate and obvious arrangements by which this duty is enforced there are two considerations which should not escape attention.

First: the value of the district in its present condition as a museum of natural science and the danger, indeed the certainty, that without care many of the species of plants now flourishing upon it will be lost and many interesting objects be defaced or obscured if not destroyed.

Second: it is important that it should be remembered that in permitting the sacrifice of anything that would be of the slightest value to future visitors to the convenience, bad taste, playfulness, carelessness, or wanton destructiveness of present visitors, we probably yield in each case the interest of uncounted millions to the selfishness of a few individuals.

It is an important fact that as civilization advances the interest of men in natural scenes of sublimity and beauty increases.

It is but sixteen years since the Yosemite was first seen by a white man [Thirty-two years. Captain Joseph Reddeford Walker saw the valley from its north rim in 1833. Ed.]. Several visitors have since made a journey of several thousand miles at large cost to see it, and notwithstanding the difficulties which now interpose, hundreds resort to it annually. Before many years if proper facilities are offered, these hundreds will become thousands and in a century the whole number of visitors will be counted by the millions. An injury to the scenery so slight that it may be unheeded by any visitor now, will be one of deplorable magnitude when its effect upon each visitor's enjoyment is multiplied by these millions. But again, the slight harm which the few hundred visitors of this year might do, if no care were taken to prevent it, would not be slight if it should be repeated by millions.

At some time, therefore, laws to prevent an unjust use by individuals, of that which is not individual but public property must be made and rigidly enforced. The principle of justice involved is the same now that it will be then; such laws as this principle demands will be more easily enforced, and there will be less hardship in their action, if the abuses they are designed to prevent are never allowed to become customary but are checked while they are yet of unimportant consequence.

This duty of preservation is the first which falls upon the state under the Act of Congress, because the millions who are hereafter to benefit by the Act have the largest interest in it, and the largest interest should be first and most strenuously guarded.

Frederick Law Olmsted (1822-1903)

Condor Literature: An Annotated List

Compiled by Sanford Wilbur
Adapted by Jerry Emory

American Ornithologist's Union. 1941. Report of the Committee on Bird Protection, 1940. *Auk* 58(2):292–298.

Estimated 50 condors in existence; Committee proposed (1) setting aside entire Los Padres National Forest for condor protection, (2) prohibiting all hunting, except for personnel killing deer for condor food, and (3) restoring the mountain lions so that lion kills would be available to condors.

American Ornithologists Union. 1971. Report of the Committee on Conservation, 1970–71. Auk 88 (4):902–910.

Notes confusing on condor data, population estimates varying from about 30 to more than 60.

Baker, J.H. 1950a. Better protection for the California condor. *Audubon Mag.* 52(6):348–354.

Recommend closing Sespe area to mining and mineral leasing.

———. 1950b. Oil and condors don't mix. *Audubon Mag.* 52(2):120.

Proposes Sespe mining closure.

———. 1951. Condor prospects improve. *Audubon Mag.* 53(2):122–123.

Passage of Public Land Order 695, and establishment of Sespe Condor Sanctuary; full text of land order.

———. 1953. Threat to the condors. *Audubon Mag.* 55(2):68.

Protests of permit to San Diego Zoo to trap condors.

Barney, Gerald O. 1980. *The Global 2000 Report to the President. Entering the Twenty-First Century.* Three vols., G.P.O.

A massive study of environmental, energy, population, and resource problems, prepared by the Council on Environmental Quality and the Department of State. Projects the extinction of up to 2,000,000 species of plants and animals by the year 2000, if present trends continue.

Bishop, R.C. 1971. Conservation of the California condor in relation to the proposed phosphate mining and processing operation in Los Padres National Forest. Calif. Agric. Exp. Stn., Contrib. to Project 1244. 25pp.

Economic analysis, concludes that "the public could legitimately question the wisdom of using public land for (a phosphate mine) . . . risking an endangered species of international significance in the process . . ."

Borneman, J.C. 1976c. The victim. *Audubon Imprint* (Santa Monica Bay Audubon Society) 1(4):4–5.

Attempted rehabilitation of condor wing broken by gun-

Buchheister, C.W. 1965a. Meeting the challenges of the "third wave." *Audubon Mag.* 67(1):18–19.

National Audubon Society proposals to save condor.

———. 1965b. Grave threat to the condor. *Audubon Mag.* 67(2):82–83.

Opposing Sespe Water Project.

California Condor Recovery Team. 1974. *California Condor Recovery Plan.* U.S. Fish and Wildlife Service. 74pp.

Proposal to maintain at least 50 condors, well distributed within their 1974 range.

———.1980. *California Condor Recovery Plan.* U.S. Fish and Wildlife Service in cooperation with the recovery team: S.R. Wilbur, D. Esplin, R.D. Mallette, J.C. Borneman, W.H. Radtkey. 81pp.

On mortality factors, captive breeding, relocation to previous habitat, and purchase of lands within present range— program through year 2020.

California Condor Advisory Committee. 1981. Recommendations to the Department of Fish and Game concerning the recovery program. D.F.G., Sacramento.

Comments on the 1981 permit request to capture condors for radiotelemetry and captive breeding.

California Condor Research Center. 1980. Report on death of condor chick. *California Condor Newsletter* Vol. 10, No. 2. report on visits to two condor nests, June 1980.

Clement, R.C. 1966. Dangers of pessimism in conservation. Trans. N. Am. Wildl. Nat. Resour. Conf. 31:378–381.

Condor as example of saving or dooming a species.

Cooper, T. 1976. Government flimflam threatens the condor. *Defenders Wildlife.* 51(3):204–205.

Criticism of government biologists for weak stand against a proposed phosphate mine.

Dawson, W.L. 1923. *The Birds of California.* 2121pp.

firsthand account of visiting condor nest. Out of print.

De Sante, D. 1980. So Gentle a Ghoul. Point Reyes Bird Observatory Newsletter. 51:1–3.

Alternative to the recovery plan proposed by condor recovery team and general commentary on condor problem.

Ehrlich, P. and A. 1981. *Extinction.* Random House, New York.

Excellent overview of endangered species. Condor program, and the June 1980 death of nestling are critically analyzed, pages 214–218.

Eissler, F. 1964. Condors and wilderness. *Sierra Club Bull.* 49(3):10–12.

Controversy over Sierra Madre Ridge road proposal.

Finley, W.L. 1906. Life history of the California condor. Part I. *Condor* 8(6):135–142.

Detailed observations at Los Angeles County nest site.

Finley, W.L. 1908a. Life history of the California condor. Part II. *Condor* 10(1):5–10.

Good compilation of distribution, and egg and skin collecting records.

Friends of the Earth. 1980–81. *Not Man Apart.*

News and feature coverage of the condors' emerging problem, in 1980 (issues dated February, March, June, July, September, and November) and 1981 (March, July, and August).

Fry, W. 1926. The California condor. *Gull* (Golden Gate Audubon Society) 8(5):1–3.

Two condors presumably killed by eating poisoned sheep carcass, 1890; proposes that killing condors, taking condor eggs, or putting out poisoned baits be made felonies.

Global 2000 Report. See Gerald O.Barney.

Hilton, J.R. 1971. What fate for Gymnogyps? California *Condor* (Society for the Preservation of Birds of Prey) 6(2):1–5.

Popular summary of recent research and management.

———. 1976. California Condor: Captive Breeding in Its Future? *Raptor Rep.* 4(3):15.

Pros and cons of captive propagation discussed.

Koford, C.B. 1953. *The California Condor.* Natl. Audubon Soc. Res. Rep. 4. 154pp.

Monographic study of condors, particularly nesting activity. First definitive work on condors. A must for those wanting to familiarize themselves with the condor.

Koford, C.B. 1979. California Condors, Forever Free? Audubon Imprint (Santa Monica Bay Audubon Society) 3(9);1–3.

Critical comments on the "Draft Recommendations for Implementing the California Condor Contingency Plan,"

Kroeber, A.L. 1906–07. Indian myths of south central California. *Univ. Calif. Publ. Am. Archeol. Ethnol.* 4(4):167–250.

Condor ("wech") as bad influence in Yokut myths.

Mallette, R.D., S.R. Wilbur, W.D. Carrier, and J.C. Borneman. 1972. California condor survey, 1970. Calif. Fish Game 58(1):67–68.

Twenty-eight condors estimated seen.

———.1973. California condor survey, 1972. Calif. Fish Game 59(4):317–318.

Thirty-six condors estimated seen.

Mallette, R.D. 1971. Results of California condor baiting effort, 1967–1969. Calif. Fish Game, Wildlf. Managmnt. Branch Admn. Report 71–76.

McMillan, I. 1953. Condors, politics and game management. *Central California Sportsman*, December. 3pp.

San Diego Zoo condor trapping controversy.

———. 1965b. Shall we save the condor or build another dam. *Defenders Wildlife News* 40(4):39–40.

Against Sespe Water Project.

———.1967. Game management vs. condor preservation. *Defenders Wildlife News* 42(4):365–369.

Criticism of current condor management.

———. 1968. Man and the California condor. Dutton and Co., New York. 191pp.

Popular treatment of condor history and management.

———. 1971. The 1971 condor survey—a return to soundness. *Defenders Wildlife News* 46(4):386.

Comments on annual survey.

Miller, A.H. 1953a. More trouble for the California condor. *Condor* 55(1):47–48.

San Diego Zoo permit to trap condors.

———. 1953b. The case against trapping California condors. *Audubon Mag.* 55(6):261–262.

Propagation and release to wild not feasible; trapping might disrupt breeding pair; condor in a cage is not a real condor.

Miller, A.H., I. McMillan, and E. McMillan, 1965b. Hope for California condor. *Audubon Mag.* 67(1):38–41.

Summary of Miller et al. 1965a.

Point Reyes Bird Observatory. 1981. Special California condor issue. Newsletter 53.

Overview of the condor controversy. Articles by: S.D. Ripley, F.A. Pitelka, T.H. Work, J.C. Ogden/S.F.R. Snyder, D. DeSante, B. Heneman, R. Stallcup.

Sibley, F.C. 1969. Effects of the Sespe Creek Project on the California condor. U.S. Fish and Wildlife Service, Laurel, Maryland. 19pp.

Effects of noise and disturbances on condors.

Sibley, F.C., R.D. Mallette, J.C. Borneman, and R.S. Dalen. 1968. Third cooperative survey of the California condor. Calif. Fish Game 54(4):297–303.

Minimum of 46 condors estimated.

———. 1969. California condor surveys, 1968. Calif. Fish Game 55(4):298–306.

Minimum of 52 condors estimated.

Smith, D. 1966. Condors and guns. *Defenders Wildl. News* 41(4):320–322.

Deer hunting seen as threat to condors.

Smith, D., and R. Easton. 1964. *California Condor, Vanishing American*. McNally and Loftin, Santa Barbara. 111pp.

Popular life history and conservation.

———. 1965a. The condor controversy : an on-the-spot report. *Defenders Wildl. News.* 40(4):40–42.

Wilbur, S.R. 1971. The condor's place. *Western Tanager* (Los Angeles Aud. Soc.) 37(11):1–2.

Philosophy of condor preservation.

———. 1972. The food resources of the California condor. U.S. Fish and Wildlife Service, Patuxent Wildlife Research Center.

———. 1973. The California condor in the Pacific Northwest. *Auk* 90(1):196–198.

Distribution, numbers, and evaluation of disappearance.

———. 1974a. California condor specimens in collections. Wilson Bulletin 86(1):71–72.

One hundred eighty-five skins, 51 skeletons, 55 eggs.

———. 1978. The California Condor, 1966-1976: A Look At Its Past and Future. United States Department of Interior, Fish and Wildlife Services.

APPENDIX 1

U.S. DEPARTMENT OF THE INTERIOR
Federal Register / Vol. 46, No. 106

Fish and Wildlife Service

Endangered Species Permit; Receipt of Application

APPLICANT: Patuxent Wildlife Research Center, U.S. Fish and Wildlife Service, Laurel, Maryland.

SPECIES: California condor (*Gymnogyps californianus*).

FILE NO.: PRT 2–8045.

PURPOSE: Recovery of the species through captive propagation, radio telemetry, and other scientific research techniques.

LONG RANGE OBJECTIVE: To establish a secure and self-sustaining wild population of California condors.

SUMMARY OF PROPOSED PROJECT: The initial recovery effort will extend over a three-year period (up to summer 1984) and will include but will not necessarily be limited to (1) Taking nine condors from the wild to establish a captive breeding population, (2) to radio-tag 12 free-flying condors and an unlimited number of pre-flight immatures, (3) to visit active and inactive nests to salvage parts, weigh and measure young birds and to remove sharp rocks from nest sites, (4) take blood samples from adult birds for various tests, and (5) take other samples of body parts (e.g., feathers) for various tests and examinations. All activities will be closely coordinated with the California Department of Fish and Game (CDF&G).

DURATION OF PROPOSED STUDY: Through the year 2015.

KEY PERSONNEL INVOLVED IN THE STUDY: See Appendix to this notice.

Outline of California Condor
Endangered Species Permit Application

I. Trapping and Handling Procedures

A. *Trapping:* Condors will be captured using cannon or rocket nets at baited trap sites. These capture methods were chosen after an evaluation of the relative merits of several trapping methods (i.e., cannon net, rocket net, walk-in trap, and clap trap) was performed on African vultures, turkey vultures, black vultures, and Andean condors in the wild. The cannon/rocket net method has an excellent record of safety.

B. *Handling:* Each trapping operation will involve at least 4 experienced bird handlers, including a veterinarian well supplied with appropriate medical equipment. No more than 3 condors will be captured during each trapping, and only 2 condors will be captured during the first trapping operation to ensure safe handling and to document the effectiveness of the trapping method. Trappings may be photographed or filmed for record-keeping purposes. Precautions will be taken to handle birds carefully and to minimize stress. Trapped birds will be held one hour or less; however, birds which are candidates for the captive breeding program may be held 1–2 days pending determination of sex.

C. *Sexing and Tissue Sampling:* The sex of all birds captured will be determined by chromosomal analysis of blood and feathers. The sexing procedure is to be performed at the San Diego Zoo.

D. *Tissue Samples:* 1. From each trapped bird, and from Topa-topa (an adult bird already in captivity), a 17cc blood sample will be drawn from a wing or neck vein for (1) heavy metal and organochlorine compound analysis (5cc for each), (2) parasite, pathogen, and DNA studies (5cc), (3) enzyme polymorphism studies (0.5cc), and (4) sexing purposes (1.5cc). The enzyme polymorphism studies are expected to give important information as to the degree of inbreeding in the wild population and may provide guidance for selection and pairing of birds for captive breeding to maximize outbreeding. The organochlorine, heavy metal, parasite, and pathogen studies will reveal current exposure to environmental stresses. The DNA hybridization studies will provide guidance to which species is/are taxonomically closest to the California condor. This will enable various tests (e.g., drug tolerance) to be conducted on surrogate species prior to using the test or procedure on California condors. The 17cc blood sample represents only 0.2% of adult condor body weight and presents no threat to the animal.

2. From each California condor trapped from the wild 3 developing feathers will be plucked for use in feather pulp sexing. Two grams of feather material from up to 20 contour feathers will be taken for heavy metal analysis.

E. *Other Examinations:* Each trapped California condor will be weighed, measured, and photographed in detail and undergo the following additional procedures: (1) tracheal and cloacal swabs for culturing bacteria and viruses, (2) checks for external parasites and molt, and (3) fecal samples (if available) for indications of parasite burdens.

II. Radio Telemetry Program

A. *Objective:* To radio-tag 12 adult or subadult free-flying condors, and to radio-tag an unlimited number of preflight immatures at nest sites.

B. *Schedule:* Trapping will begin in September 1981. Initially only two condors will be trapped to determine, over a one month period, if the radio equipment produces any adverse effects on the birds. If no adverse problems arise, 4 more birds will be radioed to make a total of six birds for the 1981–82 trapping season. Known breeding birds will not be trapped after February 1 of any year to preclude disturbance during the breeding season. During the 1982–83 and 1983–84 trapping seasons, 4 and 2 condors, respectively, will be trapped and radioed. In addition, between June 1982 and January 1983, one pre-flight immature condor will be radioed at a nest site. This should generally involve only one visit to the nest; however, an initial brief visit may be made to determine the age of the bird. Any preflight immature condor found after January 1983 may be radioed. If the numbers of condors scheduled for telemetry are not radioed during the scheduled seasons, the deficiency will be made up in following years. Changes in the number of birds to be radioed in any particular season may be made with consent of the CDF&G. Throughout the duration of the recovery effort, all phases of the radio telemetry program will be coordinated closely with the CDF&G.

C. *Materials:* Wing-mounted solar-powered transmitters, weighing about 60 grams each and known to last 3–4 years or more, appear to be the best design for the birds and for this long-term study. The overall weight of the radio packages for each bird is about 120 grams which represents approximately 1.3% of body weight, well below the 4% body weight limit usually recommended in avian telemetry. No detrimental effects of similar patagial radio tags have been noted on numerous turkey vultures and black vultures tagged and monitored by other scientists. These tags have been tested on wild and captive Andean condors and have shown no signs of associated tissue damage or impairment of behavior.

Monitoring of radioed California condors will be from ground vehicles and a small airplane. In addition, an array of 10–12 mountain-top radio receivers with directional antennae will be established to provide automatic, unmanned coverage of essentially all of the condor range. This system is expected to plot gross movements of the birds except when they descend into canyons, and will be partially operational sometime in 1982. Regular mapping of bird movements will allow identification of important flyways, feeding areas, roosting areas, and nest sites, and will provide a means to find injured or dead animals.

III. Entry into Nest Sites

A. *Inactive Nests:* Entry into inactive nests will be made to collect addled condor eggs, eggshells, and feathers, and to remove sharp rocks and other debris which may cause egg breakage if the nest site is used by breeding birds. Eggshells and feathers will be collected and analyzed for organochlorines and heavy metals, respectively.

B. *Active Nests:* Entry into active nests will be to (1) remove potential egg breakage objects, (2) attach radio-transmitters to pre-flight immature condors, and (3) examine and measure pre-flight birds to determine whether growth-rate or parasite problems exists. Pre-flight birds are partially feathered and are large enough for safe attachment of radio equipment but are not so large as to pose a risk of premature fledging or difficult capture.

Beginning 20 days after hatching, growth data will be collected monthly from nestlings and pre-flight birds beginning with the 1984 breeding season.

IV. Formation of a Captive Population

A. *Objective:* To take four males and four females from the wild, and one bird of the opposite sex to the one adult (Topa-topa) now in captivity to provide a captive breeding stock of 5 pairs.

B. *Schedule:* During the first trapping season (September, 1981–May, 1982), 3 reproductively inactive free-flying condors (i.e. potential breeders) will be taken from the wild. At least one will be of a sex opposite to that of Topa-topa for pairing purposes.

Determination of reproductive status of adults will be made through radio-telemetry; adults will be considered reproductively inactive if they remain unpaired during the normal courtship and egg-laying period (through the end of March).

Four and two reproductively inactive wild condors will be taken during the second (September, 1982–May, 1983) and third (September, 1983–May, 1984) trapping seasons, respectively. Breeding adults, eggs, or nestlings, will be taken in the event of a drastic population decline and only upon agreement with CDF&G.

If the number of condors approved for captive propagation is not taken during the scheduled period, the deficiency will be made up during remaining trapping seasons. Injured or sick birds salvaged from the wild may also become part of the captive breeding group.

The CDF&G will be consulted closely in all phases of the captive breeding project, including work to be done after the initial 3 year period (i.e. after the 1983–84 season) and will be provided with monthly, mid-year, and annual reports.

C. *Breeding Facilities:* Captured condors will be held, cared for, and bred at new facilities to be built at the 1,800 acre San Diego Wild Animal Park. Husbandry procedures will be similar to those used at the Patuxent Wildlife Research Center (PWRC) for Andean condors.

The park is directly associated with the San Diego Zoo which has a modern propagation center, full curatorial staff, veterinary hospital, and research section. The San Diego Zoo has had extensive experience with captive propagation of Andean condors.

The facilities will be patterned after the Andean condor complex at the PWRC which measures about 12m x 12m x 5m for each pair of birds. The pens have roosting and nesting compartments and perches, and are covered with 5 x 10cm welded wire. Condors will be fed a standard diet of such items as livestock, big game, rabbits, mice, rats, guinea pigs, and other similar foods. Birds will be given regular physical examinations and medical treatment as required.

Transport of captured condors from the field to the breeding facility will be by air or car with individual fiberglass sky-kennels (70 x 64 x 91cm) floored with indoor-outdoor carpet. A veterinarian will be in attendance during transport (5 hrs. by car, 2.5 hrs. by air).

APPENDIX 2

Prepared by David Phillips

	1980 USFWS Condor Recovery Plan	Present CRC Program	Friends of the Earth Proposal	
1. Land Acquisition	*Tejon ranch preservation *Hopper Mountain *Mantilija *Blue Ridge *Pothole	*Land and Water Conservation Act funding has been diverted; no habitat for endangered species will be acquired	*Restore Land and Water Conservation Fund and acquire key parcels of condor habitat *Formulate list of important parcels for acquisition using FY82 Energy Resources Fund; Califor-	nia State funding available, in part, for natural resource enhancement *Strengthen ties with private organizations interested in acquiring habitat and/or easements for the condor.
2. Management of federal lands, i.e. Los Padres National Forest	*Develop fire management program *Minimize animal damage control	*No evidence of program	*Act upon California Fish and Game Commission recommendation to designate the Sespe-Frazier Wilderness	*Implement management to improve habitat for condors: controlled burns, etc. *Confront excessive use of off-road vehicles in condor area
3. Law Enforcement	*Further closures in area *Restrict firearms use at Mt. Pinos *Relocate problem campgrounds *Patrol sanctuary	*USFWS domestic endangered species investigations deleted *No agent with primary responsibility for condor protection *No USFWS agent between Sacramento and Long Beach *Wholly inadequate funding	*Undertake extensive sign posting campaign immediately *Provide shooting area for hunters outside of condor use area *Ban firearms possession in off-season *Implement neglected	recommendations of Condor Law Enforcement Strategy and fund as high priority *Advertise DFG hotline in condor area for reporting violations *Press for firearms closure on Mt. Pinos

	1980 USFWS Condor Recovery Plan	Present CRC Program	Friends of the Earth Proposal	
4. Research	*Sample food items for contamination *Determine effects of poisons and pollutants on captive vultures	*Program emphasizes hands-on work to the exclusion of other important and long neglected studies	*Protect all active nesting, roosting, feeding, and watering areas from disturbance by biologists, photographers, and the public *Expand observation program; investigate additional historic nest sites *Prohibit removal of any condor eggs or nestlings *Require independent biologic assessments of population status, repro-	ductive activity, estimated nesting success, and surrogate research data (see Condor Research Center [Ventura, CA.] Draft fact sheet) *Require evaluation of turkey vulture telemetry in condor range before judging permit *Intensify study of the effects of 1080 and use patterns on raptors; burden of proof should be on users
5. Comprehensive habitat protection	*Fragmented responsibilities between USFWS, Forest Service, Bureau of Land Management, California Department of Fish and Game, and the National Audubon Society	*No visible effort	*Consolidate efforts by appointing habitat protection team; separate from research function *Thoroughly examine land use questions and rancher application of pesticides	*Monitor conflict between condor recovery and planned exploitation (i.e. Los Padres oil & gas leasing) *Explore tax incentive for protection of range land
6. Additional priorities	—	—	*Require preparation of an Environmental Impact Statement before judging permit request *Existing assessment is erroneous in suggesting	a finding of no significant impact *Require USFWS to honor commitment to fund biologist from DFG to work on recovery effort
7. Permit process	—	*Permit presently applied for would cover all handling between now and 2015	*Reject any open-ended permits	

APPENDIX 3

SUPPLEMENTARY BIOGRAPHIES

PAUL R. EHRLICH is professor of Biological Sciences and Bing Professor of Population Studies at Stanford University. An expert on ecology and evolution, he is the author of more than one hundred scientific papers, and several popular books including *The Population Bomb*, *The End of Affluence*, and *The Golden Door*.

ANNE EHRLICH is senior research associate in the Department of Biological Studies at Stanford University. She was a consultant on the United States government's *Global 2000* project and has co-authored many books with her husband, including *Ecoscience: Population, Resources, and Environment*. Their most recent book, *Extinction*, describes the threats to the survival of all wildlife.

FRED EISSLER is president of the Scenic Shoreline Preservation Conference, a long-time member of the Sierra Club, serving several years on its board of directors, a long-time resident of Santa Barbara, author of several articles about the California condor, a teacher, and member of Friends of the Earth.

DAVID PHILLIPS, Wildlife Program Coordinator for Friends of the Earth, received his bachelor's degree in biology from Colorado College in 1977. He has attended and reported upon three meetings of the International Whaling Commission in Europe. His interest in the recovery of the California condor began with his letter to Secretary of the Interior Cecil Andrus in November 1978 and has steadily intensified since then. He was the principal questioner in the several interviews published herein. He is a regular contributor to *Not Man Apart*.

HUGH NASH has served many years as Senior Editor of the Friends of the Earth periodical, *Not Man Apart*. Prior to that he was editor of the

Sierra Club Bulletin, to which he came when Time-Life discontinued *Architectural Forum*. He previously edited three Friends of the Earth books: *Cry Crisis: Rehearsal in Alaska*, by Harvey Manning; *The Energy Controversy: Soft Path Questions & Answers*, by Amory Lovins and his critics; and *Progress As If Survival Mattered: A Handbook for a Conserver Society*.

S. DILLON RIPLEY is a zoologist and museum director. Dr. Ripley has served as Secretary of the Smithsonian Institution since 1964.

Condors are specialized for long range soaring flight. Such flight is possible only where air currents are proper. The nature of the air currents is determined by the complicated interaction of sun, wind, and other climatic factors on the mountains, plains, and other surface features of the land. Because of their large size, condors require unobstructed spaces for alighting and taking off. There remain few areas which satisfy the requirements of condors for flight in addition to those for feeding, nesting, and roosting. The maintenance of the remaining favorable areas in their present state is of prime importance for the maintenance of the species.

For perching, condors require steady places with good footing which are easy to reach or to leave by air and where there is little disturbance by man or enemies. Roosts, in addition, must be high above the ground yet protected from strong winds, utterly free from disturbance, and suitably located with respect to food, water, nests, and perhaps to other condors. Any adequate program for conserving this species must provide for the preservation of a sufficient number of perching and roosting places as well as for the protection of nest sites.

Only a few sites are well suited for the drinking and bathing of condors. In addition, the birds are very cautious when performing these actions. Therefore, the protection of frequented watering places from disturbance is highly essential to the welfare of condors.

—CARL KOFORD

APPENDIX 4

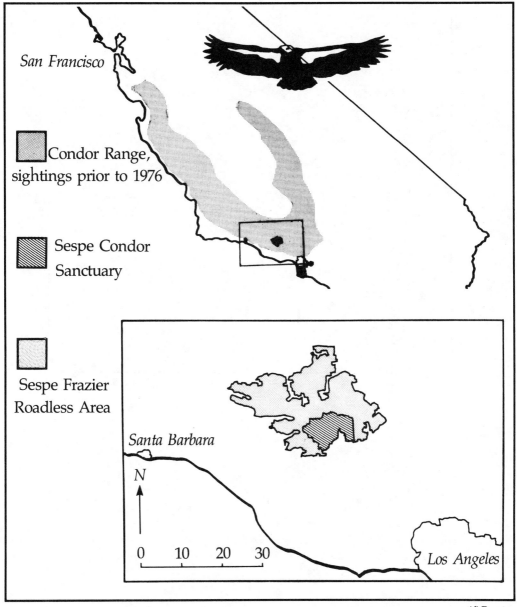

San Francisco

Condor Range, sightings prior to 1976

Sespe Condor Sanctuary

Sespe Frazier Roadless Area

Santa Barbara

N

0   10   20   30

Los Angeles

Ali Pearson

Map prepared by Dr. Steven Herman

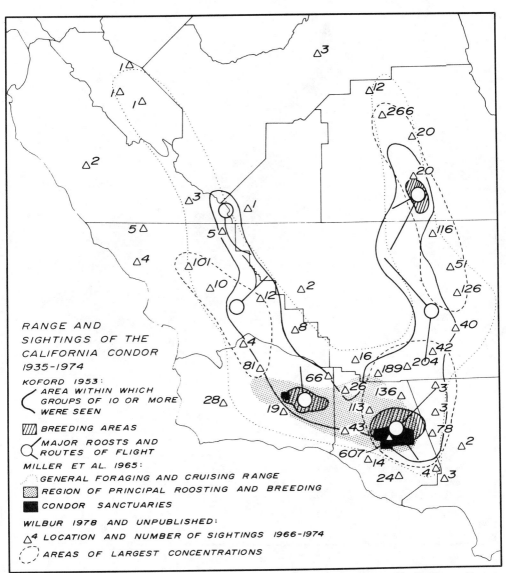

RANGE AND
SIGHTINGS OF THE
CALIFORNIA CONDOR
1935-1974

KOFORD 1953:
⌐ AREA WITHIN WHICH
⌐ GROUPS OF 10 OR MORE
⌐ WERE SEEN

▨ BREEDING AREAS

○⌐ MAJOR ROOSTS AND
○⌐ ROUTES OF FLIGHT

MILLER ET AL. 1965:
⣿ GENERAL FORAGING AND CRUISING RANGE
▨ REGION OF PRINCIPAL ROOSTING AND BREEDING
■ CONDOR SANCTUARIES

WILBUR 1978 AND UNPUBLISHED:
△⁴ LOCATION AND NUMBER OF SIGHTINGS 1966-1974

⌒ AREAS OF LARGEST CONCENTRATIONS

Map prepared by Dr. Steven Herman

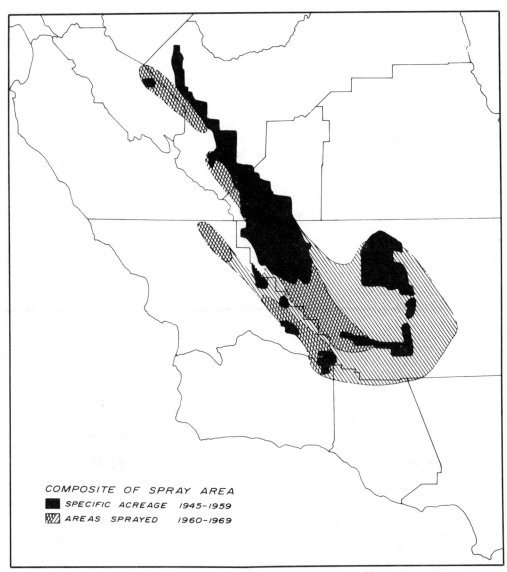

COMPOSITE OF SPRAY AREA
SPECIFIC ACREAGE 1945-1959
AREAS SPRAYED 1960-1969

Map prepared by Dr. Steven Herman

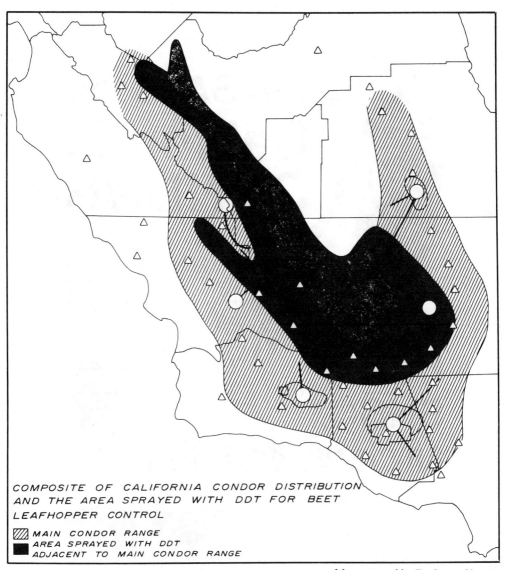

COMPOSITE OF CALIFORNIA CONDOR DISTRIBUTION
AND THE AREA SPRAYED WITH DDT FOR BEET
LEAFHOPPER CONTROL

MAIN CONDOR RANGE
AREA SPRAYED WITH DDT
ADJACENT TO MAIN CONDOR RANGE

Map prepared by Dr. Steven Herman

Help SAVE the California CONDOR

CONDORS, HAWKS, OWLS, EAGLES AND TURKEY VULTURES ARE PROTECTED BY FEDERAL AND STATE LAWS.

DON'T SHOOT
any large dark bird

10 FEET

IMMATURE CONDOR